Series Editors:
Steven F. Warren, Ph.D.
Marc E. Fey, Ph.D.

Communication
and Language
Intervention
Series

Also in the Communication
and Language Intervention Series:

Communication
and Language
Intervention
Series

VOLUME 11

Dual Language Development and Disorders

A Handbook on Bilingualism and Second Language Learning

by

Fred Genesee, Ph.D.
Professor
Department of Psychology
McGill University
Montreal, Canada

Johanne Paradis, Ph.D.
Assistant Professor
Department of Linguistics
University of Alberta
Edmonton, Canada

and

Martha B. Crago, Ph.D.
Professor
School of Communication
Sciences and Disorders
McGill University
Montreal, Canada

·P A U L·H·
BROOKES
PUBLISHING C⁰ ®

Baltimore • London • Sydney

Paul H. Brookes Publishing Co.
Post Office Box 10624
Baltimore, Maryland 21285-0624

www.brookespublishing.com

Typeset by International Graphic Services, Newtown, Pennsylvania.
Manufactured in the United States of America by
Versa Press, Inc., East Peoria, Illinois.

The cases described in this book are composites based on the authors' actual experiences.
Individuals' names have been changed, and identifying details have been altered to protect confi-
dentiality.

Library of Congress Cataloging-in-Publication Data

Genesee, Fred.
    Dual language development and disorders: a handbook on bilingualism and second language
learning/by Fred Genesee, Johanne Paradis, Martha B. Crago
        p   .cm.—(Communication and language intervention series; v. 11)
    Includes bibliographical references and index.
    ISBN 1-55766-686-5 (pbk.:alk. paper)
    1. Bilingualism in children.   2. Second language acquisition.   3. Language disorders in chil-
dren.   I. Paradis, Johanne.   II. Crago, Martha B., 1945–   III. Title.   IV. Series
P115.2.G458 2004
404'.2'083—dc22   2004002508

British Library Cataloguing in Publication data are available from the British Library.

Contents

Series Preface

The purpose of the *Communication and Language Intervention Series* is to provide meaningful foundations for the application of sound intervention designs to enhance the development of communication skills across the life span. We are endeavoring to achieve this purpose by providing readers with presentations of state-of-the-art theory, research, and practice.

In selecting topics, editors, and authors, we are not attempting to limit the contents of this series to viewpoints with which we agree or that we find most promising. We are assisted in our efforts to develop the series by an editorial advisory board consisting of prominent scholars representative of the range of issues and perspectives to be incorporated in the series.

Well-conceived theory and research on development and intervention are vitally important for researchers, educators, and clinicians committed to the development of optimal approaches to communication and language intervention. The content of each volume reflects our view of the symbolic relationship between intervention and research: Demonstrations of what may work in intervention should lead to analysis of promising discoveries and insights from developmental work that may in turn fuel further refinement by intervention researchers. We trust that the careful reader will find much that is of great value in this volume.

An inherent goal of this series is to enhance the long-term development of the field by systematically furthering the dissemination of theoretically and empirically based scholarship and research. We promise the reader an opportunity to participate in the development of this field through debates and discussions that occur throughout the pages of the *Communication and Language Intervention Series*.

Editorial Advisory Board

About the Authors

Fred Genesee, Ph.D., Professor, Department of Psychology, McGill University, Stewart Biological Sciences Building, 1205 Doctor Penfield Avenue, Montreal, Quebec H3A 1B1, Canada

Dr. Genesee is the author of nine books and numerous articles in scientific, professional, and popular journals and publications. He has carried out extensive research on alternative approaches to bilingual education, including second/foreign language immersion programs for language majority students and alternative forms of bilingual education for language minority students. This work has systematically documented the longitudinal language development (oral and written) and academic achievement of students educated through the media of two languages—their home language and another language. Along with Donna Christian and Liz Howard, Dr. Genesee is currently involved in a longitudinal national study of a number of two-way immersion programs in the United States of America. He has consulted with policy groups in Canada, Estonia, Germany, Hong Kong, Italy, Japan, Latvia, Russia, Spain, and the United States on issues related to second language teaching and learning in school-age learners.

Dr. Genesee is also interested in basic issues related to language learning, representation, and use in bilingual children. His work in this domain focuses on simultaneous acquisition of two languages during early infancy and childhood; his specific interests include language representation (lexical and syntactic) in early stages of bilingual acquisition, transfer in bilingual development, structural and functional characteristics of child bilingual code-mixing, and communication skills in young bilingual children. A new line of research will examine the language/speech processing skills of preverbal bilingual and second language infants. Collectively, this work seeks to extend understanding of the limits of the human faculty for language acquisition, which, to date, has been based primarily on studies of monolingual acquisition.

Johanne Paradis, Ph.D., Assistant Professor, Department of Linguistics, University of Alberta, 4-46 Assiniboia Hall, Edmonton, Alberta T6G 2E7, Canada

Dr. Paradis completed her doctorate in psychology and pursued postdoctoral studies in communication disorders, both at McGill University. She has published numerous articles in scientific journals on bilingual and second language children, both typically developing and with specific language impairment (SLI). Before completing her doctorate, she taught English as a Second Language to adults and children for 10 years. Dr. Paradis is currently pursuing two lines of research. One line is concerned with bilingual children with SLI (e.g., Do bilingual children with SLI exhibit difficulties equally in both of their languages? Do bilingual children with SLI exhibit more severe difficulties than monolingual children with SLI?). Her second line of research consists of comparisons between typically developing children learning a second language (minority children in particular) and monolingual children with SLI (e.g., How is their oral language similar and different? Are there aspects of language use particular to children with SLI and not to children learning a second language?). Both lines of research are aimed at developing ways to identify the clinical population among children in multilingual settings.

Martha B. Crago, Ph.D., Professor, School of Communication Sciences and Disorders, McGill University, Beatty Hall, 1266 Pine Avenue West, Montreal, Quebec H3G 1A8, Canada

Dr. Crago has bachelor of arts, master's of science, and doctoral degrees from McGill University. Prior to becoming a professor in communication sciences and disorders at McGill, she worked as a speech-language pathologist. At present, Dr. Crago is McGill's Dean of Graduate and Postdoctoral Studies and Associate Provost (Academic Programs). Her research has focused on cross-linguistic and cross-cultural studies of the acquisition of Inuktitut, French, English, and Arabic across a variety of learners, including bilingual children as well as children with language impairments. Her research has been published in numerous articles, books, and book chapters.

Dr. Crago has been the President of the Association des Doyen(nes) des Etudes Supérieures du Québec and President of the Canadian Association of Graduate Studies (CAGS) and a member of the Executive Board of the Council of Graduate Studies (USA). She also serves on a number of Canadian national committees and review boards, including the Standing

Committee on Fellowships and Career Development of the Social Sciences and Humanities Research Council of Canada, Le Chantier du Relève des Fonds Québecois de Recherche en Nature et Technologie, and the Steering Committee for the Evaluation of the Strategic Training Initiative in Health Research of the Canadian Institutes for Health Research.

Foreword

It is well known that millions of children around the world learn more than one language. Although we know that young children acquire second (and even third) languages more readily than do adults, it is easy to imagine that there is some cost to learning more than one language. As a result of learning a second language, shouldn't children be less well-versed in each language than their monolingual peers? Or pay a price in some other area of cognitive development? When it comes to children who have difficulties acquiring a single language—children with language impairment—we might think that adding a second language would be too much of a burden to bear. If the first language is weak, the second language is sure to be weaker. Is this true?

A volume covering important questions such as these can easily find an audience among scholars, policy makers, educators, or parents. But preparing a single volume that will be easily read by all of these types of readers is quite another matter. An accomplishment of this sort requires that the authors know the material so well they can communicate it in a manner that is understandable to all. No easy feat, yet, this is what we have in *Dual Language Development and Disorders.*

In preparing this book, Genesee, Paradis, and Crago have struck a rare balance. They review scientific evidence, yet present case studies of fictional children; they declare their professional biases, yet are quick to point out instances in which a direction opposite to their view is most appropriate. As a result of reading this work, an educator will be able to argue the evidence for different models of schooling, and policy makers will be able to address big questions such as whether bilingual programs can enable children to learn a second language as quickly as programs conducted exclusively in the second language. From the pages of this book, speech-language pathologists will have a means of determining whether a child's grammatical profile reflects some universal feature of language impairment or simply a pattern that is characteristic of the specific language being acquired. And, crucially, parents will have a clearer understanding of the factors to consider when deciding if they should use more than one language with their child in the home or enroll their child in a school where another language is spoken.

To deal with such issues in a coherent manner, the authors must set the stage for the reader. They do so by making distinctions between bilingual language learners and second language learners on the one hand, and between members of a majority ethnolinguistic group and members of a minority ethnolinguistic group on the other. The conjunction of these two distinctions leads to the four-way split that serves as one of the major organizing principles of the book. Fictional (but realistic) children are described who can be placed in each of the resulting four quadrants. This organization is a sure way of keeping track of the important issues while avoiding oversimplification.

Given that this volume will attract readers with diverse backgrounds and goals, each reader is sure to be surprised by some piece of evidence or line of argument. This was certainly true for me. For example, I had assumed that code-mixing—the use of two languages between or even within sentences—probably reflected limitations in the speaker's proficiency with the nondominant language. However, the changes from one language to another seem to obey linguistic boundaries at the clause or even phrase level. It seems paradoxical that one needs a fair degree of linguistic sophistication even when bailing out of a language in the middle of a sentence! Also news to me was the fact that even children acquiring a second language with relative ease will sometimes employ a syntactic construction permitted only in the first language (e.g., showing the relative clause order of Cantonese when speaking in English). The importance of this finding is that the occasional presence of such errors should not be taken as a signal that a child cannot cope with two languages.

The surprises also came from areas of the book that covered topics in which I claim some expertise. As one who studies monolingual children with specific language impairment (SLI), I was surprised to see so few differences between bilingual children with SLI and their monolingual counterparts in each language. The surprise did not come in the fact that the same child with SLI will show two different grammatical profiles depending on the language being spoken. (I had often assumed that the same child, born and raised in a different country, would show a different pattern of linguistic strengths and weaknesses.) Rather, the surprise came in learning that bilingual children with SLI do not appear to acquire language more slowly than monolingual children with SLI. Along with rather profound implications for education and treatment, these findings have important implications for theory. For example, they suggest that our usual way of thinking about the allocation of linguistic and related cognitive resources might require modification.

The authors have done us a great service in writing this volume. The book can be used as a reference or as a springboard for future research. It can be used for science or for policy. However, I believe its greatest contribution will rest at the level of the individual. Many parents will be in a better position to make sound decisions about their children's language experiences thanks to reading this book.

Laurence B. Leonard
Department of Audiology and Speech Sciences
Purdue University

Acknowledgments

We would like to thank the following people (in alphabetical order) for helpful comments on earlier versions of this volume and on the research that has been reported in it: Naomi Holobow (Montreal), Leila Ranta (University of Alberta), Mabel Rice (University of Kansas), Gail Venable (San Francisco), and Lydia White (McGill University).

We would also like to acknowledge the generous support we have received from the following granting agencies that have funded our research on bilingual and second language learners: The Social Sciences and Humanities Research Council of Canada, Ottawa; The Hospital for Sick Children's Foundation, Toronto; The Alberta Heritage Foundation for Medical Research, Edmonton; and the Kativik School Board, Montreal.

VOLUME 11

Dual Language Development and Disorders

SECTION I

Foundations

Introduction

Children come in all shapes and sizes. They differ in myriad ways that delight, puzzle, and challenge their caregivers. These differences make children unique individuals and make parenting a challenge and a joy. For educators, doctors, language development specialists, and other adults who provide professional support to children, these differences are a professional responsibility that can be particularly challenging when the child's differences are not part of the professional's background. In this book, we focus on children who, in addition to having the differences that all children embody, are different linguistically and culturally. They are **dual language learners**—preschool and school-age children who have learned two languages simultaneously from infancy and children who are in the process of learning a second language.

Simultaneous acquisition of two languages or learning a second language after a first language has been learned does not in itself make children different; there are probably as many dual language children in the world as monolingual children (Tucker, 1998). But being bilingual or learning a second language during infancy and childhood introduces variation among children that enhances their individual differences. Dual language children are often treated as if they are different, especially in communities where monolingual children are treated as the norm. When monolingual children are taken as the reference point for understanding all children's language development, then dual language children present differences that must be interpreted from a different perspective, one that encompasses different ways of learning language. The bias toward monolingual children is reinforced by the preponderance of

---

BOX 1.1

Simultaneous bilingual children—children who learn two or more languages from birth or at least starting within the first year after birth. In effect, simultaneous bilingual children have two first languages. They can be exposed to languages in different ways, from their parents or siblings in the home, from child care workers in the home or in child care centers, or from grandparents or relatives, to mention the most common patterns. We also sometimes refer to these learners as *bilingual children*.

Second language learners/children—children who begin to learn an additional language after 3 years of age; that is, after the first language is established.

Dual language learners/children—both simultaneous bilingual children and second language learners. They may be preschool or school age.

---

research and theory on monolingual acquisition and the relative paucity of work on bilingual and second language learning children.

This book focuses on the typical language development of dual language children and the identification of children with disordered or impaired patterns of development that warrant clinical attention. A discussion of these children is found in the next section, Who Are Dual Language Children? The book also discusses the adults who care for these children because their care will make a difference in these children's lives. Appropriate identification of language impairment and effective treatment of impairment in bilingual and second language learning children are our ultimate concerns. Our goal is to present a comprehensive and up-to-date synthesis of what we know about typical and impaired bilingual and second language acquisition for professionals who work with children with language disorders and for parents of these children so that they are better able to make appropriate diagnoses and plan effective interventions in cases of impaired dual language development.

Our primary audience is speech-language pathologists who are on the frontline in caring for these children, but our audience also includes early childhood educators, special education professionals, school teachers with bilingual or second language learners in their classrooms, teacher educators who educate teachers who work with these children, and pediatricians and community health care professionals who may be consulted on the status of these children. Last, but not least, parents of bilingual and second language learning children are also part of our intended audience because parents have the utmost interest in knowing what we know about language impairment among such children. Most important, parents must ultimately interpret the advice given by professionals, and they must make important decisions on behalf of their children.

We believe that the identification and treatment of impaired language development is a process in which parents and language, education, medical, and child care professionals all play a role. These groups, however, do not play the same role. For example, parents and child care workers play a critical initial role in bringing children whom they suspect of impairment to the attention of language development specialists. Once identification has occurred, then the language development specialist's role is to diagnose the specific nature of the impairment and to recommend treatment. In other words, different people play different roles during the extended process that characterizes identification, treatment, and education of these children. It is critically important that each person in this chain be as well informed as possible, given the state of knowledge in the field, if he or she is to be effective.

Because our audience is broad and varied with respect to their formal background in research, theory, and clinical practice, we have sought to be as nontechnical as possible; however, when technicalities are important, we have not avoided them. Key concepts or big ideas are defined in boxes throughout the text. We define terms and ideas in a glossary at the end of the book to aid those readers who are less familiar with some of the terms we use. The terms appear in bold throughout the book as a guide for information found in the glossary.

Our background is in research on dual language learning in preschool and school-age children. We are also educators who bring specific interests and experience to the book. Fred Genesee's educational background is in psychology. He has conducted extensive research on the effectiveness of immersion and bilingual forms of education for language majority and language minority students. Since 1988, his research has focused on the language development of children acquiring two languages simultaneously during the preschool years. He is interested in identifying typical patterns of language development in simultaneous bilingual children with a view to discovering the capacity of the brain for language learning. He has authored and edited a number of professional books for educators working with bilingual and second language learners. Johanne Paradis started her professional career as an English as a second language teacher. She subsequently earned a doctoral degree in psychology and since then has conducted research on the grammatical development of bilingual and second language children, including typically developing children and children with specific language impairment (SLI). Her research has focused on the similarities and differences in language learning among different types of learners, such as those with disorders and those who are learning a second language. Martha Crago worked for a number of years as a speech-language pathologist and was responsible for clinical training in speech-language pathology at McGill University before getting her doctorate in communication sciences and disorders at McGill

University. Her research interests have focused on language development and cultural identity as well as on the cross-linguistic nature of acquisition by children with typical language development and those with SLI.

WHO ARE DUAL LANGUAGE CHILDREN?

We use the terms *dual language children* and *dual language learners* generically throughout this book to refer to a diverse group of language learners. Before proceeding, we describe who these learners are and why they need to be considered as distinct groups at times. For our purposes in this book, dual language children differ from one another in two very important respects: 1) whether they are members of a majority ethnolinguistic community or a minority ethnolinguistic community, and 2) whether they have learned two languages simultaneously from infancy or have learned a second language after their first language is established.

A **majority ethnolinguistic community** is one in which the language is widely used and valued and thus has high social status, is associated with socioeconomic power, and typically has institutional support from governments. Speakers of mainstream English in most parts of the United States and Canada form a majority ethnolinguistic community. German speakers in Germany form a majority ethnolinguistic community in that country. A **minority ethnolinguistic community** is one in which the language is less widely spoken and valued and, thus, has lower social status, may be associated with less or no socioeconomic power, and may receive less or no institutional support. Examples of minority ethnolinguistic communities would be speakers of Cantonese (Chinese) in Canada and the United States, Spanish-speaking children in the United States, or Turkish-speaking children in Germany.

The majority–minority distinction is not binary but reflects end points along a continuum. For instance, some minority linguistic communities are more minority than others. The Spanish-speaking minority community in California is closer to the middle of the continuum than the Korean-speaking community there because the sheer number of Spanish speakers in California confers on them a certain status and power that Koreans, who are much fewer in number, lack. The status of a language can differ according to the region in which speakers of the language live; for example, in Canada as a whole, French speakers are a minority ethnolinguistic community, but in the province of Quebec, French speakers are the majority community. Or, as pointed out previously, the status of Spanish speakers varies considerably in the United States, from southern Florida and Texas, where it is relatively high, to the Midwest or Northwest, where it is relatively low.

When we refer to **simultaneous bilingual children** (or just **bilingual children**), we mean children who are exposed to and given opportunities

BOX 1.2

Majority ethnolinguistic community—a community of individuals who speak the language spoken by most of the members of the community and/or are members of the ethnic/cultural group that most members of the community belong to. The community may be as large as a country, or it may be a state or province within a country or some smaller unit. The majority language and culture usually have special recognition as the official language and culture of the community. In other cases, they are regarded unofficially as the high-status language and culture in the community. The majority language is the language used by most newspapers and other media and in the courts and by political bodies in the community. Examples are Anglo Americans in the United States, English Canadians in Canada, and native German speakers in Germany. We also use the term *majority group* synonymously.

Minority ethnolinguistic community—a community made up of individuals who speak a minority language and who belong to a minority culture. The language and culture may be in the demographic minority or have relatively low social, economic, and political power. Examples are Spanish speakers or individuals of Hispanic background in the United States, speakers of Inuktitut or Chinese in Canada, speakers of Navajo or Hopi in the United States, and Turkish speakers in Holland and Germany. We also use the term *minority group* synonymously.

to learn two languages from birth. Ideally, bilingual children are exposed to both languages equally from the outset, but this is not always the case, and we discuss the implications of exposure where relevant. When we refer to **second language learners,** we mean children who have already made significant progress toward acquisition of one language when they begin the acquisition of a second language. As we have already noted, we use the terms **dual language learners** or **dual language learning** to encompass both of these groups. There is no definitive point in development that demarcates bilingual from second language acquisition, although many researchers have accepted the cut-off to be 3 years of age because a first language can be well established at that point.

Thus, dual language children comprise four subgroups of language learners:

1. Children from a majority ethnolinguistic group who have learned or are learning two languages simultaneously from the outset (see the profile of James)

2. Children from a majority ethnolinguistic group who have learned or are learning a second language after their first language is established (see the profiles of Samantha and Trevor)

	Majority group	Minority group
Simultaneous bilinguals	James	Bistra Pasquala
Second language learners	Samantha Trevor	Carlos Bonnie Pauloosie

Figure 1.1. Types of dual language learners.

3. Children from a minority ethnolinguistic group who have learned or are learning two languages simultaneously from the outset (see the profiles of Bistra and Pasquala)

4. Children from a minority ethnolinguistic group who have learned or are learning a second language after their first language is established (see the profiles of Carlos, Bonnie, and Pauloosie)

   We have represented these subgroups graphically in Figure 1.1. In order to put personal faces on these children, we describe each group with reference to individual, fictional children who have the primary characteristics of their subgroup. Like other kinds of caricatures, however, our fictional examples gloss over some individual differences that are important to clinicians. We refer to these children throughout the book to exemplify the kinds of children we are talking about.

PROFILES OF SIMULTANEOUS BILINGUAL CHILDREN

James

James lives in Montreal, Quebec. His mother (Marie-Claire) is French Canadian and although she speaks English and French fluently, she uses only (or primarily) French with James and has done so since he was born 5 years ago. James's father, Eric, is English Canadian. Eric is functionally bilingual in English and French, but he uses only (or primarily) English with James. James's parents decided to speak their respective native languages to him so that he will grow up bilingual. In effect, James has two first languages—he is a simultaneous bilingual child. James hears and uses both French and English on a daily basis at home. He also uses both languages outside the home with schoolmates and friends of his family, some who speak only English or only French and some who speak both. His French is a little stronger than his English because his family lives in a neighborhood of

Montreal that is predominantly French speaking, but he is functionally proficient in both languages. James is a **majority group** simultaneous bilingual child because he is growing up in a family that is part of Quebec's two dominant cultural groups—English and French. This means not only that there is strong support for both his languages in the family but also that both have widespread utility in the community at large—in stores, with friends, at the movies, and eventually in the job market.

A growing number of children around the world are like James; they are children of parents from the majority group who learn two first languages. In James's case, he is learning his two languages from his parents. In other cases, the sources of language input might be different—from grandparents or child care workers. Box 1.3 shows an excerpt from *The New York Times* (2002) about English-speaking parents who are choosing to employ Spanish-speaking au pairs (nannies) who take care of the children while the parents are at work; by entrusting the care of their children with Spanish-speaking child care providers, these parents are seeking to give their children the opportunity to learn Spanish along with English. Psycholinguistically speaking, simultaneous bilingual children like James are robust language learners who are likely to acquire full proficiency in both languages because the environment in which they live supports the learning of additional languages with no cost to either language.

Bistra

Bistra is 4 years old and lives in Iowa. Her parents are both graduate students completing their doctoral degrees in the same Slavic studies department, which is where they met. Bistra's father, an American, is a native speaker of English who is also a proficient second language speaker of Russian and knows some Bulgarian. Bistra's mother is a Bulgarian who immigrated to the United States. She is a fluent second language speaker of both English and Russian as well as a native speaker of Bulgarian. Bistra's mother has spoken to her exclusively in Bulgarian from birth, and her father uses exclusively English with her. The parents speak to each other in English or sometimes in Russian. Bistra attends a child care center where only English is spoken. Like James, Bistra is a simultaneous bilingual child because she has been exposed to two languages consistently since birth. But, unlike James, one of her two languages is not widely spoken outside her home, so she would be considered a member of a minority ethnolinguistic community.

Bistra's mother considers it a high priority for her daughter to speak and eventually read and write Bulgarian fluently; however, achieving this goal will be a challenge. There is no Bulgarian-speaking community in Bistra's city, so aside from her family and a few of her parents' friends, Bistra has no exposure to Bulgarian, and, in particular, she has no opportunity on

---

BOX 1.3

The New York Times
September 19, 2002
"Hello Mommy, Hola Nanny:
Immigrant Baby Sitters Double as Language Teachers"
by Mireya Navarro

When Daniel Etkin first spoke, he said words like "mommy" and "vac-uum," perhaps not what his daddy most wanted to hear but a reflection of his fascination with the vacuum cleaner.

But Daniel's first words also included "agua" (water) and "bonito" (pretty), taught to him by the Salvadoran nanny who has been at his side since he was a week old.

The nanny, Morena Lopez, does not speak English and his parents are not fluent in Spanish, so at the tender age of 2, Daniel is the only person in the household with the facility to communicate between them. And as with many other children in New York City and other areas with large immigrant populations, the nanny in Daniel's case not only feeds him and watches after him but has become his language instructor.

The rising demand for nanny services by working parents over the last decades and the niche that new immigrants have found in such work have combined to make nannies de facto language teachers to children of English-speaking parents. That trend, along with many children whose immigrant parents speak other languages, has given higher visibility to a cultural phenomenon in many playgrounds: the bilingual toddler. (p. B1)

---

a day-to-day basis to use Bulgarian with peers. In addition, Bistra's child care center uses English, and her schooling will be in English. Even at 4 years of age, she speaks English more proficiently than she speaks Bulgarian, and sometimes she switches to English when speaking with her mother.

Maintaining the **heritage language,** or the language of the country of origin, is often a struggle for many immigrant families. Children like Bistra may go through a stage where they refuse to speak the minority language and insist on using only English, even with people with whom they have used their heritage language most of the time. Some children will lose most or all of their fluency in their heritage language once they attend school. Sometimes, it is impossible for parents to find resources such as cultural events or books and videos in the heritage language in order to give their children a broad and rich range of experience with the language. But, the more parents persist in speaking the heritage language, and the more contexts they expose their children to where that language is used, including traveling back to the country of origin, the more likely their children will retain an ability to speak that language after school entry. It is especially important to give minority language children opportunities to interact with other children the same age in the heritage language to promote full, native-like fluency in it. Bistra is a simultaneous bilingual child at age 4, but whether she will become a fully proficient bilingual adult is not entirely certain. We discuss this issue further in Chapter 6.

Pasquala

Pasquala is 6 years old, and, like Bistra and James, she is a simultaneous bilingual child because she has been exposed to both Spanish and English from birth. Pasquala was born in the New York City area, like both of her parents, and her family still lives near New York City. Her mother is a nurse, and her father works for an insurance company. Pasquala's grandparents on both her mother's and her father's side moved to New York from Puerto Rico when they were young adults. Pasquala's parents and grandparents all speak both Spanish and English in the home and in the community, although they try to speak more Spanish than English in the home. Pasquala lives in a neighborhood where there are many families of Puerto Rican heritage, so she is exposed to Spanish not just in the context of her family but also at local businesses, in church, and with other children on the playgrounds and at school. She is in grade 1 in a bilingual school. We talk in greater detail about language and academic development in bilingual programs in Chapter 7.

Pasquala is unusual among bilingual children in that she is a third-generation immigrant, yet she still speaks the heritage language. Many second-generation immigrants lose their heritage language. Pasquala's family has managed to maintain Spanish because of their pride in their heritage and their belief in the importance of passing on that heritage. In addition, New York Puerto Ricans can easily travel back and forth between Puerto Rico and the United States. As a result, Spanish is a prevalent minority language in New York City, and Pasquala's family lives in an entire community in which Spanish is used every day.

Unlike James and Bistra, Pasquala is exposed to English and Spanish from both her parents, so neither parent is associated with only one language and both parents speak Spanish and English fluently. For some families raising simultaneous bilingual children, it is difficult to maintain the child's bilingualism if one parent is monolingual. For example, Bistra's father speaks some Bulgarian but not well enough to have an extensive conversation with his daughter. In contrast, Pasquala can speak either English or Spanish freely with both parents. Because Pasquala's parents speak both English and Spanish, they sometimes mix words from the two languages together in one conversation, even within one sentence. This phenomenon, called **code-mixing,** is common in bilingual communities across the globe. Details about how code-mixing works and how bilingual children code-mix are covered in Chapter 5.

It might seem that Pasquala is growing up in a similar environment to James; however, in Figure 1.1 we have considered her a minority simultaneous bilingual child, like Bistra. This is because even though Spanish is widely spoken in New York and in many regions of the United States, it does not have the same high status that French does in Canada. However, even though Pasquala is a minority bilingual child like Bistra, because Spanish is widely spoke in her community and she will grow up with many opportunities to use Spanish, she has a good chance of maintaining her bilingualism throughout her life. Contrasting Bistra's and Pasquala's situations exemplifies another point made previously that the concept of minority language is on a continuum. Some languages are much more in the minority than others, and this can affect children's exposure to and attitudes toward those languages and, in turn, can affect their chances of becoming bilingual adults.

PROFILES OF SECOND LANGUAGE LEARNERS

Samantha

Samantha is 7 years old and lives in Tucson, Arizona. Samantha's parents are both monolingual English speakers, and consequently, Samantha learned and used English in the home during her preschool years. Samantha's parents, however, decided to send her to a Spanish-speaking child care center when she was 3 years old and then to a Spanish **immersion program** when she turned 5 so that she could become bilingual. They felt that it would be good for her to be bilingual in Spanish and English because there is a large Hispanic community in the southwestern United States, as well as other regions of the country, and because Spanish is one of the most widely spoken languages in the world. Knowing Spanish would afford Samantha opportunities for travel and professional work on a global scale.

Like James, Samantha is also considered a majority group dual language learner because her family and the community in which they live are members of the majority ethnolinguistic group. As a result, Samantha also has all of the linguistic and cultural advantages of being part of a high-status ethnolinguistic group. There is no question of her losing her English even if she has extensive exposure to Spanish in preschool and later, in elementary school. She has intensive exposure to English and mainstream American culture at home and in the community, and she will undoubtedly learn the values and orientations of that group at the same time as she learns Spanish and some of the cultural ways and values of Spanish-speaking cultural groups in her community.

In contrast to James, Samantha is a second language learner for the obvious reason that she began acquiring her second language after her first language had been established. Samantha is a fortunate second language learner because, with a little bit of effort on her parent's part, she has access to many native Spanish speakers, including adults and children, and this will greatly enhance her probabilities of acquiring full functional proficiency in Spanish. Other second language learners are not so fortunate because there are no or few native speakers of the second language in the community. For example, some children in the state of Oregon begin to learn Japanese at 5 years of age, when they begin their primary schooling in one of the Japanese immersion programs in that state. Because all of the other children in the Japanese immersion program are native English speakers and there is no sizable Japanese-speaking population in Oregon, the Japanese immersion students have relatively little access to native speaking models, and thus, they have a much greater challenge in acquiring full proficiency in Japanese. In response to this challenge, the Japanese immersion schools have arranged for exchange visits with schools in Japan so that the immersion children can spend part of their summer vacation living with Japanese families. Many parents around the world are choosing to send their children to second language immersion schools so that they will become functionally proficient in two languages (see Christian & Genesee, 2001, and Johnson & Swain, 1997, for case studies of such programs). We discuss second language learning in school settings in greater detail in Chapter 7.

Trevor

Trevor is 6 years old. He was born in a small suburban community north of Chicago. Trevor's parents are both native-born Americans who speak English. Trevor's father works for a large pharmaceutical company that has extensive international business dealings, and he was relocated to Berlin, Germany, 2 years ago to head up the European office. Trevor had not yet started school in America when they moved. Trevor's parents could have sent him to the American International School in Berlin, where English is used to teach other American and English-speaking children of relocated parents, but they decided to send him to a German public school so that he could learn German and socialize with other children from Germany. Trevor found the first 6 months of schooling in German difficult because of his lack of competence in German, so his parents arranged for him to have a German language tutor who helped him learn German and keep up with his school work. In addition, Trevor's teachers met with his parents and developed an individualized program of instruction for him so that he had time to learn German before he was exposed to the same curriculum of studies as native German-speaking students.

The transition to the all-German school, although a challenge for Trevor, went smoothly because he had a number of advantages that helped him adapt. First, he was already well on his way to learning to read and write in English when he entered the German school because he had advanced emergent literacy skills. This is common among children in families of professional parents who read and write a lot. Most children who can read and write in one language make the transition to reading and writing in another language relatively easily. Above all else, Trevor was highly motivated to learn German in order to fit in and make friends with his German-speaking classmates.

Although German has become Trevor's primary language in school and outside school when he is with his friends, English continues to be a dominant force in his life; indeed, there is no question of Trevor giving up his English as he learns German. Although Trevor is learning German as a second language in Germany and is surrounded by the German language all day, every day, he is considered to be a member of a majority ethnolinguistic group because of the status of English in his family and internationally. Trevor, like Samantha, has a lot of advantages that help him become bilingual. He is an example of additive bilingualism.

Carlos

Carlos is an example of a second language learner from a **minority group**. Carlos is 6 years old and lives in California with his parents, both of whom speak Spanish and very little English. They are migrant workers who maintain contact with family and friends in Mexico but spend most of their time living and working in the United States. Carlos was born in the United States but has grown up speaking only Spanish. Carlos's first real contact with English came when he started kindergarten in a rural school in southern California. All of Carlos's teachers speak only English, and all of their instruction is in English. Carlos is faced with a triple challenge: to learn English for purposes of schooling; to keep up with his school work in English; and to begin to integrate into the larger Anglo American culture. Because Carlos has grown up in a Spanish-speaking, largely Mexican enclave in California, he is most comfortable and competent in cultural contexts that are Mexican in orientation. In fact, he has some difficulty knowing exactly how to behave with monolingual English-speaking children because their cultural norms for interacting with one another and with adults are different. The educational challenges that Carlos, and children like Carlos, face are considerable, not simply because his education is in English, but also because his parents' literacy skills in Spanish are not well developed and, as a result, they do not read and write in either English or Spanish. This means that Carlos has not had the benefits of family literacy, unlike many children from more socioeconomically advantaged, English-speaking homes, who have plenty of books at home, are read to at home, and observe their parents reading and writing for both work-related and personal reasons. Research shows that family literacy facilitates children's acquisition of literacy skills in school (Goldenberg, 2003).

Despite his lack of full functional proficiency in English, Carlos is often referred to by teachers and educational authorities as bilingual. This is misleading because, in fact, he was really monolingual in Spanish upon school entry. The situation is even more complicated because, in reality, there is no single way to classify all Hispanic American children; the homes and communities in which they live are incredibly diverse. The same is true for children of Asian and Southeast Asian backgrounds. Of particular importance to our concerns in this book is that not all children of Hispanic background necessarily speak Spanish or are bilingual, even though there is a tendency to label all such children bilingual. Many children of Hispanic background, but not all, come to school speaking only Spanish (like Carlos); some come to school speaking only English; and some come to school speaking both (like Pasquala). Those who speak only Spanish at school entry will learn English only once they have begun schooling. Thus, some children of Hispanic background would fall into the simultaneous bilingual learner group, whereas others would be considered second language learners.

Valid information about the language background and status of minority language children is important because there are different patterns of development and different challenges for simultaneous bilingual children versus second language learners. Labeling minority language children bilingual at school entry may be misleading because not all such children are in fact bilingual; indeed, some might never achieve advanced levels of proficiency in both English and their heritage language if English is promoted at the expense of the heritage language (see Chapter 6).

The important point here is that the language situation for children from **minority language** backgrounds can be complicated and the terminology used to refer to them misleading. For this reason, we have included profiles of three children from language minority backgrounds.

Bonnie

Bonnie is 8 years old and was born in Taiwan. Her parents are both speakers of Mandarin (Chinese), and the family immigrated to Vancouver, Canada, when Bonnie was 4½. Both of her parents are professionals with well-paying jobs in the private sector, and unlike many immigrant families, they both spoke English reasonably well before arriving in Canada, although Bonnie did not. She is a second language learner like Samantha because her first language, Mandarin, was well established before she began learning her second language, English. When Bonnie began kindergarten after having been in Canada a few months, she spoke very little English.

Bonnie belongs to a minority ethnolinguistic community like Bistra, but Mandarin is much more available to her than Bulgarian is to Bistra. Vancouver is a large, cosmopolitan city on the west coast of Canada with a substantial Asian community. Bonnie's parents rarely socialize with non-Chinese people, so she has a great deal of social contact with adults and other children her own age who speak the heritage language. Her parents rent videos in Mandarin, buy Chinese newspapers, and plan to hire a Chinese-speaking private tutor to teach Bonnie piano lessons. There are restaurants and shopping centers where mainly Mandarin and Cantonese are spoken. Thus, even though English is the **majority language**, there is every reason to believe that Bonnie will grow up to be bilingual in both Mandarin and English. Bonnie is fortunate because knowing these two languages fluently will maximize her educational and professional choices.

Not all minority second language learners are as fortunate as Bonnie. Many immigrant families do not have easy access to other speakers and resources in their language; nor do they enjoy the kind of social status that Chinese Canadians and Chinese Americans have in cities like Vancouver and San Francisco, respectively. Moreover, in contrast to Bonnie's parents, many immigrant parents struggle to earn a living, work at several jobs at the same time, and cope with difficult issues of integration into their new communities. These challenges all add to the complexity of raising children and supporting their education. Carlos's parents are an example of immigrant parents who are facing these challenges. Also, as we mentioned previously for minority group simultaneous bilingual children like Bistra, without strong support outside the home, many minority second language children lose their ability to speak their first language.

Pauloosie

Pauloosie is an 8-year-old Inuk boy who lives in a small community (population: 500 Inuit, 15 non-Inuit) in Northern Quebec (Nunavik). He is the fourth child in a family of six children. Both of his parents and all of his siblings speak Inuktitut as their first language. Although Inuktitut is the language of his home and of the community, many people in his settlement, including Pauloosie's parents and all of his nuclear and extended family members, speak some English. Two of his brothers have received second language schooling in French so that they speak Inuktitut, French, and whatever English that they have picked up from watching television and overhearing English-language interactions with non-Inuit who live in or visit the settlement. Pauloosie's community is many hundreds of miles and a prohibitively expensive airplane ride from the cities of southern Canada.

He is not likely to go to a non-Inuit community unless he becomes very ill and needs medical services or until he goes to postsecondary school. There are, however, numerous television channels available that broadcast in English and French. In comparison, there is only one Inuktitut-language television channel.

Pauloosie attends a school in which he was taught in Inuktitut exclusively in kindergarten, grade 1, and grade 2. As a result, he is not only a fluent native speaker of Inuktitut, but he can also read and write it. This year, he entered grade 3. His family had to choose whether he would be educated in French or in English. They chose English for Pauloosie because they knew the grade 3 English teacher and liked her teaching style. From this year until the end of secondary school, Pauloosie will have only 1 hour of instruction each day on the Inuktitut language, the Inuit culture, or the Inuit religion.

Pauloosie, like many of his classmates, finds grade 3 an unsettling year. For the first time, he has a non-Inuit teacher. In fact, for Pauloosie this is his first sustained contact with an adult who is not an Inuk. This is also the first time that Pauloosie has had to speak English on a regular basis and for a number of hours each day. His teacher is in her second year of teaching. Her teacher education program had no courses in second language or multicultural education. Pauloosie has been surprised by many things, even in these first weeks at school. In his previous classes, he was never asked to speak alone in front of others, to raise his hand when called on by his Inuit teachers, or to look a teacher in the eye. His classmates and he answered together as a group, shared their work, and often copied the work of the smartest girl in class to learn from her. These ways of learning were considered appropriate by his Inuit teachers, but his grade 3 teacher wants all of his work done alone. He was surprised when she called what he considered to be sharing work with others as *cheating* or *copying*. Pauloosie finds it uncomfortable to be called on and to have his answers to the teacher's seemingly incessant questions evaluated. He feels ashamed, even if he knows the correct answer, and he misses the comfort of answering as one voice in a group of other children's voices. Pauloosie, like the other children in his community, has the special challenge of encountering another culture and language for the first time in school at age 8.

Summary

In these profiles, we have tried to present a broad cross-section of different kinds of dual language learners. These children vary with respect to their sociocultural status, community, and family circumstances and whether they are simultaneous bilingual children or second language learners. In the chapters that follow, we refer to these children as we describe typical patterns of

---

BOX 1.4

Specific language impairment (SLI)—a developmental disorder in which children have delayed or deviant language development; however, children with SLI have typical intelligence, hearing, and social-emotional behavior as well as no frank neurological impairment.

---

dual language development. It is important to understand the typical patterns in order to better identify children with impairments that affect their capacity for language acquisition.

WHAT IS SPECIFIC LANGUAGE IMPAIRMENT?

This book addresses dual language development in children with typical development as well as those with difficulty learning language. There are a number of reasons that can cause children to have difficulty learning language. For instance, their difficulties can be a result of autism or pervasive developmental disorders. Or the children can be hearing impaired and experience difficulty in learning oral language without adequate auditory input. The particular developmental learning problem that concerns us in this book is most frequently referred to as **specific language impairment,** or **SLI**. Over the years, a variety of other terms have been used to describe the same phenomenon, including *childhood aphasia* and *dysphasia*.

SLI affects approximately 7% of 5-year-olds in North America (Leonard, 1998). The incidence of the disorder depends to some degree on how it is defined and the criteria for diagnosis. Like dyslexia, SLI is a developmental disorder that is defined by exclusionary criteria. Children with SLI have typical hearing and intelligence. They are not children with pervasive developmental delay, nor do they have any apparent neurological damage, such as epilepsy or traumatic brain injury. They also do not have social and emotional disorders, such as autism or autism spectrum disorders. In short, these children experience typical development in every area but one: learning to speak and use language.

No one is sure what causes SLI. It is a developmental disorder that has been found in children who speak any language that has been studied to date, and it affects boys more than girls. There is also evidence that it occurs in certain families, which has led to research about its genetic basis (Crago & Gopnik, 1994). Over the years, a number of theories have been posited about the causal nature of the impairment. Some research has indicated that it might be due to a problem in auditory processing (Tallal, 1993). Other theories contradict this finding and attribute the causality to difficulties in certain cognitive abilities, in particular, to those that have to do with either the mental representation of language in the brain or the cognitive processing load of language in a developing brain (Ellis-Weismer, 1996; Johnston, 1999; Rice & Wexler, 1996).

The onset of language is delayed in children with SLI. They can have problems with both speaking and understanding language that is spoken to them. Furthermore, particular aspects of language development cause them special difficulty. Some of these difficulties give their language certain properties that are similar to language spoken by younger children or even to children in the early stage of learning a second language. For this reason, sometimes a second language learner will be misdiagnosed as having SLI. Such misdiagnosis has sometimes led to an overidentification of second language learners as impaired language learners. In any case, some aspects of the language acquisition of children with SLI reveal a pattern of delay. Other aspects of their language development are different from the language of younger children and second language learners. Therefore, their language has been characterized as having certain "deviant" patterns of development.

In general, children with SLI have problems in mastering the specifics of the grammar of their language. This is true no matter which language they speak; however, certain grammatical forms are more difficult for them than others. Exactly how difficult a specific grammatical form is for one child with SLI can differ from what is problematic for another child with SLI. In other words, children with SLI are a fairly heterogeneous group; there is variation among them. There are also various degrees of severity of SLI. Furthermore, in much the same way that there are different patterns of typical acquisition across various languages, the patterns of impairment of children with SLI can differ depending on the language that they speak. For instance, English-speaking children with SLI have particular problems with marking tense on their verbs (Rice & Wexler, 1996). For example, they may say, "He go to school," even though they are able to use a similar /s/ sound to mark the plural or the possessive form, as in *the boy's shirts*. Our own work with French-speaking children with SLI has shown us that children speaking that language often omit object pronouns (*le, la, les*) in the middle of a sentence (Paradis, Crago, & Genesee, 2003), thereby creating ungrammatical sentences. Interestingly enough, they do not have the same problem with *le, la,* and *les* when they are used as articles before a noun.

In addition to grammatical problems, children with SLI have smaller vocabularies than children with more typical development. As they grow older, speaking and understanding complex sentences is problematic for them. Once in school, children with SLI often have trouble with reading. By grade 2, approximately 42% of children with SLI have reading disabilities. This has been shown to persist into grade 4, where research has shown that approximately 36% of children with SLI continue to have reading difficulties

(Catts, Fey, Tomblin, & Zhang, 2002). The reading and writing problems of children with SLI can affect their performance in other school subjects. For instance, word problems in math are difficult for them due to the complexity of language used in such problems. Overall, the language of children with SLI improves with time and with treatment. Some children's linguistic abilities even develop into the typical range for their age. Others never resolve all of their grammatical difficulties, even into adulthood. One study showed that 60% of children with SLI at 5 years, 6 months of age continued to have language learning disabilities at 15 years of age (Stothard, Snowling, Bishop, Chipchase, & Kaplan, 1998). Sometimes the terminology associated with having a language disorder changes when a child reaches school age. Even though a preschool child's SLI may be diagnosed, by the time that same child is in school, the label for the disorder may change. School-age children's language problems are often referred to as *learning disabilities* or, more precisely, as *language learning disabilities.*

A great deal is left to be learned about SLI, and many questions are yet to be answered. However, despite their difficulties in learning language, children with SLI have a remarkable set of linguistic abilities. They can and do acquire many complicated aspects of language. Moreover, many individuals with SLI lead very productive lives, often working in fields that do not emphasize verbal skills. We contend that a number of children with SLI can and do become dual language learners.

OUR APPROACH

We believe that competent treatment of impaired language development in dual language children requires an understanding of the typical course of bilingual and second language acquisition. Dual language children are clearly different from monolingual children, who are often used as the norm for judging what is typical or atypical. The challenge of providing effective services to dual language children with possible language disorders is to identify the differences in their language development that are cause for concern and that justify special intervention versus those that simply reflect different paths to normal language development. Consequently, we approach issues in language impairment first and foremost from the perspective of what we know about typical development in dual language children. Thus, we review research that has examined typical bilingual and second language learning children in a number of the chapters of this book.

We also believe that although language is the primary focus of concern when responding to the needs of children with language impairment, other domains of development are implicated and should be considered. In particular, cognitive, sociocultural, and educational aspects of development are relevant to a thorough understanding of language impairment in children who are still making major developmental transitions from infancy to childhood and from childhood to adolescence. Although a holistic approach is important in responding to all children with impaired language development, it is especially important in cases of dual language learning children because there are sociocultural, cognitive, and educational complexities in their lives that have significant bearing on their language development and status. Some of these complexities may not be apparent, especially to professionals who are themselves monolingual or are from different cultural backgrounds, but their implications are nevertheless consequential in the process of identifying and treating children with language impairment. In this book, we identify and discuss issues relevant to these other aspects of development along with language-specific issues.

Our approach is also characterized by an emphasis on scientific knowledge balanced by professional experience and judgment. The ability to acquire language is part of every child's natural, innate endowment. Our understanding of the nature of that endowment and of the details of language development that flow from it have been enriched enormously by scientific investigations since the 1980s (Genesee, 2003). This knowledge base should be familiar to those concerned about dual language children. At the same time, we recognize that there are gaps in our scientific knowledge base and that scientifically based knowledge is constantly growing and evolving. This is particularly true when it comes to impaired patterns of dual language learning because it is a relatively young and very complex field of scientific inquiry. Thus, although we are able to provide some clear descriptions of typical patterns for some aspects of development, we are compelled to make "best guesses" with respect to other aspects in order to provide as comprehensive coverage as possible.

Our best guesses are informed by our scientific knowledge and professional experiences working in the field for many years, but they are still open to scrutiny. It is not possible to be prescriptive about the diagnosis and treatment of dual language children because each child is different and, as we have just noted, our knowledge base is simply too inadequate at this time for us to confidently prescribe what to do in every case. We are as definitive as we can be, when appropriate; otherwise, we suggest guidelines or ways of thinking about critical issues in the field. We encourage readers to be critical in their own thinking about these issues and, when appropriate, to develop their own knowledge base from their clinical experiences and professional reading.

Finally, we believe that knowing two or more languages and being able to use them appropriately and effectively is a personal, social, professional, and societal asset. For many children, bilingualism is a fact of life linked to family and community circumstances. The children are born into families where more than one language is used, and thus needed, for day-to-day living. This situation can arise from having parents with different language backgrounds or grandparents who speak other languages (as experienced by James and Bistra). It can arise from growing up in a community where the dominant societal language differs from the language of the parents and the home (as experienced by Pasquala, Carlos, Bonnie, and Pauloosie). This situation affects children of immigrant families as well as children of parents who are living in a foreign country for a short time. In both cases, the children may need or simply want to learn the dominant language of the larger community. In other cases, bilingualism is a result of personal choice—when parents decide to expose their children to other languages so that the children will acquire and benefit from another language (as Samantha's parents chose to do).

More and more parents from majority group families in different regions of the world want their children to learn other world languages so that they can participate fully in the emerging global village. (Trevor and Samantha are examples of such cases.) They have organized their lives to give their children dual language experiences through special child care, preschool, or school programs. These parents are motivated by the recognition that individuals who know additional languages will be able to take real advantage of our growing interconnectedness with other people around the world.

ORGANIZATION OF THE BOOK

This book is organized into three sections that, in turn, are broken down into chapters, each with a specific focus. Section I, Foundations, includes Chapters 1–3. In Chapter 1, we define who dual language learners are and offer a definition of SLI. We also describe our approach to thinking and making decisions about dual language learners who are suspected of having impaired language development. Our approach is decidedly multidimensional; it involves many stakeholders and requires knowledge of typical as well as impaired patterns of development. In this chapter, we also seek to put faces on dual language learners so that readers have the same reference points as we do.

In Chapter 2, we discuss the language–culture connection; that is, the process that links language learning with becoming a member of a cultural group or groups. This developmental process shapes the lives of all children and is especially important in the case of dual language learners because they often have exposure to more than one culture and must learn to live in and mediate between these cultures. Interacting with multiple cultures has important implications for our understanding of dual language learners' language acquisition and ultimate language use.

We continue to consider the foundations of language learning in Chapter 3 by examining the language–cognition connection. In this chapter, we consider both the cognitive prerequisites and the cognitive consequences of dual language learning. More specifically, we consider whether infants and children have cognitive abilities that limit language learning to one language at a time or whether they are equally capable of learning two languages. We also examine whether the acquisition of additional languages, simultaneously or in succession, affects cognitive development—for better or for worse.

Section II, Understanding Bilingual and Second Language Acquisition, consists of Chapters 4–7. In this section, we discuss language-specific aspects of dual language learning in detail. Specifically, in Chapter 4, Bilingual First Language Acquisition, we review current research and theory concerning language development among children who acquire two languages simultaneously during infancy, that is, from birth to about 3 years of age. The emphasis in this chapter is on typical patterns of language development by children raised bilingually. Chapter 5 continues this focus by discussing an aspect of bilingual acquisition that is often controversial, poorly understood, and yet very important for our understanding of children who grow up with two languages—code-mixing.

Chapter 6 addresses issues in second language acquisition in children. Second language acquisition differs from bilingual first language acquisition in that it is the acquisition of another language after the first language has taken root and is functional. After 3 years of age, dual language learning is really second language learning and not simultaneous bilingual acquisition.

Chapter 7 discusses schooling in a second language. Here we extend the scope of our discussion to include children who are exposed to two or more languages in the context of schooling. These may be children who come to school speaking the dominant societal language (e.g., English in the United States) or who speak a minority language (e.g., Spanish in the United States). For the former group, dual language learning is usually a choice, whereas for the latter, it is a necessity. Each entails important educational as well as language-related issues that can be relevant to language development specialists.

The final section of the book—Section III, Diagnosis and Intervention—includes Chapter 8, in which we discuss issues related to the diagnosis and treatment of dual language children suspected of an impaired capacity for language development. Chapters 4–8 include a Summary and Implications section to draw readers' attention to the clinical implications of the material reported in each of these chapters.

There are some limitations to the scope of this book. We do not consider children who know or are acquiring a third or fourth language. This does not mean that multilingual children are unimportant; rather, too little scientific or systematic professional information exists about these children to permit adequate coverage. We further limit our discussion to children acquiring oral languages, although, in principle, bilingual or second language acquisition also includes the acquisition of signed along with oral languages. Again, this decision has been made for practical reasons—the lack of information about bilingual individuals who use sign language.

Finally, to avoid sexist terminology and the cumbersome use of *he or she* or *s/he,* we have randomly used *he* and *she* when we could not use the generic *they.*

REFERENCES

Catts, H.W., Fey, M.E., Tomblin, B., & Zhang, X. (2002). A longitudinal investigation of reading outcomes in children with language impairment. *Journal of Speech, Language, and Hearing Research, 45,* 1142–1157.

Christian, D., & Genesee, F. (Eds.). (2001). *Bilingual education.* Alexandria, VA: Teachers of English to Speakers of Other Languages.

Crago, M.B., & Gopnik, M. (1994). From families to phenotypes: Theoretical and clinical implications of research into the genetic basis of specific language impairment. In S.F. Warren & J. Reichle (Series Eds.) & R.V. Watkins & M.L. Rice (Vol. Eds.), *Communication and language intervention series: Vol. 4. Specific language impairments in children* (pp. 35–51). Baltimore: Paul H. Brookes Publishing Co.

Ellis-Weismer, S. (1996). Capacity limitations in working memory: The impact on lexical and morphological learning by children with language impairment. *Topics in Language Disorders, 17,* 33–44.

Genesee, F. (2003). Rethinking bilingual acquisition. In J.M. de Waele (Ed.), *Bilingualism: Challenges and directions for future research* (pp. 158–182). Clevedon, England: Multilingual Matters.

Goldenberg, C. (2003). Making schools work for low-income families in the 21st century. In S.B. Neuman & D.K. Dickinson (Eds.), *Handbook of early literacy research* (pp. 211–231). New York: The Guilford Press.

Johnston, J. (1999). Cognitive deficits in specific language impairment: Decision in spite of uncertainty. *Journal of Speech-Language Pathology and Audiology, 23,* 165–172.

Johnson, R.K., & Swain, M. (1997). *Immersion education: International perspectives.* New York: Cambridge University Press.

Leonard, L. (1998). *Children with specific language impairment.* Cambridge: MIT Press.

Navarro, M. (2002, September 19). Hello mommy, hola nanny: Immigrant baby sitters double as language teachers. *The New York Times,* p. B1.

Paradis, J., Crago, M., & Genesee, F. (2003). Object clitics as a clinical marker of SLI in French: Evidence from French–English bilingual children. In B. Beachley et al. (Eds.), *Proceedings of the Boston University Conference on Language Development* (pp. 638–649). Sommerville, MA: Cascadilla Press.

Rice, M., & Wexler, K. (1996). Toward tense as a clinical marker of specific language impairment. *Journal of Speech, Language, and Hearing Research, 39,* 1236–1257.

Stothard, S.E., Snowling, M.J., Bishop, D.V.M., Chipchase, B.B., & Kaplan, C.A. (1998). Language-impaired preschoolers: A follow-up into adolescence. *Journal of Speech, Language, and Hearing Research, 41,* 407–418.

Tallal, P. (1993). *Temporal information processing in the nervous system: Special reference to dyslexia and dysphasia.* New York: New York Academy of Sciences.

Tucker, G.R. (1998). A global perspective on multilingualism and multilingual education. In. J. Cenoz & F. Genesee (Eds.), *Beyond bilingualism: Multilingualism and multilingual education* (pp. 3–15). Clevedon, England: Multilingual Matters.

CHAPTER 2

Language and Culture

Children who speak two languages are exposed to two cultures. These cultures, like languages, may be relatively similar or different from one another. Children who are learning the languages of two very different cultures have a double learning task. They not only have to learn both of their languages, but they also have to learn how to use each language in culturally appropriate ways. Children are brought up to become members of their cultural group in part by the way the people of their culture interact and use language with them. They learn their cultural norms by observing and being exposed to the behaviors of the people who live with them, talk to them, parent them, and educate them. Language plays a central role in all of these socialization experiences. Children are also sometimes directly instructed in the culturally appropriate means of interacting and speaking, for example, when children are told that they should wait their turn before talking. The idea that culture and language are interwoven in the upbringing of a child has been called **language socialization.** Children are socialized into their culture through language, and, in turn, cultural patterning socializes children in how and with whom to use the language or languages they are learning.

Think for a moment about the dominant North American culture. Parents from this culture treat their children as conversational partners from birth (Ochs & Schieffelin, 1984). Tiny infants' cries and burps are interpreted as conversational turns; it is not uncommon for mainstream North American parents to respond to such bodily noises by saying such things as "Oh sweetie, listen to you. You are just so hungry. Mommy will give you some milk."

BOX 2.1

Language socialization—the study of language socialization has as its goal the understanding of how children become competent members of their social groups and the role language has in this process. Language socialization, therefore, concerns two major areas: socialization *through* the use of language and socialization *to* the use of language (Schieffelin, 1990).

Parents from the mainstream North American culture eagerly await their children's first words, attributing meaning to even early approximations of words. Parents label objects for children, then quiz them by asking the child to point to or name objects. Later, when the children in this culture can speak in words and small sentences, parents and relatives frequently address questions to them and ask children to recount events that have happened to them, including events where the adult has been present. In doing so, they are requesting that children display their ability to talk.

Children's verbal displays are greeted with enthusiasm by adults and older children. Many mainstream, middle-class adults believe that practicing and displaying talk in this way will help children become better talkers. Furthermore, young children are explicitly taught to use politeness words such as *thank you* and *please*. For instance, after giving her child something, a mother from with a middle-class, mainstream cultural background may ask the child to say "the magic word" (i.e., *thank you*).

In addition, children from mainstream North American culture are exposed to literacy activities well before they are expected to be able to read. In a sense, the children are being prepared to participate in a valued cultural and educational practice—reading. Even before children are 1 year old, parents show them books at bedtime, labeling pictures or reading stories in simple language. Parents often ask small children to point to pictures in the book. Later, they ask children questions about the story as they read it aloud. These specific language socialization practices seem like ordinary, expected, typical behaviors to many of our readers who consider them desirable ways to raise a child. They are, in fact, ways that socialize children to fit into the norms of the middle-class, mainstream North American culture; however, people from cultures with different belief systems and socialization practices may find these norms and behaviors to be peculiar and even untoward.

Contrast our description of the language socialization practices of the middle class, mainstream North American culture with some behaviors that we learned about during our research in certain Canadian First Nation and Inuit homes (Crago, 1988). The Inuit people who live in the north of

Canada inhabit small, remote villages. Until recently, they enjoyed a hunting and gathering society, where people lived nomadically, inhabiting tents and igloos. Traditionally, extended families lived together, with multiple generations interacting with each other on a daily basis. Although much has changed in their society, children in many homes of the eastern Arctic still grow up speaking Inuktitut. Babies are carried on their mothers' backs in the pouch of a long wool parka called an *amautiq*.

Typically, Inuit mothers do not converse with their babies. Instead, the children look out of their mothers' parkas, overseeing and overhearing their mothers' interactions with older children and adults. They become adept lookers and listeners. Inuit mothers address their babies using a rhyming, cadenced, affectionate talk. They do not interpret their babies' early vocalizations and bodily noises as talk and do not respond to them verbally. When their children are toddlers, Inuit parents do not often address the children directly. Instead, the children's needs are met silently, without requests for display, labeling, frequent questioning, or rehearsals of politeness terms. Book reading with young children is infrequent, and parents may actually frown on a school-age child who reads extensively because the child is sitting quietly instead of developing physical prowess.

Children learn many skills simply by watching the behavior of a competent member of the culture. Girls learn to sew boots and parkas by watching their mothers and older relatives. Boys learn how to hunt from their fathers and other men. Children are not expected to converse with adults or to interrupt adult conversations. Instead, they are expected to play and talk with their peers.

It is easy to see why English- or French-speaking people from the Canadian mainstream cultures find Inuit socialization patterns strange. The silence of Inuit interaction patterns can be disquieting for people from other cultures; however, Inuit find the talkative ways that non-Inuit interact with their children equally unsettling. An Inuk woman once said that white people must really hate their food because "they talk so much while eating," an indication of the different value that Inuit place on this kind of conversation.

Each of these cultures brings their children up in accordance with certain beliefs, using very different patterns of language socialization. Inuit, for instance, believe it is demeaning for an adult to sit on the floor and play with children or to talk with children as though they were adults. Inuit do not believe children have "reason" or *isuma* until they are about 5 years of age. Therefore, they consider it strange to engage in conversation with an "unreasonable" child, who does not have experience with life. Talking with children is left to other children. Children are oriented to interact with other children and not with adults. Inuit believe that children learn language by overhearing it and comprehending it. Listening to adults is emphasized more than speaking with adults. Similarly, activities that strengthen the body and teach children about the physical world are valued more than activities that prepare children for literacy.

In contrast, middle-class North American parents believe that children learn to talk by talking. They also believe that children should be talked to directly and should engage with adults in conversation and play. Individual accomplishment is valued, and display of an individual's ability is applauded in the mainstream culture. Parents' ways of guiding their children toward the accomplishment of culturally specified goals can vary widely (Rogoff, 1990). Who a child talks with, who talks to a child, what to talk about, when to talk about it, and in what ways to talk about it can and do differ across cultures. Such differences correspond to different sets of underlying beliefs.

A study of Chinese Canadian mothers' beliefs about **child-directed talk** revealed that this cultural group held beliefs that were quite different from the beliefs held by mainstream Canadian mothers (Johnston & Wong, 2002). The Chinese Canadian mothers believed that teaching rather than playing with their children was the more appropriate way to help their children learn new words. The Chinese Canadian mothers were less likely than the mainstream Canadian mothers to prompt their children to tell about nonshared events, and they did not permit the intrusion of children into adult conversations, particularly with adults who were not family members. Yet, this study, like others before it, found that no one culture is totally unique. Language socialization practices vary within a cultural group, and they also overlap with the practices of other cultural groups. Despite their marked dissimilarities, the two Canadian groups of mothers had a number of beliefs about other aspects of parent–child communication in common. For instance, they both believed that babbling could be interpreted as meaningful communication, and they also both reported that children understand words before they speak.

Shared language socialization practices have been pointed out for other cultural groups. Vasquez, Pease-Alvarez, and Shannon (1994) studied Mexicano homes in California, where they found that certain interaction patterns found in Mexicano homes were similar to those found in mainstream American homes. For instance, in certain Mexicano homes, mothers would scaffold their children's talk with what are called **contingent queries,** questions that promote a conversation. A Mexican American mother, like a mainstream North American mother, might ask her child, "What did you do in school today?" Furthermore, even within the Mexican American group, there was variation in how various parents socialized their children to use language.

These findings indicate that cultures are not monolithic, with totally unique and singular social practices, and that although cultures are different from one another, they often share some social practices. The similarities and differences in cultural beliefs lead to similarities and differences in language socialization practices and cultural membership. Integral to this process is language itself, complete with its meanings, grammatical structures, and patterns of social interaction. Consequently, when children learn more than one language, whether from birth or later, they are being socialized into more than one culture.

CULTURES IN CONTACT

What happens when children are exposed to different cultural ways through multiple languages? How about if they are exposed to languages with different cultural patterns? What happens when different cultures come in contact with each other? These questions have relevance to educational and clinical intervention practices with children. Many children around the world have parents who come from two different cultures and speak different languages. Some children have pediatricians, child care workers, school teachers, or speech-language pathologists from different cultures who speak different languages. As people interact across their different languages and cultures, whether at home, in schools, or at clinics, certain dynamics influence the patterns of their interaction.

In many bilingual, bicultural homes, there are social forces such as gender and power differentials that influence language use and the participants' sense of cultural membership. For example, we found that in homes where two parents speak different languages (e.g., Inuktitut and English) there is likely to be a power differential (Crago, Chen, & Genesee, 1998). The more politically powerful culture is, of course, the mainstream culture. This means that there can often be pressure on the minority culture parent to adopt the languages and socialization patterns of the dominant culture. An Inuk mother is likely to speak to her children in English in the presence of their English-speaking, mainstream father. Interestingly, a small number of white women from the mainstream culture in Canada have married Inuit men. Some of these women have learned to speak Inuktitut. The same cannot be said for most of the men from the mainstream culture who marry Inuit women.

Power differentials are particularly noteworthy in educational and medical environments, where a doctor or teacher has an even more evident power status. The situation is aggravated when such professionals have not been educated about the many forms that language socialization can take. In this next example, we once again draw on our experience in Northern Canadian Inuit communities to describe what can result from misunderstandings and power differentials (Brophy & Crago, 2003; Crago, Eriks-Brophy, Pesco, & McAlpine, 1997).

First of all, most mainstream North American teachers who come to Inuit communities believe that they know what is appropriate classroom behavior for themselves and their students. The behaviors they expect are, unfortunately, almost always premised on the cultural patterns of their own culture. These are not, of course, the beliefs and patterns of the Inuit culture. To cite a noteworthy example, when Inuit teachers who teach in Inuktitut in the early elementary grades ask a question of their class of Inuit children, they do not expect the children to raise their hands and to be chosen one at a time to respond. They expect any or all of the children to volunteer an answer if they wish to. Often several children reply at the same time.

In grade 3, Inuit children switch into English second language classes taught by middle-class southern Canadian teachers. Picture the first day that one of these teachers asks a question of the class. She expects hands to go up and children to wait to be called on. Instead, any number of Inuit children simply call out the answer. This behavior appears rude and uncivilized to a mainstream teacher. Mainstream teachers consequently struggle with changing the children's behavior and persist in calling on individual students to display their knowledge in front of the class. If the child who is responding is wrong, the teachers will negatively evaluate his response. Inuit children find it very hard to give individual responses and very humiliating to be evaluated, either negatively or positively, in front of their peers. They have been, as mentioned previously, brought up in a culture where people believe that peer group interaction and collaboration are more valued behaviors than individual displays of competence.

It is easy to see how different the teacher's beliefs are and how uncomfortable these differences can become for both the children and the teachers; however, it is important to be aware that the teachers from the mainstream culture have the power to evaluate and, in the worst-case scenario, to punish the children whose language-use patterns they find unusual. The educational history of the native people in North America and elsewhere in the world is filled with devastating examples of the deleterious effects of a lack of respect for cultural and linguistic differences that became ensnared in power differentials. Similar dynamics have been played out in numerous classrooms of immigrant children around the world with equally unfortunate educational and social consequences. When teachers do not understand the particular cultural patterns of their students, there will be less than successful outcomes.

Shirley Brice Heath described the different educational abilities of children from Cantonese families and those from Hispanic backgrounds (Heath, 1986). The Hispanic children she studied were particularly good at collaborative work with their peers and at speculating on hypotheses. Their Cantonese counterparts performed better in teacher-led lessons and were particularly proficient at answering precisely and accurately. These different abilities were directly related to the language socialization practices of the children's different cultural groups. Clearly, teaching strategies that stressed collaborative work were not as comfortable nor as successful for Cantonese children, and those that stressed teacher-led lessons were not as comfortable nor as successful with the Hispanic children.

It is important for teachers from the mainstream culture to learn about and be aware of the various abilities that have been instilled in their students through their families' particular language socialization. Ignorance of these different patterns of interaction will reduce teachers' effectiveness and children's learning. In contrast, educational programs that build on the cultural bases established in the children's homes can be more successful for both the teachers and the learners.

In many instances, when children learn two languages they are also learning about membership in the two cultures that go with their languages. When the two cultures are premised on very different beliefs, the contact between them is not always easy and, indeed, has the potential to become exceptionally difficult, with the threat that the minority culture will be obliterated or, at least, overwhelmed by the dominant culture. Practitioners of all kinds who are responsible for the care of dual language children have the duty to be aware of the fragility and importance of certain cultures' practices and their susceptibility to domination and disappearance. Because of the interwoven nature of language and culture, dual language children are particularly at risk for both cultural and linguistic identity displacement.

Erasing a child's language or cultural patterns of language use is a great loss for the child. Children's identities and senses of self are inextricably linked to the language they speak and the culture to which they have been socialized. They are, even at an early age, speakers of their languages and members of their cultures. Language and culture are essential to children's identities. All of the affectionate talk and interpersonal communication of their childhoods and family life are embedded in their languages and cultures.

Many North American immigrants have lost their language and cultural patterns of interaction within one generation. Lily Wong Fillmore (1996), the child of Chinese immigrants, has described the sense of loss that she and other Chinese immigrants felt when they could not communicate with family members and the shame they felt about their culture's practices. She has pointed out the irony that North America is a continent of immigrants, but at the same time, North America, as a whole, has been particularly disrespectful of cultural and linguistic diversity.

CHANGING PATTERNS OF LANGUAGE AND CULTURE

Despite the potential for problematic results, new and positive forms of diversity can evolve from the contact between languages and cultures. In some bilingual, bicultural homes, children learn the cultural ways of both their parents. In certain instances, language and culture separate from each other, creating a new and different combination of behaviors. There are, for instance, a number of mixed marriages in Inuit communities. In these homes, we have seen Inuit parents reading aloud to their toddlers, in much the same manner that English-speaking parents from the mainstream culture do (Chen, 1997). The only difference is that the Inuit parents read the story in Inuktitut. Changes such as this indicate that the Inuit culture is evolving and language socialization patterns are changing. Literacy skills are becoming increasingly important to Inuit now that schooling is a customary part of their children's lives.

Such cultural change has also been documented in immigrant populations. One language socialization researcher, Elinor Ochs, first studied Samoans' ways of talking with their children in Samoa. A number of years later, she studied Samoans who had moved to the United States and discovered that they were now socializing their children with a mixture of traditional Samoan and recently acquired American interactional patterns.

There can also be a distinctive richness to the complex dynamics of bilingual and bicultural children's lives. In their study of Mexican American homes, Vasquez and her colleagues (1994) described how young children become linguistic interpreters and cultural brokers for their communities, translating and explaining mainstream North American institutions and practices to adults in their community. These children's skills in juggling multiple roles, languages, and cultures are remarkable. They develop skills and knowledge that children from mainstream English-dominant communities have limited access to because of their relative cultural and linguistic isolation.

Sometimes children who live in close contact with other cultures will mix their cultural patterns, much as they code-mix their languages (see Chapter 5). In doing so, they create a new identity out of their new, mixed patterns of language use and cultural practices. Ben Rampton (1995) has described what he called **language crossing** in a school in London, England. Teenagers of British, Punjabi, Caribbean, and Bangladeshi descent shared expressions in each other's languages, creating a striking multiethnic way of interacting and talking. This kind of friendly trading and crossing of language boundaries served to strengthen the boys' friendships and created a set of peer group interactions and new shared identities that reflected the multicultural diversity of these boys' lives.

Other instances of culture change in language socialization practices have been less positive. Shirley Brice Heath first studied the language socialization that occurred in two working-class American communities, one of black Americans and one of white Americans, in the 1970s. Twenty years later, she studied the offspring of the children in her first study (Heath, 1990). Heath found that in certain homes, the rich interactional language socialization patterns found in the original communities had diminished and were replaced by increased television watching and reduced language input to the children. Social institutions such as welfare laws and housing had created very different and less interpersonal home lives for this second generation of children, many of whom were being raised in apartments by single parents rather than in single-family homes and on the porches and streets of a close-knit, multigenerational community. Even though Heath's work does not focus on second language learners, it provides a haunting picture of the speed with which culture-based interaction patterns can change and of the societal and institutional forces that unwittingly lead to their demise.

The power and impact of social institutions on children's cultures serves as a reminder that any intervention with children, be it medical or educational, needs to take into account cultural differences in language use. In addition to finding ways to assess dual language children in their two languages, interventionists need to have culturally sensitive diagnostic procedures and interview techniques. Not only are there culturally varying attitudes to developmental impairment, but there are also culturally varying norms for who talks to whom about what. Without realizing it, professionals working with dual language learners who are language impaired may set up testing and diagnostic routines that violate certain cultural norms.

For instance, one of us attempted to have Inuit adults elicit samples of Inuit children's language. At first glance, it seemed appropriate to us to have fluent speakers talk with the children in Inuktitut; however, we had made one very significant oversight in setting up this procedure. Inuit children are not accustomed to, nor are they comfortable with, talking to adults. The end result was that the language samples collected by the teachers contained very limited language and were terribly misleading. Later, we remembered the pioneering work of William Labov (1972), who, by altering the circumstances in which he had African American children talk, elicited very different kinds of language. His landmark work showed that social settings and adult interlocutors have a profound influence on the language that children use. This led us to elicit language from Inuit children by putting them in a room with interesting things to play with, such as furry puppies and ugly fish. Talking with other children was comfortable and customary for them. They used vocabulary and grammatical structures that were much more complicated than they had used when talking with Inuit teachers.

Time and attention also need to be given to developing intervention strategies that do not contravene children's or their parent's cultural norms. Intervention with children with language impairments is a language-based activity. Because language is rooted in culture, it is also a culturally based activity. We can remember mistakenly asking Inuit parents to sit on the floor to play and talk with their children with language impairments. We also requested that Inuit mothers keep diaries about their children's vocabulary, never stopping to realize that many homes did not have pencils and paper in them. Such inappropriate requests are not likely to be met, and, moreover, they reveal an insensitivity that will erode the clinical relationship. Inappropriate intervention signals to parents and children that their cultural ways are not suitable and are not valued. In the long run, these sorts of signals can create confusion and even feelings of shame and insufficiency. They disrupt natural parent–children interactions, and over time, they risk contributing to cultural loss.

Pediatricians, nurses, child care workers, teachers, speech-language pathologists, second language specialists, and other professionals who work with dual language learners need to be aware of the connection between linguistic and cultural competencies because it is susceptible to disruption. This connection has incredible importance; the link between children's languages and cultures helps the world maintain one of its greatest riches—the diversity of its peoples.

SUMMARY

This chapter describes how different cultures socialize their children in terms of language use and language interaction. Cultures in contact may often misunderstand each other's norms for language socialization, which can lead to misunderstandings and, in the case of children, to unfortunate educational and clinical outcomes. Nonetheless, cultures in contact influence each other and evolve. Children in multicultural environments have even found ways to share their cultural interaction patterns, thereby erasing the strength of the boundaries that can exist between them. To be successful and respectful, language education and language intervention need to take the cultural patterns of socialization into consideration.

REFERENCES

Brophy, A.E., & Crago, M. (2003). Variation in instructional discourse features: Cultural or linguistic?: Evidence from Inuit and non-Inuit teachers of Nunavik. *Anthropology and Education Quarterly, 34*(4), 1–25.

Chen, C. (1997). *Language use and language socialization in bilingual homes in Inuit communities.* Unpublished master's thesis, McGill University, Montreal, Canada.

Crago, M.B. (1988). *Cultural context in communicative interaction of young Inuit children.* Unpublished doctoral dissertation. McGill University, Montreal, Canada.

Crago, M., Chen, C., & Genesee, F. (1998). Power and deference: Decision making in bilingual Inuit homes. *Journal of Just and Caring Education, 4*(1), 78–95.

Crago, M., Eriks-Brophy, A., Pesco, D., & McAlpine, L. (1997). Culturally-based miscommunication in classroom interaction. *Language, Speech, and Hearing Services in the Schools, 28*(3), 245–254.

Heath, S.B. (1986). Sociocultural contexts of language development. In *Beyond language: Social and cultural factors in schooling language minority children* (pp. 143–186). Los Angeles: Evaluation, Dissemination and Assessment Center.

Heath, S.B. (1990). The children of Trackton: Spoken and written language in social change. In J.W. Stieler, R.A. Schweder, & G. Herdt (Eds.), *Cultural psychology* (pp. 496–519). New York: Cambridge University Press.

Johnston, J., & Wong, M.-Y.A. (2002). Cultural differences in beliefs and practices concerning talk to children. *Journal of Speech, Language, and Hearing Research, 45,* 916–926.

Labov, W. (1972). *Language in the inner city: Studies in the Black Vernacular English.* Philadelphia: University of Pennsylvania Press.

Ochs, E., & Schieffelin, B.B. (1984). Language acquisition and socialization: Three developmental stories and their implications. In R.A. Schweder & R.A. LeVine (Eds.), *Culture theory: Essays on mind, self, and emotion* (pp. 276–322). New York: Harper & Row.

Rampton, B. (1995). Language crossing and the problematisation of ethnicity and socialization. *Pragmatics, 5*(4), 485–513.

Rogoff, B. (1990). *Apprenticeship in thinking: Cognitive development in social context.* Oxford: Oxford University Press.

Schieffelin, B.B. (1990). *The give and take of everyday life.* New York: Cambridge University Press.

Vasquez, O.A., Pease-Alvarez, L., & Shannon, S.M. (1994). *Pushing boundaries: Language and culture in a Mexicano community.* New York: Cambridge University Press.

Wong Fillmore, L. (1996). What happens when languages are lost? An essay on language assimilation and cultural identity. In D. Slobin, J. Gerhardt, A. Kyratzis, & J. Guo (Eds.), *Social interaction, social context, and language: Essays in honor of Susan Ervin-Tripp* (pp. 435–446). Mahwah, NJ: Lawrence Erlbaum Associates.

CHAPTER 3

The Language–Cognition Connection

In this chapter, we explore links between language and cognition and their implications for understanding language impairment. The links between language and cognition are complex and multidirectional. There has been a very rich history of scholarship that has explored these links, including such eminent theoreticians as Jean Piaget, Benjamin Whorf, Jerome Bruner, and Lev Vygotsky. Clearly, considering all that has been written about this fascinating topic is unnecessary because our objectives are more limited than those who seek to map the relationship between language and cognition in complete theoretical detail. Rather, we focus on those aspects of language and cognition that are clinically related to dual language development and impairment. Two primary developmental links between language and cognition that we explore are 1) the cognitive foundations of language acquisition and use, and 2) the consequences of dual language learning for cognitive development. More specifically, we organize our discussion of this topic around two general questions:

- Do infants and children have cognitive limitations that make dual language learning burdensome?

- Does dual language learning influence cognitive development?

These two questions can be thought of as two sides of the same coin, one that views cognitive capacity as setting limits on language development and the other that views language development as limiting or expanding the cognitive or intellectual capacities of the child. Both have been the subject of some controversy among researchers and theoreticians, and both are often of concern to parents, teachers, and other professionals who care for dual language learners. We explain each of these controversies and present evidence pertaining to each in the sections that follow.

Before proceeding, it is useful to provide a definition of *cognition*. Here is a useful one given by Laura Berk in her book *Child Development*: "Cognition refers to the inner processes and products of the mind that lead to 'knowing.' It includes all mental activity—attending, remembering, symbolizing, categorizing, planning, reasoning, problem solving, creating and fantasizing" (2003, p. 218).

WHY IS THE LINK BETWEEN LANGUAGE AND COGNITION IMPORTANT?

Why is it important to examine the developmental relationship between language and cognition? At first, this could seem like a largely academic issue of interest to theoreticians and researchers, not professionals concerned with dual language children. There are a number of reasons why these issues are of some importance for professionals who work with dual language learners. First, there is the matter of expectations. Professionals, parents, and others who are in a role where they can influence the course of children's language development—and whether they learn two languages instead of one—must have a solid, scientifically grounded understanding of the capacity of infants and young children for language learning. They need to understand whether infants and children have the capacity to learn two languages simultaneously or successively to the same extent as one language or whether there are cognitive limitations to infants' or children's capacity to learn more than one language.

The belief that dual language learning exceeds infants' or children's typical developmental capacities could bias professionals to interpret the behaviors of dual language learners that differ from monolingual learners as signs of impairment when, in fact, they might simply reflect individual differences or typical development for dual language learners. For example, some children are faster language learners than others. This is equally true of dual language learners. A professional who believes that dual language learning is burdensome might well interpret the language development of a slow dual language learner as a sign of impairment due to dual language learning rather than simply a sign of a particular child's aptitude for language acquisition. It is not uncommon for language specialists to claim that learning two languages is ill-advised in the case of children with language learning difficulty. In Chapter 5, we consider in detail a specific aspect of dual language learning (code-mixing) that is typical among bilingual individuals but is often misinterpreted by professionals and parents who are not familiar with the scientific literature on this topic.

Second, an understanding of the cognitive foundations of dual language learning can help professionals provide advice to concerned parents or other professionals when asked whether children with cognitive challenges should or should not be encouraged to learn more than one language. Evidence that dual language learning exceeds the cognitive capacity of children could justify recommendations to limit children who experience difficulty to one language only or to successive instead of simultaneous dual language learning; however, such recommendations may not be warranted. Nevertheless, we regularly hear from parents and professionals who believe that a child's cognitive abilities set limits to language development, and, thus, dual language exposure should be curtailed for children with cognitive challenges. Decisions about whether dual language learning is possible have serious lifelong repercussions for some children, especially those who need to know more than one language to interact with family members and others in the community.

Finally, an understanding of the links between language and cognition can help professionals identify appropriate language outcomes in children with cognitive disabilities. In other words, understanding the nature of a child's cognitive capacities, especially those that might be manifest in her language behavior, helps clinicians set realistic expectations about the outcomes of remediation. In a related vein, professionals who understand the relationship between language and cognitive development may be better able to design intervention programs to match each child's cognitive abilities. Language embodies children's thoughts and ways of thinking, and it is important that individual differences in these regards be considered when designing intervention programs and when evaluating the progress of children with language impairment following intervention.

IS DUAL LANGUAGE LEARNING BURDENSOME FOR INFANTS AND CHILDREN?

Are infants and children cognitively equipped to learn two languages, either simultaneously or successively, without costs to their ultimate language competence? The fact that humans possess the cognitive capacity to learn one language without difficulty is easy for people to accept. In contrast, early

BOX 3.1

Los Angeles Times
October 7, 2002
Judy Foreman

"Kids who grow up in bilingual homes may be slower to speak than other kids, but once they've learned both languages they appear to have a number of intellectual advantages" (p. S.1).

Although Foreman acknowledges the positive attributes of later bilingualism, she describes the negative effects of early bilingualism (i.e., bilingual children learn language slower than monolingual children).

bilingualism (i.e., dual language acquisition for preschool and young school-age children) is often seen as problematic and is thought to challenge developing children. Writers for newspapers and magazines often describe the uncertain, problematic aspects of the learning phase of bilingualism (see Box 3.1).

Scientists are also susceptible to such pessimistic thinking. For example, in an early influential theory, Macnamara argued that language acquisition in bilingual children is like an old-fashioned balance scale with development in each language represented by each pan on the balance. As proficiency in one language increases, proficiency in the other falls behind (Macnamara, 1966). Such pessimistic views of bilingualism conceptualize the child's underlying mental capacity for language learning as a balloon that can only contain so much air; when the balloon expands as a result of acquisition of one language, acquisition of the other language is limited by the remaining space. Too much air (or too many languages) will burst the balloon. We refer to these views of dual language learning as the **limited capacity hypothesis** because they argue that dual language acquisition is problematic because the language faculty has a limited capacity.

In the following sections, we discuss two different aspects of this issue:

1. The innate capacity of infants and young children to acquire two languages at the same time

2. The relationship between general intelligence and second language learning

Are There Innate Limitations to Simultaneous Dual Language Learning?

The limited capacity hypothesis raises important fundamental questions about the innate ability of the human language faculty—are infants biologically predisposed to acquire only one language, and, as a consequence, does

BOX 3.2

Limited Capacity Hypothesis—theory that infants and children have the ability to acquire one language completely, but learning two or more languages exceeds children's innate ability. As a result, it is argued, acquisition of two languages simultaneously during infancy and early childhood or the acquisition of a second language in childhood after a first language has been learned will result in reduced levels of first and/or second language proficiency. The parents of a child who is suspected of having specific language impairment are often counseled to limit the child to one language on the assumption that the child's impairment is related to (and perhaps even caused by) excessive demands on the child's language learning ability.

simultaneous dual language exposure and acquisition entail certain costs, either in cognitive or linguistic development? A more optimistic view is that infants possess the biological ability to acquire two languages as typically as one. The metaphor of a computer is useful here. A computer is an electronic device that has enormous processing capacity that is commonly referred to as *hardware*. The hardware of a computer relies on the help of programs called *software* to perform many complex operations at the same time. People can purchase additional software to load onto their computers in order to perform new functions. Infants' brains are like the hardware of computers because they have vast amounts of processing capacity, and infant development is like purchasing additional software that relies on the brain's hardware to perform functions. The question is this: Can the brain support the acquisition of only one language comfortably or, like a computer, can a number of languages be learned (i.e., loaded in the computer) without exceeding the processing capacity of the brain? We consider research evidence pertinent to this question in the next sections. Although all of the details are not known, we think that the evidence supports this optimistic view.

Speech Perception and Production in Preverbal Children

Minimally, infants must possess two critical capacities to acquire two languages simultaneously: the ability to discriminate important language-related differences in the auditory input and the ability to remember language-related information. In the absence of these fundamental abilities, infants cannot distinguish one language from another or one sound from another and cannot remember linguistically relevant acoustic information from the input. Memory for language-relevant acoustic information is critical for the construction of distinct language systems. Research since the 1980s indicates that infants possess these abilities and, moreover, that they are operational very early in development (see Boysson-Bardies, 1999, for a review). Thus, critical processes that are essential for bilingual acquisition begin earlier than previously imagined. The scant evidence available on preverbal language processing by bilingual infants reassures us that, indeed, infants can cope with dual language input.

The evidence we review in this section comes from investigations of the neurocognitive abilities of infants from the prenatal stage of development to the end of the first year of life, before most children produce their first words. This research was designed to see how neonates and preverbal infants experience language before they actually begin to produce their first words. Collectively, this research is often referred to as "speech perception research," but in fact, it encompasses research on children's processing abilities with respect to different aspects of language. For example, some studies look at infants' ability to discriminate between different languages during the first months of life. Others look at infants' ability to discriminate words from continuous speech. Still others look at infants' perception of speech sounds. We include in our discussion research that has looked at children's early verbal productions and, specifically, their babbling, to see if their babbling resembles the sounds in the language used by parents and others in the child's language environment.

This research, like most research on children in the verbal stages of language acquisition, has been carried out primarily with children acquiring only one language. There is only limited work on preverbal infants exposed to two languages simultaneously. Nevertheless, the results of research on monolingual children can help us understand the capacity of the language faculty and, in particular, whether there are innate limits to coping with dual language learning. We review this literature in some detail because we believe that it is important for parents and clinicians who care for simultaneous bilingual children and because it is not easily available to speech-language professionals otherwise. Moreover, we believe that the results from this research teach valuable lessons about young language learners, namely that they have far greater language learning capacity than previously imagined and that the process of language learning begins very early, probably even prenatally. A brief and simplified view of some key studies follows, but please see Chapters 1, 2, and 3 in Golinkoff and Hirsh-Pasek (1999) for a nontechnical discussion of this work and Jusczyk (1999) for a more technical review.

Within 24 hours of birth, newborns prefer to listen to the voice of their mothers more than the voice of another woman speaking to her baby (DeCasper & Fifer, 1980; see also Mehler, Jusczyk, Lambertz, Halsted, Bertoncini, & Amiel-Tison, 1988, for evidence concerning older infants). Infants show that they prefer their mother's voice by visually fixating longer on an image (like a bull's-eye) that has the mother's voice coming from it than an image with an unfamiliar woman's voice. Preference for the mother's voice is not demonstrated if the voice samples that the infant hears are played backward, suggesting that the infants' preference is tied to perception of the rhythmic or prosodic features of language and not to the specific sounds that make up the language. **Prosody** refers to the intonational contours of language—the changes in pitch and stress that occur during talking. This is important because prosody is a likely cue to early discrimination of dual language input because different languages have different prosodic characteristics.

Jacques Mehler and his colleagues in Paris (1988) have shown that infants who are only 2 months old can distinguish utterances in their native language from those in a foreign language; native language here refers to the language used by the parents and overheard by the infant pre- and postnatally. When the language samples were acoustically filtered so that only prosodic cues remained, the infants continued to differentiate between the native and foreign language, again reinforcing the notion that prosody is important in the early discrimination of language. Infants' ability to distinguish a familiar, previously heard language from an unfamiliar, foreign language implies that they have formed a neural representation of the familiar language that then acts as a template against which other languages (familiar or unfamiliar) can be compared. The ability to recognize a familiar language (or languages) also directs the child's attention to input that is relevant to the language to be acquired. Bosch and Sebastián-Gallés (2001) reported that bilingual (Spanish-Catalan) infants as well as monolingual infants demonstrate a similar pattern of discrimination between Spanish and Catalan, suggesting that bilingual infants are not delayed in this particular perceptual milestone as a result of dual language exposure.

Infants' impressive auditory discriminatory and memory capacities are based on language experiences in utero. More specifically, DeCasper and Spence (1986) found that fetuses who were read prose passages by their mothers on a daily basis 6 weeks prior to birth demonstrated a preference for these passages after birth in comparison to new passages. The infants demonstrated a preference for the previously heard passages even when they were read by another female, indicating that it was not simply familiarity with the mother's voice but rather the general acoustic properties of the speech signal that the infants were responding to. By monitoring changes in fetal heart rates, these researchers also noted that fetuses in the 37th week of gestation distinguished between familiar and new poems following previous exposure to the familiar poem.

Additional evidence of newborns' innate preparedness for dual language learning comes from extensive investigation of children's perception of the individual sounds that make up human language, for example, /b/, /l/, and

/a/. These individual phonetic units are referred to as the sound **segments** of language. Infants begin life with the ability to discriminate between all sound segments found in the world's languages on which they have been tested, and the perceptual mechanisms they employ to do so, such as categorical perception, appear to be the same ones adults use (Jusczyk, 1985; Werker & Peg, 1992). The acoustic differences between some sound segments can be very subtle, yet these sounds can be **phonemic** in a language, which means that changing the sound segment changes the meaning of a word. For example, /l/ and /r/ in English are phonemic because *lice* and *rice* and *lot* and *rot* are separate words differing in only the first segment. The segments /l/ and /r/, however, are not phonemic in Japanese. Instead, they are two acoustic variations on one phoneme, and there are no words in the language that contrast in meaning based only on a change between /l/ and /r/.

It is widely believed that the infant's impressive discriminatory perceptual capacities reflect the innate hardwiring of the auditory system and its sensitivity to acoustic information that is fundamental to the **segmental features** of all human languages. Most important, these findings demonstrate that infants can discriminate virtually all of the phonemic contrasts that languages use, and they can do so from birth, regardless of whether they have had exposure to a language that uses those contrasts. By 10 months of age, infants continue to discriminate contrasts that are phonemic in the input language but no longer discriminate contrasts that are not phonemic in that language. In other words, experience with a specific language has begun to shape their perceptual sensitivities.

Although we lack evidence at this time about the discriminant perceptual capacities of bilingual infants, the available evidence indicates that infants' initial capacity for sound discrimination is virtually unlimited and, thus, they should have no problem distinguishing the sounds of two languages. In short, the results from monolingual children indicate that there is nothing in infants' initial perceptual capacities that would limit them to discriminating between, and thus learning, the phonological characteristics of more than one language. At the same time, there is a lack of detailed evidence about the time course and pattern of their actual acquisition of the phonologies of two languages at the same time.

Taken together, these findings on speech-language perception in monolingual infants are important because they indicate that newborn infants are innately prepared to discriminate language-related signals, both segmental (individual sounds/phonemes) and **suprasegmental** (prosody). This means that infants begin to focus attention on acoustic information in the input that is relevant to the acquisition of language early in development. Timing is important because infants must begin early if they are to analyze and make sense of dual language input. To quote Boysson-Bardies, "We now know that not only is the brain of the baby not empty, but in a certain sense it is fuller than that of the most brilliant scientist" (1999, p. 13). No research of monolingual acquisition leads one to believe that bilingual acquisition is inherently problematic or burdensome.

Unfortunately, only a few studies to date have systematically examined language development in preverbal infants who are exposed to two languages. The few that have been carried out are reassuring in suggesting that infants exposed to two languages process them in language-specific ways, in some significant respects. Research by Linda Polka at McGill University has shown that 7½-month-old children who were exposed to French and English simultaneously from birth were able to recognize both English and French words in continuous spoken speech before they produced recognizable words (Polka & Sundara, 2003). This is the same age that monolingual children begin to recognize words in their input languages. Monolingual control children whom Polka also tested who had been exposed to English only or French only were able to recognize words from their input language but not from the other language; that is, English monolingual infants could recognize English words but not French words in continuous speech, and, similarly, French monolingual infants could recognize French words but not English words. The fact that the bilingual infants could recognize both English and French words suggests that their language processing abilities were sensitized to both French and English input. These results are important because they indicate that infants exposed to two languages simultaneously are able to parse the speech stream into words in their two respective input languages at the same age as monolingual children do, indicating that dual language input does not retard this critical accomplishment in early language development.

Researchers working with monolingual children have found that the babbling of infants exposed to only one language begins to reflect certain features of the input language around 10–12 months of age, indicating that the children are able to produce some of the language-specific sounds of the target language. Maneva and Genesee (2002) determined that the same was true for bilingual children. They systematically recorded then analyzed the babbling of an infant who was exposed to English and French in the home in order to ascertain whether his babbling reflected specific features of each language. They found that the babbling of the young bilingual infant was distinct when with his French-speaking father in comparison to his English-speaking mother. Moreover, the distinctive features of his English and French babbling reflected phonetic features of the target languages and were the same kind of language-specific features that monolingual English and monolingual French infants have been shown to produce during the babbling stage.

The results of these studies indicate that infants with dual language exposure demonstrate the same critical milestones in word segmentation and babbling as monolingual children and at approximately the same age as monolingual infants. However, more research needs to be done to examine all aspects of early language and speech processing. Infants exposed to two languages from birth will not necessarily behave as monolingual infants do in all respects. Indeed, work by Chris Fennell and Janet Werker (2003) at the University of British Columbia suggests that there may be some aspects of sound discrimination that are delayed in bilingual, in comparison with monolingual, infants. Whether these differences between monolingual infants and bilingual infants represent clinically important differences needs to be explored.

Language Development Milestones

Another way to examine if dual language learning is burdensome is to examine developmental milestones in the language of simultaneous bilingual children. If the language faculty is not equipped to acquire two languages simultaneously, then one would expect to see delays in critical milestones in dual language development, for example, in the discrimination of speech sounds, the emergence and time course of **canonical** and **variegated babbling**, the emergence of first words and word combinations, and the emergence of particular syntactic structures (e.g., finite verb forms, question forms, negatives). These kinds of milestones have been studied extensively in monolingual children, and the results from such research often serve as a basis for ascertaining whether children are on course.

Unfortunately, no such normative database exists for bilingual children, and collecting such data would not be easy. Bilingual children differ considerably from one another in ways that might be expected to affect their rate of development without implicating an underlying impairment. For example, as we discuss in some detail in Chapter 4, bilingual children often have different amounts of exposure to each language, which could affect their rate of development in each language (see Pearson, Fernandez, Lewedag, & Oller, 1997, for a study on levels of exposure and vocabulary development). Also, it is possible that acquisition of different language pairs could affect rates of development insofar as acquisition of languages that are similar to one another (e.g., Spanish and Italian) might be facilitated, whereas acquisition of languages that are different (e.g., English and Thai) might be delayed as the child must acquire different (and at times disparate) properties for each language. In addition to the variation in rates of development that might reflect differences in exposure and language similarities/differences, there is always individual variation among learners to consider, making the task of deciding whether a bilingual child's development is on track even more difficult.

The question remains: Does the current research have anything to say about critical milestones in bilingual acquisition? More specifically, are the milestones of bilingual acquisition similar to those of monolingual acquisition? Evidence that they are would argue for an underlying capacity for language acquisition that encompasses two or more languages, not just one. A number of studies are relevant, provided one keeps the caveats mentioned previously in mind. The sample sizes in studies of bilingual children are often small and, in some cases, involve case studies of one or several children. Consequently, the results of these studies cannot be interpreted as normative. Truly normative data require large samples of children who have been studied longitudinally over the first 2 or 3 years of acquisition; such data do not exist for bilingual children.

Notwithstanding these problems, the current research on bilingual children follows. Oller and his colleagues examined the **canonical babbling** of a group of Spanish-English infants being raised in the Miami area. There were 73 infants (monolingual and bilingual) in their study, and they were examined longitudinally from 4 months of age to 1½ years of age. These researchers found that the onset of canonical babbling for bilingual infants did not differ significantly from that of monolingual infants and, likewise, specific infraphonological features that they examined (i.e., canonical babbling ratio, full vowel ratio, volubility) were the same for the bilingual and monolingual infants (Oller, Eilers, Urbano, & Cobo-Lewis, 1997).

In a related vein, Maneva and Genesee (2002) reported that the French-English bilingual infant they studied exhibited **variegated babbling** that resembled in certain respects that of monolingual French and English infants of the same age. Petitto and her colleagues reported that first words, first two-word combinations, and acquisition of the first 50 words occurred within the same age range for three French-English bilingual children they studied as has been reported for monolingual children (Petitto, Katerelos, Levy, Gauna, Tetreault, & Ferraro, 2001). Three of the children that Petitto and her colleagues studied were hearing children who were learning French oral language and French sign language simultaneously. They noted that the children's milestones also resembled those of monolingual hearing children learning French, suggesting that the milestones in bilingual acquisition are not different for those learning oral or signed languages.

Finally, Padilla and Liebman (1975) reported that three Spanish-English bilingual children being raised in southern California exhibited the same rate of development, as measured by **mean length of utterance (MLU),** as has been reported for monolingual children. The children were between 1 year, 7 months and 2 years, 2 months of age at the onset of the study, and naturalistic language samples were collected longitudinally over a period of at least 5 months.

Clearly, caution must be used when interpreting so few studies with such small sample sizes. It is not possible to interpret these results to represent the typical pattern for bilingual children because the sample sizes are too small, the domains of acquisition examined too limited, and replicability has not been established. Nevertheless, such findings suggest that bilingual acquisition is not necessarily burdensome because some bilingual children are able to traverse critical milestones in dual language development within the same time frame as most typical monolingual children do when they acquire a single language. We return to this issue in Chapter 4 with respect to the emergence of grammatical structures in the two languages of simultaneous bilingual children and the ways the timing and developmental patterns of grammatical structures resemble those of monolingual children.

WHAT IS THE RELATIONSHIP BETWEEN GENERAL INTELLIGENCE AND SECOND LANGUAGE LEARNING?

In this section, we consider yet another aspect of the language-cognition connection, namely, the link between general intelligence and second language learning. By general intelligence, we mean the kinds of intellectual skills that are evident to parents and others in children's day to day behavior: their ability to think analytically, to learn new skills and knowledge, to solve problems, and to be creative. These kinds of skills are generally thought to be critical for success in school. They are measured by IQ tests or other tests of general ability, such as the Peabody Picture Vocabulary Test, Third Edition (Dunn & Dunn, 1997), and Raven's Coloured Progressive Matrices Test (1965). These conceptualizations of intelligence are controversial and even objectionable to some people; however, this notion of intelligence is widely held and has significant influence on many people's thinking and decision making. For example, many parents are reluctant to enroll their children in bilingual school programs if they think that they are intellectually challenged. Moreover, speech-language professionals often assess children's level of general intelligence in order to better understand the nature of their suspected language impairment. Children who show typical levels of general intelligence but poor language skills are thought to have language-specific problems. Thus, because of its practical importance, we include a discussion of general intelligence and its relationship to dual language learning.

The link between general intelligence and dual language learning has been investigated most extensively in the case of second language learners (like Samantha, Trevor, and Bonnie, from Chapter 1) and primarily second language learners of school age (we consider this issue further in Chapter 7). One of the reasons for this focus stems from the fact that there are many tests of general intelligence for school-age children but relatively few for preschoolers. Moreover, tests of general intelligence for school-age children have better long-term predictive validity than those for preschoolers; in fact, such tests are notoriously unreliable in the case of young preschool children. Tests of general intelligence for infants (and thus for simultaneous dual language learners) are virtually nonexistent because of the psychometric problems in defining and assessing this form of intelligence among such young children.

There has been a focus on the link between general intelligence and bilingualism in school-age children because parents and educators are often concerned that children of below-average intelligence are not able to learn a second language successfully and that they are hampered if they are educated through the medium of a second language. This has spawned applied research to address this concern.

General intelligence is usually correlated with those aspects of language proficiency that are linked to reading and writing, so that monolingual children who score high on tests of general intelligence also usually score relatively high on tests that assess reading, writing, and spelling skills, for example. This pattern of correlations is to be expected because tests of general intelligence are usually validated against children's school grades, which, in turn, are heavily influenced by their reading and writing skills.

The same pattern of correlations is equally true in the case of second language proficiency (see Genesee, 1976, 1987). Children who score high on tests of general intelligence also tend to score relatively high on tests of reading and writing in the second language; however, of particular importance to this book, children with relatively low levels of intellectual ability are not differentially challenged in learning their first language as a result of learning a second language. This has been documented by showing that students with low levels of general intelligence who are participating in second/foreign language **immersion programs** score at the same level as comparable students with low levels of intellectual ability in native language programs on standardized tests of reading, writing, and spelling administered in their native language.

At the same time, students with below-average intelligence participating in immersion programs can acquire reading and writing skills in the second language to the extent one would expect given their intellectual abilities. Their literacy skills are not as advanced as those of average or above-average students in immersion, but they are impressive. We discuss these findings in greater detail in Chapter 7.

When it comes to acquisition of spoken language, the picture is different. Correlations between measures of general intelligence and measures of speaking and listening comprehension in the second language are typically quite low, especially among elementary school–age children (Genesee, 1987). Low correlations in this case indicate that general intelligence is not a significant predictor of proficiency in second language speaking and listening comprehension. This is most likely to be the case if the test assesses speaking and listening skills of the type that are common in most face-to-face social conversations. It is less likely to be true when assessing second language skills related to academic tasks, such as comprehending a science lecture or giving an oral science report. Genesee (1976) found few differences among immersion students with below-average, average, and above-average levels of general intelligence in their oral second language development at the elementary school level; this work is discussed in more detail in Chapter 7.

The differential effects of intelligence on different kinds of language learning (spoken versus written language) may be due, in part, to the importance of other factors. In particular, one might expect children's motivation to fit in and communicate with peers who speak the second language to have a powerful influence on their acquisition of that language. Indeed, most young children, regardless of their general intellectual ability, are successful in acquiring a second language if surrounded by same-age peers who speak the language, given sufficient exposure to the language. In Chapter 6, we examine more carefully the rate at which young children learn a second language.

At the same time, some children can take longer to learn a second language than others, perhaps because they have poor aptitude for language learning or, in the case of immigrant and especially refugee children, they may have been traumatized in their home country and are having trouble with sociocultural adaptation. From a practical, clinical perspective, it is important to examine the social and personal circumstances surrounding a child learning a second language when trying to understand the source of the child's difficulties. Circumstances of second language learning might explain why a child is exhibiting difficulty or delay in learning language.

Children with Severe Cognitive Challenges

Although research clearly indicates that children with typical capacities for learning—and even children with nonclinically low levels of ability—usually do not experience difficulty acquiring two languages, questions still remain: How well can children with severe cognitive challenges, such as **Down syndrome** or **Williams syndrome,** learn a second language? How well can children with severe sensory or perceptual difficulties, such as hearing or visual impairment, learn a second language? Unfortunately, there is no systematic research on such children, so we can only conjecture how well these children would do if exposed to two languages simultaneously or to a second language after the first language has been acquired. Based on everything else we know about language acquisition, we believe that such children are capable of acquiring some proficiency in a second language, but we cannot assert with any precision how successful they would be and in what domains.

The answers to these questions might be quite different for simultaneous exposure versus sequential exposure (i.e., second language learning) especially if second language learning takes place primarily in school. The success of children who learn a second language in school can be influenced by pedagogical factors. Such factors, along with the cognitive challenges that some children face, can impede second language acquisition. An elementary school teacher with 25 (or more) students has difficulty providing the kind of intensive, individualized attention that a student with a cognitive or sensoriperceptual problem would need to learn to her full potential. In contrast, the success of preschool simultaneous bilingual learners is dependent primarily on their own inherent abilities. From everything we know about language learning in natural contexts, these abilities, even when compromised by cognitive disabilities, are considerable. At the same time, it is important to point out that even simultaneous bilingual preschool children may be slowed down in their language development if they are not given sufficiently consistent and rich exposure to both languages. All things considered, we suspect that children with severe cognitive or sensoriperceptual challenges are likely to experience more success with dual language learning if they are preschool age and have more language exposure outside school than similar children whose second language learning is dependent on school experiences; however, we caution that this speculation is not based on systematic empirical evidence.

DOES DUAL LANGUAGE LEARNING INFLUENCE COGNITIVE DEVELOPMENT?

Theoreticians and laypersons alike have long been fascinated with the possibility that bilingual children are different from monolingual children in ways that go beyond knowing two languages. Some people think that bilingualism is a threat to the child's typical social, cognitive, and personality development. We saw the same view expressed about the linguistic consequences of learning two languages. The challenges facing children who are raised or educated bilingually (a topic we explore in detail in Chapter 7) are often thought to be far reaching and detrimental. There is no significant theoretical reason to believe that learning, knowing, or using two languages should jeopardize children's development, yet this fear is harbored by some people.

This fear does have some empirical support. For example, in an early review of research on bilingualism and personality, Diebold (1968) concluded that bilingualism leads to emotional maladjustment and, in particular, to psychodynamic conflict (e.g., schizophrenia in the extreme case). Closer to the issue at hand, a number of early researchers also reported that bilingual children exhibited lower levels of verbal intelligence and/or general intellectual ability (Arsenian, 1945; Darcy, 1946; Macnamara, 1966). As noted previously, these effects were often explained in terms of children's limited linguistic and cognitive capacities.

Closer examination of these early studies, however, reveals that many of them had serious methodological shortcomings. In some cases, the performance of bilingual children was compared to that of monolingual children, but the two groups were not from the same socioeconomic stratum. The bilingual children were often from lower socioeconomic backgrounds and on those grounds alone would be expected to perform worse on the standardized tests used to assess their abilities. In addition, the bilingual children's level of proficiency in the language of the tests was not always controlled so that some of the children were evaluated using tests in their weaker language. As a result, their performance on tests that were supposed to measure intelligence was really a reflection of their level of second language proficiency.

Most important, many of the bilingual children in these early studies were living in **subtractive bilingual environments.** This term was coined by McGill University psychologist Wallace Lambert to describe the circumstances under which many minority language children learn the majority language of their community. Subtractive bilingualism occurs when acquisition of the majority language comes at the cost of loss of the native language. The prototypical case of a subtractive bilingual environment is that of immigrant children or the children and grandchildren of immigrants (like Bonnie, Pasquala, or Carlos). Such children are often expected to learn the dominant language of the wider community and to give up their native language. In fact, it is widely believed that the best way for immigrant children to learn the majority language is to abandon their heritage language altogether. The parents of immigrant children are often encouraged to use only the majority language in the home during the preschool years as a way of facilitating the child's integration into majority language schools.

Immigrant children are not the only children subjected to subtractive bilingual environments. Children who speak an indigenous language in a community that is otherwise dominated by another language also often experience subtractive bilingualism; native Inuktitut-speaking children in Canada (like Pauloosie) or Hopi-speaking children in the United States are examples of such cases. Yet other cases include the children of migrant workers who continue to learn and use the language of their national origin but live in communities (full time or part time) where another language is the majority language; children of Turkish descent in Germany or children of Mexican descent (like Carlos) in the United States are examples. Bistra might have experienced a subtractive bilingual learning environment except that her parents went to great trouble to promote the acquisition and use of both her mother's language (Bulgarian) and her father's language (English).

In contrast, **additive bilingual environments** are contexts in which there is substantial support for children to maintain their native language as they acquire an additional language. Children like Samantha or Trevor, for example, are expected to continue to learn English at the same time as they learn Spanish and German, respectively. There is no question of their giving up their native language for their second language. Dual language children from majority ethnolinguistic groups often enjoy the benefits of living in additive bilingual environments. In a related vein, additive bilingualism supports dual cultural identities so that children can identify with and enjoy the cultures connected with both of the languages they are learning. They are not made to feel that they have to be a member of only one cultural group.

There was a significant turn of events in the history of research on the cognitive consequences of bilingualism in the early 1960s with research by Elizabeth Peal and Wallace Lambert of McGill University. Peal and Lambert (1962) corrected many of the methodological weaknesses of earlier work. They compared the performance of English-French bilingual children who were fully proficient in both languages with that of monolingual English- and French-speaking children from the same socioeconomic backgrounds and with the same level of education. What is particularly important about the Peal and Lambert study, and many subsequent studies, is that the bilingual children under investigation were raised in social settings that supported and valued their bilingual skills; that is, they were living in additive bilingual environments. In contrast to previous studies, the study by Peal and Lambert found that the bilingual students they tested exhibited a number of cognitive advantages in comparison to their monolingual comparison group. More specifically, they found evidence that the bilingual students had a greater number of independent cognitive strategies at their disposal and exhibited greater flexibility in the use of these strategies to solve problems.

With stronger methodological controls, many studies since Peal and Lambert's (1962) landmark study have reported advantages for bilingual children in comparison to monolingual children on a variety of cognitive tasks (see Bialystok, 2001; Cummins, 1976; and Hakuta, 1986, for reviews). Among those studies that have found a bilingual superiority, it has often been found that bilingual children are advantaged on tasks that called for **metalinguistic awareness.** Metalinguistic awareness is the ability to reflect on and manipulate the elements of language independently of their communicative use. There are numerous types of metalinguistic tasks, from those that focus on the sounds of language, to words, to grammar, and to language use itself. For example, the child might be asked to identify whether specific words (e.g., *if, cat*) are words or to identify which words have the same final, medial, or initial sound (e.g., *bat, boss, car*). He might be asked to say what sound is left if the first sound is removed from a word (e.g., remove the first sound from *cat*).

Awareness of these aspects of language is not particularly important when using language for most day-to-day communicative purposes; however, it is important when it comes to acquiring written language. There is a strong positive correlation between learners' metalinguistic skills, especially in phonology, and the acquisition of reading and writing (Adams, 1990). Good readers and writers are aware of the structural properties of the language and how the language functions as a system for communication.

Some of the most significant advances in our understanding of the cognitive consequences of bilingualism and the conditions in which they are evident have come from the laboratory of Ellen Bialystok of York University in Toronto. Bialystok (2001) has provided compelling evidence that there is a bilingual advantage when selective attention is required during the processing of information so that misleading information is inhibited in favor of relevant information in the performance of a variety of cognitive tasks. Bialystok has argued further that the bilingual advantage is most evident under conditions of moderate cognitive demands and less likely when cognitive demands are very high or very low; in the latter cases, there are no differences between bilingual children and monolingual children (see Chapter 7 in Bialystok, 2001, for more details).

It is important to point out that even some methodologically sound studies have failed to find a difference between bilingual children and monolingual children (see, e.g., Rosenblum & Pinker, 1983, and Cummins, 1976). Thus, contrary to the simplistic notion that bilingualism confers unconditionally positive or negative cognitive consequences, contemporary research has demonstrated a variety of outcomes—some showing a bilingual advantage; some a monolingual advantage; and some no differences between monolingual and bilingual children. We should not be surprised that bilingualism can be associated with different patterns of outcomes. Children become bilingual for very different reasons and under very different circumstances— some that might favor bilingual children, others that might favor monolingual children, and still others that might result in comparable patterns of cognitive ability.

Jim Cummins, from the Ontario Institute for Studies in Education at the University of Toronto, recognized this important point in the formulation of his **threshold hypothesis.** According to Cummins (2000), the cognitive consequences of bilingualism are dependent, in part, on the levels of language proficiency that bilingual children attain in their two languages; see Figure

3.1 for a schematic representation of this hypothesis. Cognitive advantages among bilingual children are usually associated with advanced levels of bilingual proficiency, whereas cognitive disadvantages (or relatively lower levels of cognitive ability relative to monolingual children) are often associated with low levels of bilingual proficiency. Bilingual proficiency that falls between these two thresholds is likely to result in neither an advantage nor a disadvantage.

Cummins has attributed these differential effects to the quality of the bilingual children's interactions with their learning environment. Children with low levels of proficiency in one or the other of their two languages could experience lowered levels of cognitive ability, as demonstrated in their ability to solve problems, critically analyze information, or identify alternative points of view, because they experience impoverished interactions with their learning environment. In contrast, children with advanced levels of bilingual proficiency are likely to experience enriched cognitive abilities as a result of enhanced metalinguistic awareness or attentional abilities of the type identified by Bialystok because of enriched learning experiences.

Taken together, these findings on language and cognitive development are important for a number of reasons.

1. They indicate unequivocally that the pessimistic view of bilingualism is not valid.

2. They indicate that the cognitive consequences of bilingualism may be positive, negative, or null, depending on the level of proficiency of the bilingual child. This makes eminent sense in view of the widely varied circumstances under which children learn two languages.

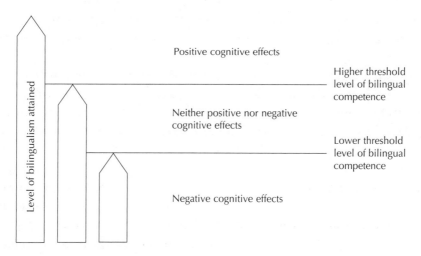

Figure 3.1. Cognitive effects of bilingual competence.

3. Clinicians should consider the cognitive advantages that can accrue from knowing and using two languages instead of considering only the possibility of cognitive disadvantages, as has been the case traditionally when consulting with parents about the pros and cons of bilingualism.

4. Most important, clinicians, educators, other professionals, and parents are advised to aim for advanced levels of bilingual proficiency for individual children in order to ensure that they benefit from all of the advantages of being bilingual.

In short, children should be fully supported in their acquisition of two languages, and the decision to raise a child bilingually should be made only if the sustained, enriched, and consistent bilingual experiences that are necessary to achieve advanced bilingual proficiency can be provided.

SUMMARY

There are two sides to the language–cognition connection. One considers the cognitive capacity of infants and children for dual language learning, whereas the other considers the cognitive consequences of dual language learning. With respect to the cognitive capacity for dual language learning, there is no scientific evidence that infants' language learning ability is limited to one language. To the contrary, research on infants with monolingual and dual language exposure suggests that they have the innate capacity to acquire two languages without significant costs to the development of either language, provided they receive consistent and adequate exposure to both languages on a continuous basis. Viewed from the perspective of intelligence, research has shown that general intelligence is often correlated with second language proficiency in domains related to reading and writing but not necessarily to oral language development. Affective and personal factors, such as attitudes and motivation, can be important, even more important in some cases, especially if a second language is being learned in school or the child is learning an additional language under difficult personal or social circumstances. These other factors deserve careful consideration when clinicians are trying to understand the source of an individual learner's difficulty with language.

The cognitive consequences of dual language learning can be varied and probably depend on the circumstances of acquisition. In particular, whether the learning environment supports additive or subtractive bilingualism and whether the child achieves advanced bilingual proficiency can have important consequences for language learning and possibly even cognitive outcomes. Positive cognitive consequences are more likely to result from additive bilingual environments in which the child achieves advanced levels of language proficiency. Negative consequences are more likely to result from subtractive environments in which the child's proficiency in one or both languages is truncated. The latter is particularly true if the child is being educated through the medium of the second language. Dual language children should be provided support—affective and linguistic—to learn both languages fully. Continuous, consistent, and rich exposure to both languages is important for full dual language development.

REFERENCES

Adams, M.J. (1990). *Beginning to read: Thinking and learning about print.* Cambridge: MIT Press.

Arsenian, S. (1945). Bilingualism in the post-war world. *Psychological Bulletin, 42,* 65–85.

Berk, L. (2003). *Child development.* Toronto: Pearson Education Canada.

Bialystok, E. (2001). *Bilingualism in development: Language, literacy, and cognition.* New York: Cambridge University Press.

Bosch, L., & Sebastián-Gallés, N. (2001). Early language differentiation in bilingual infants. In J. Cenoz & F. Genesee (Eds.), *Trends in bilingual acquisition* (pp. 71–94). Amsterdam: John Benjamins.

Boysson-Bardies, B. (1999). *How language comes to children.* Cambridge, MA: MIT Press.

Cummins, J. (1976). The influence of bilingualism on cognitive growth: A synthesis of research findings and explanatory hypotheses. *Working Papers on Bilingualism, 9,* 1–43.

Cummins, J. (2000). *Language, power and pedagogy: Bilingual children in the crossfire.* Clevedon, England: Multilingual Matters.

Darcy, N. (1946). The effect of bilingualism upon the measurement of the intelligence of children of preschool age. *Journal of Educational Psychology, 37,* 21–44.

DeCasper, A.J., & Fifer, W.P. (1980). Of human bonding: Newborns prefer their mothers' voices. *Science, 208,* 1174–1176.

DeCasper, A.J., & Spence, M.J. (1986) Prenatal maternal speech influences newborns' perceptions of speech sounds. *Infant Behavior and Development, 9,* 133–150.

Diebold, A.R. (1968). The consequences of early bilingualism in cognitive and personality formation. In E. Norbeck, D. Price-Williams, & W.M. McCord (Eds.), *The study of personality: An interdisciplinary appraisal* (pp. 218–245). New York: Holt, Rinehart & Winston.

Dunn, L.M., & Dunn, L.M. (1997). *Peabody Picture Vocabulary Test–Third Edition.* Circle Pines, MN: American Guidance Service.

Fennel, C.T., & Werker, J. (2003, May 1). *Does exposure to multiple languages affect infants' use of phonetic detail in a word learning task?* Paper presented at the 4th International Symposium on Bilingualism, Tempe, AZ.

Foreman, J. (2002, October 7). Health sense: The evidence speaks well of bilingualism's effect on kids. *Los Angeles Times,* p. S1.

Genesee, F. (1976). The role of intelligence in second language learning. *Language Learning, 26,* 267–280.

Genesee, F. (1987). *Learning through two languages: Studies of immersion and bilingual education*. Rowley, MA: Newbury House.

Golinkoff, R., & Hirsh-Pasek, K. (1999). *How babies talk*. New York: Dutton/ Penguin Putnam.

Hakuta, K. (1986). *Mirror of language*. New York: Basic Books.

Jusczyk, P.W. (1985). On characterizing the development of speech perception. In J. Mehler & R. Rox (Eds.), *Neonate cognition: Beyond the blooming, buzzing confusion* (pp. 199–229). Mahwah, NJ: Lawrence Erlbaum Associates.

Jusczyk, P.W. (1999). *The discovery of spoken language*. Cambridge, MA: MIT Press.

Macnamara, J. (1966). *Bilingualism and primary education*. Edinburgh, Scotland: Edinburgh University Press.

Maneva, B., & Genesee, F. (2002). Bilingual babbling: Evidence for language differentiation in dual language acquisition. In B. Skarabela et al. (Eds.), *The Proceedings of the 26th Boston University Conference on Language Development* (pp. 383–392). Somerville, MA: Cascadilla Press.

Mehler, J., Jusczyk, P.W., Lambertz, G., Halsted, N., Bertoncini, J., & Amiel-Tison, C. (1988). A precursor of language acquisition in young infants. *Cognition, 29,* 143–178.

Oller, D.K., Eilers, R.E., Urbano, R., & Cobo-Lewis, A.B. (1997). Development of precursors to speech in infants exposed to two languages. *Journal of Child Language, 24,* 407–426.

Padilla, A.M., & Liebman, E. (1975). Language acquisition in the bilingual child. *Bilingual Review, 2*(1, 2), 34–55.

Peal, E., & Lambert, W.E. (1962). The relation of bilingualism to intelligence. *Psychological Monographs, 76,* 1–23.

Pearson, B.Z., Fernandez, S., Lewedag, V., & Oller, D.K. (1997). Input factors in lexical learning of bilingual infants (ages 10 to 30 months). *Applied Psycholinguistics, 18,* 41–58.

Petitto, L.A., Katerelos, M., Levy, B.G., Gauna, K., Tetreault, K., & Ferraro, V. (2001). Bilingual signed and spoken language acquisition from birth: Implications for the mechanism underlying early bilingual language acquisition. *Journal of Child Language, 28,* 453–496.

Polka, L., & Sundara, M. (2003). Word segmentation in monolingual and bilingual infant learners of English and French. In M.J. Solé, D. Recasens, & J. Romero (Eds.), *Proceedings of the International Congress of Phonetic Sciences, 15,* 1021–1024.

Raven, J.C. (1965). *The Coloured Progressive Matrices Test*. London: Lewis.

Rosenblum, T., & Pinker, S.A. (1983). Word magic revisited: Monolingual and bilingual children's understanding of the word-object relationship. *Child Development, 54,* 773–780.

Werker, J.F., & Peg, J.E. (1992). Infant speech perception and phonological acquisition. In C.A. Ferguson, L. Menn, & C. Stoel-Gammon (Eds.), *Phonological development: Models, research, implications*. Timonium, MD: York Press.

Understanding Bilingual and Second Language Acquisition

CHAPTER 4

Bilingual First
Language Acquisition

This chapter addresses the language development of simultaneous bilingual children, who acquire two languages from birth or from early on in the preschool years. James, Bistra, and Pasquala, profiled in Chapter 1, are all simultaneous bilingual children because they have been consistently exposed to dual language input from birth in their homes. One difference between them is the minority/majority status of the two languages they are learning. James is learning French and English in a city where both languages have high status and are widely used. Bistra, however, is learning Bulgarian and English in the United States in a city where there are very few Bulgarian speakers other than her mother. Thus, Bulgarian is a minority language. Pasquala falls between the two because one of her two languages is Spanish, which is not a high-status language like French in Canada, but it is much more widely spoken than Bulgarian in the United States.

The importance of this minority/majority language distinction is how it can influence children's ultimate success at learning both languages. Many simultaneous bilingual children like Bistra may be proficient in both languages when they are 3 years old, but shift **dominance** sharply to the majority language, typically the language of schooling, when they are older, and they may even end up not being bilingual adolescents and adults. Much of the research on bilingual preschool children is based on children like Bistra, who are the offspring children of so-called "linguistically mixed marriages," in which the parents have different native languages and each parent speaks his or her native language to the child. One language, however, is not frequently used in the community outside the home. This kind of situation is called **family bilingualism.**

In contrast, our own research, which we present in this chapter, is based on children like James and Pasquala, who grow up in both a bilingual family and a bilingual community where they are expected to develop their bilingualism past their childhood years. Regardless of whether simultaneous bilingual children are destined to become bilingual adults, educators and health practitioners should be aware of the impact of simultaneous dual language exposure on children's language development. They may be asked to give advice about both majority and minority bilingual children who speak two languages at the age of school entry, when the children's language abilities are being assessed.

The contexts in which James, Bistra, and Pasquala are growing up are the most common, but they are not the only routes to simultaneous bilingualism. Some parents expose their children to another language from birth via a full-time caregiver who speaks another language. An example of this is an English-speaking family living in Los Angeles who hires a live-in, Spanish-speaking nanny when their child is an infant (see page 11). If this child's exposure to Spanish is frequent and sustained over the preschool years, she could be considered a simultaneous bilingual, like James and Bistra, even though the parents do not speak Spanish. Children of parents who travel or live outside their home country for business or personal reasons might also experience simultaneous bilingual acquisition.

Our primary goal in this chapter is to provide information about what is typical in the preschool language development of simultaneous bilingual children. We use monolinguals as a reference point in our descriptions. In so doing, we highlight the similarities and differences between bilingual and monolingual children that will permit professionals to learn what to expect of simultaneous bilingual children and, thus, better identify atypical language development in bilingual children. The global question in the minds of professionals that we would like this chapter to answer is, When should the differences bilingual children present relative to monolingual children be cause for concern? More specifically,

1. Do children exposed to two languages from birth learn bilingually at first? That is, do they have one single language system or two separate language systems?

2. Do bilingual children show the same stages in their language development as monolingual children? If bilingual children display some unique developmental stages, should this be cause for concern?

BOX 4.1

E-mail message from a concerned parent to Fred Genesee:

Dr. Genesee,
We hope you can shed some light on a question about infant bilingualism. My Russian wife and I hope to raise our soon-to-be-adopted 10-week-old infant bilingually. (The infant comes from Georgia, a former Russian republic.) My wife insists on the importance of almost exclusively speaking Russian. I was born and raised in California and have only begun to learn Russian. I would like my wife mostly to speak English to our infant when I am around. My question: Will my wife's speaking Russian almost exclusively increase the chances of our child becoming bilingual? I suspect there are both cognitive and affective factors.
Thank you for any assistance,
A Father

Parents often ask us what is the best way to raise infants bilingually. Although many different methods can work, the one that people use the most is the one parent–one language method. In this case, each parent speaks his or her native language exclusively with the child. This ensures that the child will get sufficient input in both languages, and this is especially important when one language is a minority language and spoken very little outside the home.

---

3. Are bilingual children slower to learn language than monolingual children? Do they show the same rate of development in both of their languages? If not, is asymmetrical development cause for concern?

4. How does specific language impairment (SLI) affect the language development of bilingual children? Does it affect their patterns and rates of development to make them look different from monolingual children with SLI? Is it a challenge for children with SLI to learn two languages?

Although there may not be as many differences between bilingual and monolingual language development as one might expect, the previous questions involve comparisons. Therefore, before we begin to answer this list of questions, we discuss alternative ways of viewing differences between monolingual and bilingual children.

Historically, bilingualism in young children was thought to put them at an intellectual disadvantage, which concerned educational policy makers (see Chapter 3). Because of this historical attitude, differences between bilingual and monolingual language development are often viewed negatively.

Bilingual children have often been considered typically developing only if they appear to be like monolingual children; they are considered not to be developing typically or to have disabilities if they show any differences. This kind of attitude results when monolingual children's development is taken as the norm even though, as discussed in Chapter 1, childhood bilingualism is most likely as common worldwide as monolingualism. Given how widespread bilingualism in childhood is, we cannot help but acknowledge that the human mind is just as capable of bilingual development as monolingual development, even if there are some differences (see Chapter 3). Any differences between the two should not be taken immediately to imply that bilingualism has pernicious effects on language development as a whole. We believe that a more appropriate attitude is that there is more than one path to acquiring language, and one of these paths is to acquire two languages at a time.

DO BILINGUAL CHILDREN HAVE ONE LANGUAGE SYSTEM OR TWO?

Some researchers support the idea that bilingual children do not acquire language bilingually at first. That is, they go through a stage when the two input languages are treated as if they were part of a single language. Proponents of this view believe that the fused language system that results from this initial process differentiates into dual language systems later in development, sometime before 3 years of age.

The most influential model of this **Unitary Language System Hypothesis** (see Figure 4.1) was put forth by Virginia Volterra and Traute Taeschner (1978). They proposed that bilingual children begin the acquisition process with a single language system that combines the words and the grammatical rules from their dual language input. At the next stage, the

Figure 4.1. Unitary Language System Hypothesis. When an infant is presented with dual language input, he does not construct two separate linguistic representations at first. Instead, he melds the dual language input into one system that must undergo a process of differentiation before age 3, after which he is considered to be bilingual. Researchers Virginia Volterra and Traute Taeschner put forth the most articulated model of this view in 1978.

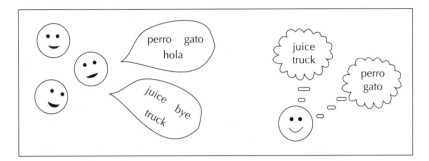

Figure 4.2. Dual Language System Hypothesis. When an infant is presented with dual language input, she constructs two separate linguistic representations from the outset (e.g., two vocabularies, two grammar systems). The child is always considered bilingual, and the language systems never have to differentiate. This has been the majority view among researchers since the 1990s.

words differentiate into two vocabularies/lexicons, but the system of grammatical rules remains the same for both languages. In the final stage, the system of grammatical rules becomes differentiated, and the bilingual child can be said to have separate linguistic systems, as bilingual adults do. See Box 4.2 for an explanation of this model in Volterra and Taeshner's own words.

An alternative view to Volterra and Taeschner's model is one put forth by Fred Genesee (1989), the **Dual Language System Hypothesis** (see Figure 4.2), which assumes that children exposed to two languages from birth establish two separate linguistic systems from the outset of acquisition. According to this view, children with simultaneous dual language exposure never go through a noticeable period where their linguistic representations are unified and later separate from one into two systems.

Both the Unitary and Dual Language System Hypotheses refer to the nature of the language representation in a child's mind, so it is relevant to ask whether this is a meaningful distinction for understanding the child's language behavior. It is meaningful because these two viewpoints make very different predictions about how young bilingual children will use their

BOX 4.2

Volterra and Taeschner's Model of Early Bilingual Development:

"Analysing the gradual learning process through which a child becomes bilingual from early infancy, three stages can be distinguished: (1) the child has one lexical system which includes both languages; (2) the child distinguishes two different lexicons but applies the same syntactic rules to both languages; (3) the child has two linguistic codes, differentiated both in lexicon and in syntax. . . . Only at the end of this stage . . . can one say that a child is truly bilingual" (Volterra & Taeschner, 1978, p. 311).

languages and what developmental stages they will go through. If young bilingual children initially have a unitary vocabulary and grammar, then one would expect them to frequently mix words and phrases from both languages together regardless of language context or conversation partners. One might also expect them to use grammar rules from one language with words from another and even blend the rules from both languages together. Furthermore, it is possible that the process of differentiating two language systems could be cognitively costly for a bilingual child, causing a slow-down in their language development between the ages of 2 and 3 years. In sum, if the Unitary Language System Hypothesis is correct, then we would expect bilingual children's early language productions to be quite different from productions of monolingual children acquiring either language, but most research in bilingual acquisition overwhelmingly supports the Dual Language System Hypothesis. We review the research on this topic according to language domain: phonology (sound system), vocabulary, and grammar.

Phonology

Some researchers present evidence to support the Unitary Language System Hypothesis with respect to the sound system of children's languages. For example, Celce-Murcia (1978) noted that the French-English bilingual child she studied had the same phonological substitution processes in both languages. Phonological substitution processes occur when a child uses an easier-to-pronounce sound segment instead of the correct sound segment. A *sound segment* is like a letter in the written system. For example, many children substitute a vowel for an /l/ at the ends of words so that the word *ball* would be pronounced "bao" or "bau." This kind of evidence for a unitary language system is problematic because these substitution processes are very common across children and languages. Therefore, two monolingual French- and English-speaking children the same age as Celce-Murcia's bilingual child could easily have displayed identical phonological substitutions in their speech.

Given that the early phonological system of children is so similar cross-linguistically, how can we tell if bilingual children have one or two phonologies? Johnson and Lancaster (1998) examined the use of sound segments exclusive to either Norwegian or English phonology in the word productions of a Norwegian-English toddler younger than 2 years of age. Even at this early age, the production and distribution of these sounds in the boy's words showed he was building separate sound segment inventories for his two languages.

Vocabulary

One of Volterra and Taeschner's (1978) sources of evidence for a unified vocabulary was the initial absence of **translation equivalents** in bilingual children's vocabularies. A translation equivalent is a word that has the same meaning in two languages, such as *zapatos* in Spanish and *shoes* in English. The two girls studied by Volterra and Taeschner had few pairs of words in their combined vocabularies. These researchers suggested that bilingual children learn lexical labels for concepts on a one-to-one basis and avoid learning words with the same meaning. For example, if a child exposed to Spanish and English acquired the word *zapatos,* she would not have *shoes* in her vocabulary right away because this concept had already been labeled.

When children start to use translation equivalents, this is considered evidence for two vocabularies, hence two language systems. While the two girls studied by Volterra and Taeschner (1978) may have had few translation equivalents, they appear to be anomalous among the many other bilingual children studied. Researchers examining Spanish-English, Portuguese-English, and French-English bilingual children have all found translation equivalents from the earliest stages, even before children have vocabularies of 50 words (Nicoladis & Genesee, 1996a; Nicoladis & Secco, 2000; Pearson, Fernández, & Oller, 1995; Quay, 1995). In a large-scale study examining 27 Spanish-English bilingual children in the Miami area, Barbara Pearson and her colleagues found that, on average, 30% of bilingual toddlers' early vocabularies are translation equivalents. Thus, there is compelling empirical evidence to suggest that bilingual children establish two vocabularies from the onset of acquisition.

It is worthwhile to ask why bilingual children would have only 30% translation equivalents in their vocabularies. Why don't bilingual children have a larger number of translation equivalents? The answer to this question becomes clear when we consider how words are learned. Children learn new words as they interact with the world around them while hearing speech. Children do not duplicate every experience in both languages. A bilingual child may acquire certain words during an activity with his Spanish-speaking grandmother and not learn the English equivalents for some time because he does not engage in that activity with his English-speaking play-mates. If English is spoken by the child mainly at child care, then he will learn many English words related to that environment, and there may be many home-related vocabulary items lacking in his English vocabulary. Even fluent bilingual adults have gaps in their vocabularies due to experiential factors.

Bilingual individuals, particularly bilingual children, should not be expected to have a translation equivalent for absolutely every word. Pearson and her research group in Miami looked at how the proportion of *singlets,* or words that do not have a translation equivalent, changes over time in a bilingual child's languages. The percentage of singlets in their dual language vocabularies was 50% in grade 1 (age 6) and declined to 30% by grade 5 (age 11) in Spanish-English bilingual children. Bilingual students attending college still had an average of 10% singlets (Pearson, 1998). In other words, these bilingual students acquired more and more translation equivalents as their language development and experiences expanded but never reached a point where they had 100% translation equivalents.

Grammar

Volterra and Taeschner (1978) claimed that the bilingual children they studied had a unified grammatical rule system for their two languages until they were 3 years old. Once the children appeared to have differentiated vocabularies (i.e., when translation equivalents emerged), they still seemed to use the same grammatical rules to make sentences in both languages, even when this resulted in erroneous sentences. For example, one child formulated most of her negative sentences in both Italian and German by putting a negative marker (e.g., *not* in English) after the verb. This word order corresponds roughly to German grammar but not to Italian grammar, in which the negative marker comes before the verb.

Since Volterra and Taeschner's study, a wealth of contrasting research has emerged that shows that bilingual children can have separate grammatical systems—in some cases even from the beginning of their first word combinations. For example, like German and Italian, French and English differ in terms of the placement of the negative marker. In French, the negative marker *pas* comes after the main verb, but in English the negative marker *not* comes in between the main verb and a verb such as *do, can*, or *is*. Compare this French sentence with its English translation where the negative markers and main verbs are italicized: Le bébé ne *boit pas* le lait/The baby is *not drinking* the milk. If French-English bilingual children had a unitary grammatical system, they might go through a stage where they adopt one of these rules for both languages, so they might say, "Le bébé ne *pas boit* le lait" in French or "The baby is *drinking not* the milk" in English—neither of which is a grammatically well-formed sentence. In language samples of 15 French-English bilingual children ages 2–4 years, Paradis, Nicoladis, and Genesee (2000) found only sporadic use of the wrong order for the placement of the negative marker in either language. There was no evidence for a stage where any of these 15 children had a unitary rule for negative marker placement in their grammars.

As of 2004, the majority of researchers in the field believe that bilingual children have two language systems very early on in their development. In other words, researchers believe that the human language faculty is perfectly capable of sorting out dual language input and establishing two linguistic systems, and there does not appear to be a stage unique to bilingual development where children's language system undergoes differentiation. Does this mean that bilingual children are like "two monolingual children in one" in their language development? Not entirely, and in the following sections we discuss the ways bilingual children can appear similar to and different from monolingual children.

DO BILINGUAL AND MONOLINGUAL CHILDREN HAVE THE SAME STAGES IN THEIR LANGUAGE DEVELOPMENT?

All children produce sentences that are **target deviant** in their developmental language. For example, an English-speaking child might say, "Me no want broccoli," instead of "I don't want broccoli." Even nonlinguists understand that these target-deviant sentences are part of a natural process as the child gradually develops adultlike language skills. Many kinds of target-deviant sentences can be very systematic across individuals acquiring the same language and can follow definable stages. When we refer to stages in language development, we are mostly talking about these target-deviant sentences that children produce as their language gradually approximates the adult system. The question we address in this section is, Do bilingual children show the same target-deviant sentences and, therefore, the same stages as monolingual children in both of their languages, or does the dual language experience cause them to produce unique target-deviant structures and go through some distinct stages?

In order to examine how monolingual and bilingual children compare with respect to stages in development, we will continue to discuss negative sentences in French and English. Let's first determine what the stages and target-deviant sentences look like in the monolingual acquisition of the two languages, then we'll move on to show some data from bilingual children.

French-speaking children go through two stages in acquiring negation. At Stage 1, they produce sentences where the negative marker, *pas,* is placed before the main verb, so the verb is in the infinitive form (e.g., "le bébé *pas boire* le lait"), which is a target-deviant sentence. At Stage 2, French-speaking children essentially have figured out the adult system because they place the negative marker after the main verb, so the verb is conjugated (e.g., "le bébé *boit pas* le lait"). French-speaking children go from Stage 1 to Stage 2 at approximately 2–2½ years of age.

In English, there are three stages children go through en route to achieving the adult system, and they often do not reach Stage 3 until they are well over 3 years of age. At Stage 1, children place a negative marker such as *no* or *not* sentence initially (e.g., *"no Leila have a turn"* or *"no me wearing mittens"*). At Stage 2, they place the negative marker sentence medially and before the verb, but they do not include a verb such as *do, can*, or *is* (e.g., "me *no want* broccoli" or "Martin *not going* to school"). In Stage 3 in English, children have acquired the target system, where they include the

BOX 4.3

Target-deviant sentences and stages—Young children produce sentences that are different from adult sentences, such as "Me no want broccoli." In this case, the adult form, "I don't want broccoli," is the target, and the child's form is target deviant because it is not identical to the adult model. Target-deviant sentences could simply be called errors because they do not follow the rules of the adult grammar, but the term *error* could imply that the child is doing something wrong, whereas producing these kinds of sentences is a typical and natural part of the process of language acquisition. All aspects of children's speech can be target deviant: children make errors in pronunciation, choice of words, as well as grammar.

Target-deviant sentences are usually systematic in that they follow a rule system particular to the grammar at that stage in the child's language development, rather than to the adult grammar rule. For example, the adult English rule to make a negative is to put the negative marker *not* after a verb such as *can, do,* and *is,* and before the main verb, as in "I *do not want* broccoli." The child's target-deviant sentence comes from a stage where the child's grammar rule is to put a negative marker *no* before the main verb only, as in "Me *no want* broccoli." Typically developing children pass through stages in which the grammar rules gradually get closer to the adult language, and the number of target-deviant sentences diminishes.

verbs *do, can,* or *is* in their sentences (e.g., "Leila *can't have* a turn" or "Martin *isn't going* to school").

As mentioned previously, we have examined the negative sentences over time in 15 French-English bilingual children and have conducted more focused analyses on three of the children, William, Gene, and Olivier, from ages 2 to 3 years (Paradis & Genesee, 1996). Each of these three boys passed from Stage 1 to Stage 2 in French before the age of 3. By the age of 3 years, more than 90% of their negative sentences in French were adultlike in grammatical form. In English, from the ages of 2 to 2½, the majority of their negative sentences were Stage 1, and from 2½ until 3 years, the majority shifted to Stage 2 sentences. During this time, none of the boys used Stage 3 negative sentences in English. Our focused analysis told us that these three bilingual children passed through the same stages at the same ages as their monolingual counterparts, and moreover, they showed separate developmental paths for their French and English.

Both bilingual and monolingual children show the same patterns when producing sentences without the target verb forms. For example, they omit verbs such as *do, can,* and *is,* and they also drop suffixes, or endings, on the verb. Some typical sentences young children say in English are "the truck going over there" or "the truck go in the box" instead of the adult version, "the truck *is* going over there" or "the truck *goes* in the box." Children learning French also produce target-deviant verb forms, but the striking difference between the two languages is that children learning French acquire the target system more rapidly in development than children learning English. So, at virtually any point in development between the ages of 2 and 3 years, French-speaking children will typically produce more adultlike verb forms than English-speaking children.

The graphs in Figure 4.3 show the use of verb forms in French and English for five bilingual children at 2 years, 2½ years, and 3 years of age. The bars represent the percentage of "correct," or adultlike, verb forms used by the children. Notice that for each child and each age the percent correct for French is higher than for English. These data illustrate how the stages in the monolingual acquisition of each of these languages are followed by the bilingual children. In other words, the bilingual children go through the same prolonged stage of producing target-deviant verb forms in English as monolingual children do, and they go through a much shorter stage of this type in French, just like monolingual children. Furthermore, very few of the target-deviant verb forms used by the bilingual children were different from the target-deviant forms monolingual children typically use.

What we have just shown about French-English negative sentences and verb forms holds true for other aspects of language and for other bilingual children. The results of research projects that have followed groups of children acquiring the same language pair over time, such as the Montreal-McGill project in Canada (e.g., Paradis & Genesee, 1996, 1997) and the DUFDE project in Hamburg, Germany (e.g., Meisel, 1989, 1994), overwhelmingly support the claim that, for the most part, bilingual children demonstrate the same stages in their developmental language—from the sound system to grammar—as their monolingual peers. This does not mean that bilingual children *never* produce developmental language that has some unique target-deviant structures that reflect their dual language systems; this is the topic of the next section on **crosslinguistic influence**. What this does mean is that when looking beyond specific instances of crosslinguistic influence and focusing on the major developmental stages, there are no significant differences between monolingual and bilingual children. Therefore, parents, educators, and health care practitioners can expect to see bilingual children go through the same kinds of stages that they have seen in monolingual children, on the whole. This point was also made in Chapter 3 with respect to early milestones in language development.

Crosslinguistic Influence in Bilingual Acquisition

The majority of researchers agree that bilingual children have dual language systems from early on, perhaps even at the onset of language acquisition, and that bilingual children acquire language following the same stages as

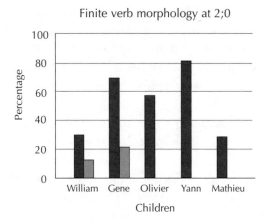

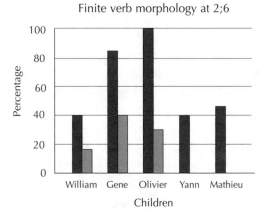

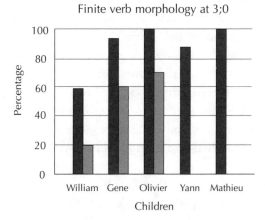

Figure 4.3. Accuracy with use of finite verb morphology in French and English for five French-English bilingual children from the ages of 2 to 3 years. *Sources:* Paradis and Genesee (1996, 1997). (Key = ■ French; ▨ English)

> **BOX 4.4**
>
> *Crosslinguistic influences*—interactions between the bilingual child's two languages during development that result in target-deviant structures in one language that reflect structural properties of the other language. Crosslinguistic influence is distinct from the concept of a Unitary Language System because the target-deviant structures do not result from across the board blending of the two languages, but instead are limited in scope. The target-deviant structures that result from crosslinguistic influence are not pervasive, and many researchers have found that they are not permanent in a bilingual child's language; they can occur as part of the bilingual development process.

monolingual children, but this does not necessarily mean that bilingual children's two languages are hermetically sealed and utterly autonomous in development. As researchers have moved beyond the Unitary versus Dual Language System debate, they have been engaged in understanding the degree of interconnectivity and separation between bilingual children's two developing languages. Knowledge to date is that bilingual children can show some target-deviant structures in their speech that appear to be influenced in their form by the other language.

To borrow from our previous discussion about negative sentences, an example of such **crosslinguistic influence** would be a French-English bilingual child producing the English sentence "the baby *drink not* the milk," in which the *not* is placed after the main verb as it would be in French. If such a sentence just occurs once, then it is most likely some kind of code-mixing, which we talk about in Chapter 5, but if we see these kinds of sentences used often for a certain period of time by a bilingual child, we assume that the child has a rule in her English grammar that allows for these kinds of sentences, and this rule reflects the rule in her French grammar. It is possible, then, that this English rule is the product of crosslanguage contact during development. As mentioned previously, we have found very few crosslinguistic structures in the form of negation in our corpus of 15 French-English bilingual children. So, not only did they not have a unified system for negation, but they also did not seem to have much crosslinguistic influence in this part of the grammar either. Other researchers, however, have found crosslinguistic structures in their studies of bilingual children.

There are two kinds of crosslinguistic influences: qualitative and quantitative. Qualitative crosslinguistic influence results in target-deviant structures that are not attested in the monolingual acquisition of the language. Quantitative crosslinguistic influences do not result in unique target-deviant structures, but instead, they result in an increased frequency in the appearance of target-deviant structures that are also evident in a monolingual child's development of that language.

Interesting instances of qualitative crosslinguistic word order structure have been documented in the bilingual acquisition of Cantonese (Chinese) and English by Hong Kong–based researchers Virginia Yip and Stephen Matthews (2000). In Cantonese, relative clauses are placed before the noun they are modifying, whereas in English, relative clauses appear after the noun they are modifying. Yip and Matthews recorded several instances of Cantonese relative clause order in a Cantonese-English child's English for a period between the ages of 2½ and 3 years, when the child was dominant in Cantonese. For example, the child asked, *"Where's the Santa Claus give me the gun?"* instead of the target English structure "Where's the gun *that Santa Claus give (gave) me?"* This kind of word order for sentences with relative clauses is not common in the monolingual acquisition of English, so this instance of crosslinguistic influence generated target-deviant structures unique to bilingual acquisition.

Several researchers have found quantitative crosslinguistic influence in the word order in sentences. To illustrate this, consider English and German. German has more complicated rules for word order in sentences; for example, a sentence can begin with the subject of the verb or the object of the verb, depending on what the speaker wants to focus on. Also, in German, there are different rules for where the verb is placed in the sentence if it is a main clause or a subordinate clause. English, however, has more straightforward rules for word order in sentences, so speakers must put the subject of the verb first, as in *"the baby* is drinking the milk," and cannot put the object first. Therefore, *"the milk* is the baby drinking" is not an appropriate way to say the previous sentence in English. In effect, English word order rules are a subset of the more complicated rules for German.

Susanne Döpke (1998, 2000) extensively examined word order in a group of German-English bilingual children from Australia. Not surprisingly, monolingual children acquiring German go through developmental stages in their acquisition of word order before they converge on the target system. Döpke found that the bilingual children also passed through these stages in German, but they produced many more target-deviant structures in their German that corresponded to the word order rules for English than monolingual German-speaking children. Döpke suggested that the English input these children were receiving was responsible for this difference between their German and that of monolingual German children. The reason why this effect is considered quantitative is that the bilingual children were not using target-deviant structures in their developmental language that had never been seen before in monolingual children. They were just using them more often and for a longer period of time.

Most researchers have found quantitative rather than qualitative forms of crosslinguistic influence, which is consistent with our point throughout this chapter that the similarities in acquisition patterns between monolingual and bilingual children far outweigh the differences. This means that crosslinguistic influence may not always be noticeable unless one is gauging the frequency with which a child is using a particular construction. Furthermore, crosslinguistic influences of any kind are not rampant in the speech of bilingual children; on the whole, they use grammatical structures appropriate for their stage in development in that language. But when professionals dealing with bilingual children come across target-deviant structures that appear to be influenced by the child's other language, it is important to bear in mind that this phenomenon is typical in bilingual development and is not a sign of confusion or difficulty coping with dual language input. In fact, borrowing a grammatical structure from one language to use with the other could be interpreted as a clever and practical strategy bilingual children use during development when they have not yet acquired the relevant target structure in the other language.

ARE THERE DIFFERENCES IN RATE OF DEVELOPMENT BETWEEN BILINGUAL AND MONOLINGUAL CHILDREN?

When examining developmental language, researchers look not only at patterns of acquisition but also at how rapidly children acquire target-appropriate patterns—in other words, their rate of development. As discussed in Chapter 3, there is no systematic evidence that bilingual children are slower than monolingual children to pass through early critical milestones such as babbling and use of their first word combinations. To put it more generally, infants have the capacity to process input from one or two languages in roughly the same amount of time. Is this also true for language development past the early months? Many parents, teachers, and health care professionals dealing with children have the impression that bilingual children go through the stages of language development more slowly than monolingual children because they have a "double burden"—twice as much language to acquire in the same amount of time—but the research does not support this impression for either the early milestones as discussed in Chapter 3 or for grammatical development after the age of 2 years.

There is very little comprehensive research on the issue of whether bilingual children are slower to develop grammar. All of the research to date is based on case studies or small groups of children. In addition, bilingual children are difficult to place in large groups for research because they are not homogenous as a population; each child can have different degrees and contexts of exposure to each language, and this can affect their rate of development in each language. Thus, the case studies and small group studies might not tell what *does* happen, normatively speaking, to rates of language development in the bilingual context, but they do tell us what *can* happen (see Chapter 3 for more discussion of this issue).

Previously in this chapter, we discussed French–English bilingual children's acquisition of negative sentences and verb forms, and we showed that they go through the same stages as monolingual children. Now, we focus on whether they go through these same stages at the same time. With respect to negative sentences, the bilingual children we studied achieved the target system in French between 2 and 3 years of age. Because 2½ years of age is typical for monolingual children, the bilingual children's development is within the same range. In English, the bilingual children were at Stage 2 by 3 years of age, whereas monolingual English children can take until 4 years of age to fully achieve Stage 3. Again, these bilingual children are not outside the monolingual norms.

Turning to verb forms, let's compare the bilingual children's performance at age 3 directly with findings from monolingual children. Ten monolingual French-speaking 3-year-olds we studied produced verb forms accurately (i.e., targetlike) in 86%–97% of their utterances (Paradis & Crago, 2001). Four of the five bilingual children in Figure 4.3 displayed accuracy rates of over 90% in their French at the same age. For English, the 21 3-year-old monolingual children studied by Rice, Wexler, and Hershberger (1998) used correct verb forms 56% on average, with a standard deviation of 22%, which indicates a lot of individual variation. Three of the five bilingual children in our group were within one standard deviation of the monolingual mean, and two fell just below one standard deviation. So, they showed a lot of variation in English and much less in French, just like monolingual children.

Overall, what these observations about negative sentences and verb forms demonstrate is that bilingual children do not cluster as a group at or below the lower bound as set by monolingual children. In fact, two of the bilingual children we examined scored at the mean or above in *both* of their languages for correct verb forms. Thus, we can conclude from this small group data that it is possible for bilingual children to exhibit the same rate of grammatical development as monolingual children. At the same time, it is important to remember that bilingual children, like monolingual children, vary considerably in their individual rates of development; some children acquire language faster than others. We now examine a couple of special aspects of language development in bilingual children that need to be taken into account when assessing whether a bilingual child is on track.

The Special Case of Vocabulary

Researchers, educators, and clinicians often measure the size of a child's vocabulary in order to assess whether that child's language is typically developing. In contrast to what we just discussed for rates of grammatical development, bilingual–monolingual differences have been consistently documented for vocabulary size. Preschool and early school-age bilingual children, approximately 3–6 years old, frequently show smaller vocabularies in each language than monolingual children on standardized tests (Nicoladis & Genesee, 1996b; Umbel, Pearson, Fernández, & Oller, 1992).

Why would bilingual children perform like monolingual children in other aspects of language development but not in vocabulary development? One explanation for this discrepancy has to do with what children are learning when they are accumulating vocabulary as opposed to learning grammar. Vocabulary accumulation can be considered distinct from other aspects of language learning because it involves novel encoding of individual items, as opposed to acquiring rules or patterns that generalize across structures. Therefore, vocabulary learning could be considered more demanding in terms of time, frequency of contextual experiences, and memory load. It is also important to consider that a bilingual child may use one language in certain contexts more than the other, so the child would not have completely parallel vocabularies, as we discussed previously for translation equivalents.

Because bilingual children have the same cognitive abilities and limitations with respect to memory load as monolingual children, one would expect that their vocabulary in each of their languages would be smaller than that of monolingual children. Viewed this way, it is not surprising that bilingual children may not have accumulated the same absolute number of novel items in two languages in the same amount of time as a monolingual child has for one language; however, Barbara Pearson and colleagues in Miami have shown that when the vocabularies from both languages of a bilingual child are combined and the translation equivalents are only counted once, this total "conceptual" vocabulary is similar in size to monolingual norms (Pearson, 1998; Pearson, Fernández, & Oller, 1993).

Language Dominance and Rates of Bilingual Development

Almost all studies of simultaneous bilingual children have found that even though the children have been acquiring two languages from birth, the two languages often do not develop in perfect synchrony. The language in which bilingual children appear to have greater proficiency is commonly referred

---

BOX 4.5

Dominance—the condition in which bilingual people have greater grammatical proficiency in, more vocabulary for, or greater fluency in one
language or simply use one language (i.e., the dominant language) more
often. The dominant language can change throughout the life span, and
a bilingual person can be just slightly dominant or highly dominant in
one language. In bilingual children, dominance potentially has effects for
language choice (see Chapter 5), and for how closely bilingual children
can be compared with monolingual children with respect to rate of development.

---

to as their **dominant language** and the other as the **nondominant language.** Most researchers of simultaneous bilingual children consider dominance to be a measure of *relative* proficiency between the two languages that
the child is learning; dominance is not typically construed as meaning a
simultaneous bilingual child is incompetent in one language or only has
passive knowledge of one language. How can one tell what the dominant
language is? The dominant language usually has a number of the following
characteristics when compared with the nondominant language:

1. Longer mean length of utterance and more advanced grammatical struc-
    tures

2. Larger number of different word types, or verb types in particular, used
    in a stretch of discourse of fixed length

3. Fewer pauses or hesitations

4. Greater volubility

Dominance is typically closely linked to the amount of input the bilingual child receives in each language, which is seldom equal. For example,
a bilingual child might hear Spanish from her mother and English from her
father on weeknights and weekends and hear English during the weekdays
at a child care center. In this case, the child is receiving much more input
in English, and it would be expected for this child to be English dominant.
Barbara Pearson and her colleagues found that Spanish-English bilingual
children who received less than 25% of their input in Spanish often did not
achieve bilingual success; in other words, they never became fluent Spanish
speakers (Pearson, Fernández, Lewedag, & Oller, 1997). Therefore, very
low input for one language could render it a passive language, rather than
a nondominant language. This means that the child does not spontaneously
speak that language but can understand, more or less, speech directed at him in
that language. Over time, passive ability in a language can disappear entirely.

Expectations of balanced development are unrealistic, and it is more likely that bilingual children will be dominant in one language. One consequence of dominance is that a bilingual child may appear to be less advanced in the development of the nondominant language than an average monolingual child of the same age. At this point, we do not know whether a bilingual child's proficiency in the nondominant language can be so low that the child would appear outside the range of performance for typically developing monolingual children in that language in an assessment context; however, it is possible that a child's proficiency in her nondominant language could be so far behind her proficiency in her dominant language that it would not be effective to clinically assess this child in her nondominant language. Also, remember that if the nondominant language is so underdeveloped that the child barely speaks it, then that child is not truly bilingual.

Dominance has another effect on bilingual children, namely their language choice. Fred Genesee and colleagues have conducted a series of studies examining the sensitivity of bilingual children to the language preferences or abilities of their conversation partners (Genesee, Boivin, & Nicoladis, 1996; Genesee, Nicoladis, & Paradis, 1995; Nicoladis & Genesee, 1996a). They found that even bilingual children as young as 2 years old can tailor their language choice to their adult interlocutor; however, bilingual children are often constrained by their dominance in that when they are speaking to an adult in their nondominant language, they often interject individual words and whole utterances from their dominant language in the conversation. Thus, even though bilingual children are very sensitive to appropriate language choice, they may not be able to adhere to one language in a conversation in their nondominant language. This should be taken into account when assessing the language abilities of bilingual children suspected of having language delay or disorder.

HOW DOES SPECIFIC LANGUAGE IMPAIRMENT AFFECT THE LANGUAGE DEVELOPMENT OF BILINGUAL CHILDREN?

The bilingual children we have been discussing until now were typically developing children, and we have pointed out aspects of bilingual children's development that may be different from monolingual children but nevertheless typical. Now, we examine a subpopulation of bilingual children with SLI. What happens to a child with SLI who is exposed to dual language input from birth? Despite the significant Spanish- and French-speaking populations in the United States and Canada and widespread immigration in these countries as well as Australia and Western Europe, surprisingly little research attention has been paid to bilingual acquisition for children with disabilities.

BOX 4.6

E-mail message from a concerned parent to Martha Crago:

Bonjour Mme Crago. J'ai un enfant dysphasique. Mon époux et moi voulons que notre enfant soit bilingue (i.e. qu'il apprenne le français et l'anglais). Toutefois, il nous a été fortement recommandé que nous choisissions seulement une langue, car notre enfant pourrait ne parler aucune des deux langues, i.e. de façon adéquate. Nous voulons savoir si vous pouvez nous éclaircir sur le sujet (nous transmettre vos connaissances ou nous référer des lectures qui pourraient aider notre choix). Nous souhaitons que notre enfant soit bilingue, mais nous voulons être certain que ce n'est pas néfaste pour lui . . . Merci de votre collaboration et de votre temps.
Une Mère

English translation
Hello Mrs. Crago. I have a child with SLI. My husband and I want our child to be bilingual (i.e., to learn French and English). However, it has been strongly recommended to us that we choose just one language, because our child would not be able to speak either of the two languages, i.e., to an adequate degree. We want to know if you could shed some light on this subject (communicate to us your knowledge, or refer us to readings that could help us in our choice). We wish our child to be bilingual, but we want to be certain that it is not harmful for him. . . . Thank you for your assistance and your time.
A Mother

There is very little research on dual language children with SLI and even less on simultaneous bilingual children with SLI.

One unfortunate outcome of this lack of research is that parents, educators, and health practitioners have little information to guide them in making decisions about this population of children. There is a widespread belief in North America and the United Kingdom that bilingualism poses too much of a burden on a child with SLI and that dual language input will slow down an already arduous learning process. Consequently, parents are often counseled to use only one language with their children and effectively arrest their children's bilingual development (see Box 4.6). This kind of decision can have irrevocable and profound costs for a child, for example, loss of educational opportunities, loss of ability to communicate fully with other family members, shift in ethnic identity, and limitations on access to an ethnic community. Moreover, for some families, the choice of using one language is simply not available; the household operates in two languages, and no one can change that. Clearly, the decision to eliminate a language from a child's environment cannot be made lightly and should not be made in ignorance.

We have conducted some of the only existing research on simultaneous bilingual children with SLI. We examined the language production of eight 7-year-old French-English bilingual children with SLI with respect to specific aspects of grammar, including verb forms and object pronouns (Paradis, Crago, & Genesee, 2003; Paradis, Crago, Genesee, & Rice, 2003). All of these children were simultaneous bilingual children from majority language backgrounds. They all had been exposed to both languages in the home from birth and resided in communities where both languages are spoken. These children were growing up very much like James (see Chapter 1). All of the children were assessed with SLI. They were all below age expectations in their linguistic abilities in both their languages; they had IQ scores in the normal range and no frank neurological damage or social-emotional disorders.

Next, we answer a list of questions that our study addressed. It is important to keep in mind that because our sample is not large and the aspects of language we analyzed are not comprehensive, our answers to these questions are tentative. We believe, however, that the information that we can give can provide a base for understanding simultaneous bilingual acquisition under conditions of impairment and for making decisions about such children's language learning environments, education, and intervention. We revisit some of these issues and questions with respect to second language learners with SLI in Chapter 6.

- **Can children with specific language impairment become bilingual?** Children with SLI can become bilingual. Each of the eight children in our study could communicate fluently in both languages. Less than half the children had a strongly dominant language, so most of them were well-balanced bilingual children.

- **Do bilingual children with specific language impairment experience difficulties in both languages?** Bilingual children with SLI experience difficulties in both languages. Each of the children in our study performed below age expectations on standardized language tests in both languages and exhibited deficits in their spoken language of the kind found in monolingual children with SLI in the same languages.

- **Do bilingual children experience more impairment in their nondominant language?** Some bilingual children experience more impairment in their nondominant language, but others do not. We found that most of the children were not strongly dominant in any language, but for those who were dominant in one language, some experienced more profound impairments in their nondominant language when compared with their dominant language. Most important, however, is that not all bilingual children do experience more impairment in one language versus the other.

- **Do bilingual children with specific language impairment show the same deficit patterns as monolingual children with specific**

language impairment? Bilingual children with SLI do show the same deficit patterns in each language as monolingual children with SLI. Monolingual English-speakers with SLI generally have difficulty using correct verb forms. French-speaking monolinguals with SLI typically have difficulty using correct verb forms and object pronouns. The bilingual children in our study displayed these language-specific patterns and, importantly, the children did not show any difficulties that could be construed as crosslinguistic influence, such as having difficulties with object pronouns in English.

• **Do bilingual children with specific language impairment acquire language slower than monolingual children with specific language impairment?** Bilingual children with SLI do not acquire language slower than monolingual children with SLI. The bilingual children we studied had deficits in their use of correct verb forms to the same extent as the monolingual comparison groups in both languages. Both sets of children had accuracy rates of approximately 82%. In the case of object pronoun use in French, the bilingual children actually scored higher than the monolingual children—70% versus 47%, respectively.

KEY POINTS AND CLINICAL IMPLICATIONS

Key Point 1

There is no scientific evidence that infants' language learning ability is limited to one language. On the contrary, research on infants with monolingual and dual language exposure indicates that infants have the innate capacity to acquire two languages without significant costs to the development of either language. Simultaneous dual language children generally experience the same milestones at approximately the same age as monolingual children, in both the early months and later on with respect to grammatical development.

Implications

• Parents and professionals should not assume that any delays or difficulties a dual language child is experiencing in language development are due to dual language exposure. Dual language exposure is not a risk factor in language development.

• In order to ensure full dual language development, it is important that children be given consistent, continuous, and rich exposure to both languages on a regular basis. What appear to be delays in the development of one or both languages could be due to inadequate exposure (see also Summary Idea 3). Input is important.

- Clinicians should use the same developmental variation that characterizes monolingual children as a benchmark for judging SLI in dual language learners; in other words, some time-related variation is typical, but extreme cases are cause for concern and call for further examination.

Key Point 2

Children exposed to two languages from birth have two separate but interconnected linguistic systems from the outset. Developmental language patterns and rates are the same *overall* for monolingual and bilingual children for phonology and grammar. For the most part, the same kinds of "errors" occur in the language of bilingual and monolingual children while they are en route to mastering the target language system. When bilingual children occasionally produce rather unique errors in their language, it is most likely the result of crosslinguistic influence.

Implications

- Parents and health care practitioners should not assume that bilingual children will be delayed in language development or that they will display unique stages or patterns in their languages because dual language input might confuse them. Bilingual children can be expected to appear as "two monolingual children in one," for the most part, and can differentiate between their two languages.

- Parents and health care practitioners should not be concerned if bilingual children sometimes produce sentences in one language that follow the grammatical rules of their other language; this kind of crosslinguistic influence is typical and temporary and is not a sign of confusion or impairment. It is simply one of the few ways in which bilingual children are not always like "two monolingual children in one" (see also code-mixing in Chapter 5).

Key Point 3

Dominance or unbalanced development of the two languages is expected and typical in bilingual acquisition. Bilingual children may appear more advanced in one of their two languages. It is important to keep in mind that when speaking their nondominant language, bilingual children may use words from their dominant language because they do not know them yet in their nondominant language. This style of language use is typical and does not indicate the presence of language or pragmatic impairment.

Implications

• Health care professionals should try to determine which of a bilingual child's two languages is the dominant language before assessing the child's language development. This can be achieved by asking the parents about the child's language environment in order to ascertain which language the child is exposed to and uses more often. The language of greatest exposure is typically the dominant language. This can be determined by asking the parents a series of questions about language use around the child. More precise measures of language dominance would include examining vocabulary size, sentence length and complexity, and volubility in each language.

• When assessing a bilingual child, the dominant language is the one to examine for the upper limits of that child's development. This can be problematic for cases where the societal or majority language is the language of the clinician, but the child's more proficient language is a minority language, because the clinician lacks competence in the appropriate language of assessment.

• Testing bilingual children in their nondominant language could result in substantial underestimation of the child's linguistic abilities overall and for vocabulary size in particular. Clinicians should be very aware of the pitfalls of testing the children in their nondominant language and be appropriately cautious in coming to conclusions from such testing.

Key Point 4

There is a discrepancy between how bilingual children's development of phonology and grammar compares with monolingual children and how their vocabulary size in each language compares with monolingual children. Bilingual children usually exhibit the same rates and stages of development with respect to phonology and grammar. In contrast, they typically have smaller vocabularies in each language than monolingual children of the same age who are learning the same language. When their two vocabularies are added together with translation equivalents counted only once, however, bilingual children typically have vocabularies of an age-appropriate size.

Implications

• For assessing level of language development in bilingual children, it is preferable not to use vocabulary tests as a central measure. Measuring the level of general language development using standardized tests of vocabulary size could lead one to erroneously conclude that a bilingual child is not at an age-appropriate level.

- When health care practitioners or educational professionals are assessing vocabulary development, it is important to expect the vocabulary size in each language of a bilingual child to be smaller than that of a monolingual child.

- It is essential to interpret the results of a standardized vocabulary test differently for bilingual and monolingual children. Pearson (1998) offered a useful guide to using and interpreting standardized vocabulary tests for bilingual populations that do not disadvantage bilingual children. We recommend that professionals who regularly use vocabulary tests with bilingual populations consult this reference.

Key Point 5

Bilingual children with SLI display characteristics of SLI in both of their languages. They do not experience more severe impairments than same-age monolingual children with SLI. Children with SLI have the capacity to become bilingual.

Implications

- Health care professionals and educators who suspect a bilingual child of having language delay or SLI should be certain that they are not basing this judgment on bilingual-specific developmental patterns, such as cross-linguistic influence or code-mixing (see Chapter 5).

- When dealing with a bilingual child who may have language delay or SLI, it is not always possible to conduct an assessment in both languages; however, if the child shows an SLI profile in one language, one can assume that she also shows an SLI profile in her other language (i.e., we have not yet come across a child with SLI in only one language). It is important, however, to distinguish between delay and impairment. If a bilingual child is suspected of having language delay based on an assessment in just one of her two languages, it is possible that the child has been assessed in her nondominant language and that this is the reason for the appearance of developmental delay.

- If a bilingual child appears to be more profoundly delayed or impaired in the language being tested than a monolingual age-mate with delay or SLI, one should not assume that dual language acquisition is causing this problem. It is possible that the language of testing is the child's nondominant language (as discussed previously), or that the child is simply more severely affected than other children with SLI. With respect to intervention, the evidence indicates that intervention in one language alone is effective for bilingual children, although slightly less effective than bilingual intervention. Intervention in both languages would be ideal, but if, for example, English is the only language that can be used, it will still be useful for diagnostics and treatment.

• It is not appropriate or recommended to suggest that a bilingual child with SLI be encouraged to use only one language. There is no reason to assume that dual language knowledge is a burden for children with SLI; in fact, children with SLI are able to learn two languages.

REFERENCES

Celce-Murcia, M. (1978). The simultaneous acquisition of English and French in a two-year-old child. In E. Hatch (Ed.), *Second language acquisition: A book of readings* (pp. 38–53). Rowley, MA: Newbury House.

Döpke, S. (1998). Competing language structures: The acquisition of verb placement by bilingual German-English children. *Journal of Child Language, 25*(3), 555–584.

Döpke, S. (2000). The interplay between language-specific development and cross-linguistic influence. In S. Döpke (Ed.), *Crosslinguistic structures in simultaneous bilingualism* (pp. 79–103). Amsterdam: John Benjamins.

Genesee, F. (1989). Early bilingual development: One language or two? *Journal of Child Language, 6,* 161–179.

Genesee, F., Boivin, I., & Nicoladis, E. (1996). Talking with strangers: A study of bilingual children's communicative competence. *Applied Psycholinguistics, 17,* 427–442.

Genesee, F., Nicoladis, E., & Paradis, J. (1995). Language differentiation in early bilingual development. *Journal of Child Language, 22,* 611–631.

Johnson, C., & Lancaster, P. (1998). The development of more than one phonology: A case study of a Norwegian-English bilingual child. *International Journal of Bilingualism, 2*(3), 265–300.

Meisel, J. (1989). Early differentiation of languages in bilingual children. In K. Hyltenstam & L. Obler (Eds.), *Bilingualism across the lifespan: Aspects of acquisition, maturity and loss* (pp. 13–40). Cambridge, MA: Cambridge University Press.

Meisel, J. (1994). *Bilingual first language acquisition: French and German grammatical development.* Amsterdam: John Benjamins.

Nicoladis, E., & Genesee, F. (1996a). A longitudinal study of pragmatic differentiation in young bilingual children. *Language Learning, 46*(3), 439–464.

Nicoladis, E., & Genesee, F. (1996b). Word awareness in second language learners and bilingual children. *Language Awareness, 5*(2), 80–89.

Nicoladis, E., & Secco, G. (2000). Productive vocabulary and language choice. *First Language, 20*(58), 3–28.

Paradis, J., & Crago, M. (2001). The morphosyntax of specific language impairment in French: An extended optional default account. *Language Acquisition, 9*(4), 269–300.

Paradis, J., Crago, M., & Genesee, F. (2003). Object clitics as a clinical marker of SLI in French: Evidence from French-English bilingual children. In B. Beachley et al. (Eds.), *BUCLD 27 Proceedings* (pp. 638–649). Somerville, MA: Cascadilla Press.

Paradis, J., Crago, M., Genesee, F., & Rice, M. (2003). Bilingual children with specific language impairment: How do they compare with their monolingual peers? *Journal of Speech, Language, and Hearing Research, 46,* 1–15.

Paradis, J., & Genesee, F. (1996). Syntactic acquisition in bilingual children: Autonomous or interdependent? *Studies in Second Language Acquisition, 18,* 1–15.

Paradis, J., & Genesee, F. (1997). On continuity and the emergence of functional categories in bilingual first language acquisition. *Language Acquisition, 6*(2), 91–124.

Paradis, J., Nicoladis, E., & Genesee, F. (2000). Early emergence of structural constraints on code-mixing: Evidence from French-English bilingual children. *Bilingualism: Language and Cognition, 3*(3), 245–261.

Pearson, B. (1998). Assessing lexical development in bilingual babies and toddlers. *International Journal of Bilingualism, 2*(3), 347–372.

Pearson, B., Fernández, S., Lewedeg, V., & Oller, D.K. (1997). The relation of input factors to lexical learning by bilingual infants. *Applied Psycholinguistics, 18,* 41–58.

Pearson, B., Fernández, S.C., & Oller, D.K. (1993). Lexical development in bilingual infants and toddlers: Comparison to monolingual norms. *Language Learning, 43,* 93–120.

Pearson, B., Fernández, S., & Oller, D.K. (1995). Cross-language synonyms in the lexicons of bilingual infants: One language or two? *Journal of Child Language, 22,* 345–368.

Quay, S. (1995). The bilingual lexicon: Implications for studies of language choice. *Journal of Child Language, 22,* 369–387.

Rice, M., Wexler, K., & Hershberger, S. (1998). Tense over time: The longitudinal course of tense acquisition in children with specific language impairment. *Journal of Speech, Language, and Hearing Research, 41,* 1421–1431.

Umbel, V., Pearson, B., Fernández, S., & Oller, D.K. (1992). Measuring bilingual children's receptive vocabularies. *Child Development, 63,* 1012–1020.

Volterra, V., & Taeschner, T. (1978). The acquisition and development of language by bilingual children. *Journal of Child Language, 5,* 311–326.

Yip, V., & Matthews, S. (2000). Syntactic transfer in a Cantonese-English bilingual child. *Bilingualism: Language and Cognition, 3*(3), 193–208.

CHAPTER 5

Bilingual Code-Mixing

Virtually all children who acquire two languages simultaneously code-mix. It is important to discuss code-mixing in some detail because it is widespread among bilingual children and is often the source of concern and misunderstanding. Fortunately, there is an extensive body of research on code-mixing that can provide practical insights about what it means from a language development point of view. In this chapter, we first define bilingual code-mixing (BCM) and then discuss adult BCM in order to get a long-term developmental perspective on child BCM. Next, we turn to research that has sought to explain why children code-mix and whether child BCM is grammatically systematic or random. Finally, we consider the clinical implications of mixing and what parents, educators, and speech-language specialists should do about it.

WHAT IS CODE-MIXING?

Code-mixing is the use of elements from two languages in the same utterance or in the same stretch of conversation. When the elements occur in the same utterance, it is called **intrautterance code-mixing,** and when they occur in two different utterances in the same conversation, it is called **interutterance code-mixing.** Some researchers talk about *intrasentential* and *intersentential* mixing, but we choose to refer to "utterances" because children—and adults—seldom speak in complete sentences. Example 1 in Box 5.1 is an instance of intrautterance mixing in Spanish and English. To facilitate your understanding of these examples, we present what was actually said in

---

BOX 5.1

Bilingual code-mixing—use of phonological, lexical, morphosyntactic or pragmatic patterns from two languages in the same utterance or stretch of conversation. Mixing within an utterance is called *intrautterance mixing.*

1. **Intrautterance mixing (from Zentella, 1999, p. 119)**
   "Alguien se murió en ese cuarto that he sleeps in." (Someone died in that room . . .)

Mixing from one utterance to another is called *interutterance mixing.*

2. **Interutterance mixing (from Zentella, 1999, p. 118)**
   "Pa, ¿me vas a comprar un jugo? It cos' 25 cents." (Are you going to buy me juice?)

---

quotation marks, with the non-English segments in italics and the English segments in roman. Translations of non-English segments are provided in parentheses following the quotations.

The mixed elements can include whole words, phrases or clauses, and even pragmatic patterns. In other words, mixing can involve small units of language (e.g., sounds, inflectional morphemes, words) as well as larger chunks (e.g., phrases, whole clauses). Examples 3–6 show each of these types of mixing.

3. **Words (from Poplack, 1980, p. 241)**

   "Estamos como marido y woman" (we are like man and . . .)

4. **Phrase (from Zentella, 1999, p. 119)**

   "I'm going with her *a la esquina"* (. . . to the corner)

5. **Clauses (from Zentella, 1999, p. 118)**

   "You know how to swim but *no te tapa."* (. . . it won't be over your head)"

6. **Pragmatic (from Genesee & Sauve, 2000)**

   "Donne moi le cheval; le cheval; the horse!" (Give me the horse; the horse; . . .) Child loudly asks for "the horse" when repeated attempts to get a toy horse from his father using French had failed.

There are individual differences in how much children code-mix. Some mix a lot, and some mix very little; children may even mix differently and at different rates with different members of their family. However, virtually all bilingual children code-mix at some time. In our work in Montreal with children who are learning French and English from their parents in the home, we generally find that children mix within utterances less than 10% of the time, although there are very large individual differences. Some of the children we have studied mix as little as 2% of the time, whereas others mixed much more frequently (Genesee, Nicoladis, & Paradis, 1995). It has been our experience that children mix much more from utterance to utterance than within the same utterances, although this clearly depends on the child's stage of development. Children in the one-word and early two-word stages mix primarily across utterances; as their competence grows and their utterances increase in length, they have more and more opportunities to mix within a single utterance. A lot of research has been conducted to identify the factors that account for why some children mix a lot and others mix less, and we discuss this research later.

ADULT CODE-MIXING: THE END POINT FOR CHILD CODE-MIXING

Before proceeding with our discussion of child BCM, it is useful to look at it in the broader developmental perspective that is afforded by examining bilingual adults. Understanding how, when, and why adults code-mix can help us better understand child BCM since the patterns we see in adults give us an indication of the developmentally typical trajectory or end point of child code-mixing.

Like bilingual children, adults mix languages both within an utterance (even switching from one grammatical system to the other to insert segments or strings of words from the other language) and from one utterance to another in the same conversation. Adults are much more likely to mix in informal settings during casual conversations than in public settings, when formal or careful language is called for (Zentella, 1999). This preference to mix under these circumstances probably reflects the general belief that mixing is a casual, even improper, form of usage. When adults switch languages from one utterance to another, each utterance is grammatically well formed according to the rules of the host language, so interutterance code-mixing (or switching) is not very controversial because each utterance is well formed according to the grammar of its respective language. Mixing that occurs in a single utterance, or intrautterance mixing, is much more controversial because it gives the appearance that the grammars are mixed, even mixed up, and, thus, that the utterance is incorrect.

There has been extensive research on the grammaticality of adult intra-utterance mixing. Without exception, all researchers agree that, in most cases, each language segment of a mixed utterance is well formed according to the rules of its respective language; the instances that are not grammatical are probably a result of performance errors. In Examples 1–6 on the previous pages, the non-English segments of each utterance are correct according to the grammar of that language, and the English segments are correct according to the grammar of English. Also, the shift from one language to the other in the examples of intrautterance mixing occurs at places in the sentence that correspond in each language—in the utterance "I'm going with her *a la esquina* (to the corner)" from Example 4, the speaker shifts from English to Spanish after the English pronoun *her* and before the Spanish preposition *a* ("to," in English). What is important to notice here is that this shift is correct according to both English and Spanish word order; in other words, it is perfectly correct to have a prepositional phrase after the first segment of this utterance whether you apply English rules or Spanish rules. If you look at the other previous examples of intrautterance mixing, you will find the same pattern.

Researchers have discovered that the types of mixing that bilingual adults and adolescents use depend to some extent on their level of proficiency in their languages. Those who are proficient in both languages can switch between languages fluently and flawlessly in the middle of the utterance, avoiding violations of the rules of each language as they do so, much like we have just described. Such patterns may sound funny and even ungrammatical to people who are not used to hearing languages mixed in this way, but, as we noted, careful analysis of such mixing reveals that these individuals clearly know the rules of both languages and are able to apply them flawlessly and in tandem in order to integrate segments from both languages in the same utterance.

Learners who are in the process of developing proficiency in a second language often mix in ways that are different from fluent bilingual learners. Generally speaking, second language learners lack the linguistic competence that is needed to engage in the fluent, flawless mixing that is characteristic of simultaneous bilingual learners or those who are already fluent in both languages. Transfer is often evident in the mixing of second language learners; that is, the structure of the host language is imposed on the mixed segments from the other language, often resulting in violations of one or both languages.

In Example 7, English grammatical structure has been imposed on the utterance, and the Spanish elements are made to conform to this structure, resulting in an incorrect utterance. *Enseñar* ("to teach," in Spanish) is inserted in its infinitival form, with the result that there is a double infinitive; *leer* ("to read," in Spanish) is inserted without the particle *a,* which is required in Spanish for infinitival compliments. This example of mixing was probably motivated by the speaker's lack of grammatical competence in Spanish.

7.   Grammar (from Zentella, 1999, p. 116)

"*Yo* have been able to *enseñar Maria leer*" (I . . . teach Maria to read.)

Filling lexical gaps in their proficiency is another common reason for mixing among second language learners. Fluent bilingual people and bilingual learners often mix to fill lexical gaps as well; however, in contrast to the fluent and generally unmarked lexical mixing of fluent bilinguals, second language learners are more likely to "flag" their mixing by pausing, asking for help in finding the correct word or expression in the target language, or interjecting in their stronger language to say that they are about to mix.

In Example 8, the speaker indicates that he knows that he is mixing and that it might not be correct by explicitly giving his reason for switching. Fluent bilingual people seldom need to do this. Flagging is a pragmatic strategy that second language learners can use to isolate the mixed elements because they may not know how to integrate them grammatically; in effect, the speaker is signaling to the listener that he is about to mix and that he might make a mistake in the process. Evidence of these strategies can be taken as an indication that mixing is motivated by proficiency issues.

8. Flagging

"Hier, je suis allé au hardware store—how do you say hardware store in French?" (Yesterday, I went to the . . .)

Finally, research on adults and adolescents has revealed that BCM serves a number of important sociopragmatic and cultural functions. Bilingual adults and adolescents might code-mix in order to express their bilingual ability to other bilingual people—a kind of identity marker (see Myers-Scotton, 1993, and Poplack, 1987). They might code-mix as an indication of intimacy and ethnic solidarity with others who share their language or culture. For example, bilingual children like James and Bistra from Chapter 1 probably code-mix a lot with friends who are also fluent bilingual children because it is something they can do and is part of who they are. Bilingual people might code-mix in order to narrate episodes that themselves were bilingual in nature or to talk about unique cultural aspects of their lives. They might code-mix out of respect for others in the conversation who are more proficient in one or the other language. Alternatively, they might code-mix in order to show they are different from the monolingual people around them. In short, BCM serves a number of important sociopragmatic functions and, thus, is part of bilingual people's communicative competence, something that makes them different:

• BCM is a typical and virtually ubiquitous feature of language use among bilingual adults.

• It serves important linguistic, communicative, social, and cultural purposes.

BOX 5.2

"The free mixing of English and German vocabulary in many of her sentences was a conspicuous feature of her speech. But the very fact that she mixed lexical items proves that there was no real bilingualism as yet. Words from the two languages did not belong to two different speech systems but to one . . . " (Leopold, 1949)

- Adult BCM is grammatically, socially, and culturally constrained; it is not random.

- Proficient bilingual people and second language learners engage in mixing with different characteristics and for different reasons, although there is overlap.

WHY DO BILINGUAL CHILDREN CODE-MIX?

In sharp contrast to the view of adult BCM that research has shown us, many people, including some parents, educators, and speech-language specialists, believe that child BCM is a cause for concern because it indicates that the child is not developing language typically or that she is confused and cannot separate her two languages (see quote from Leopold in Box 5.2) and, in the extreme, that the child has actually formed a single language system made up of elements from both languages. According to this view, the child is actually like a monolingual child (with a blend of two languages) rather than a true bilingual child. In this section, we review research that examines this interpretation of child BCM and the more general questions of why and when children code-mix. The focus of this discussion will be on children who are in the process of acquiring two languages, children between 2 and approximately 4 years of age, because this age range is so controversial.

Unitary Language System Hypothesis

A common explanation of child BCM is that young bilingual children mix words and other elements (e.g., inflections, phrases, grammatical rules) from their two languages in the same utterance because their languages are not differentiated in the early stages of development. This is referred to as the **Unitary Language System Hypothesis**. According to this point of view, children in the process of learning two languages initially represent the languages in a single (or unitary) neurocognitive system. Differentiation takes place later in development, around 3 years of age. We consider this explanation in some detail here because it is widespread, even among some researchers. Because this interpretation views the bilingual child's code-mixing as a symptom of confusion and, in the extreme, incompetence, it has serious clinical implications. Thus, it is important to determine whether this view is valid.

There are many problems with this argument, the chief one being that it is entirely circular—children's code-mixing is taken as evidence of lack of differentiation of their developing languages, and lack of differentiation is used to explain BCM. In order to substantiate this explanation, it is necessary to provide independent evidence that bilingual children cannot differentiate their languages. One way to test this is to document how children use language with others to see if they use their languages without regard to the language of their conversational partners. Finding evidence that they use their languages appropriately with others can rule out the confusion argument. When addressing this issue, most early research on language differentiation focused exclusively on how often bilingual children code-mixed and ignored how often they used the appropriate language with others. Looking at appropriate language use along with BCM is critical for examining whether bilingual children mix because they are confused or because they have a single language system.

In order to examine how bilingual children use language with others, we observed English-French bilingual children from Montreal during naturalistic interactions with their parents in their homes (Genesee, Nicoladis, & Paradis, 1995). The parents, who spoke different native languages, used primarily their native language with their children—exhibiting the so-called **one parent–one language rule.** Thus, the parents presented different language contexts. The children were observed on three separate occasions: once with their mothers alone, once with their fathers alone, and once with both parents present. By observing the children with each parent individually and when both parents were present, we were able to observe the children's ability to keep their languages separate in different language contexts. The children were between 22 and 26 months of age and were in the one- and early two-word stage of language development. We examined not only the frequency of the children's mixing (within and between utterances), but also the frequency with which they used single language utterances that were appropriate to each parent (e.g., French utterances with the French-speaking parent, English utterances with the English-speaking parent).

Even at this young age, these children were able to use their two languages in a context-sensitive manner. They used more French with their French-speaking parent than with the English-speaking parent and more English with their English-speaking parent than with their French-speaking parent. When the parents were together with the children, the children likewise used more of the father's language with the father than with the mother, and vice versa for the mother's language; see Figure 5.1 for the results of five children. The fact that these children used their two languages

BOX 5.3

One parent–one language rule—pattern of parental language use in bilingual families in which each parent uses only, or primarily, one language (usually his or her native language) with the child. This pattern is often recommended to parents on the assumption that by keeping the languages separate, parents will make it easier for children to distinguish between the two languages and to keep them separate as they learn them. In fact, there is little systematic evidence in support of or contrary to this possibility. Nevertheless, this pattern of language use helps parents manage language use in the family. Parents still need to decide which language to use with one another and with visitors in the home.

appropriately with each parent, whether alone or together, is incompatible with the Unitary Language System Hypothesis. According to the Unitary Language System Hypothesis, one would expect random use of each language, regardless of language context.

At the same time, you will notice from Figure 5.1 that most of the children tended to use one language more than the other with both parents. In every case, this was the child's more proficient language, and the child was simply using that language more because she knew it better. Because the parents in these families themselves knew both languages and sometimes used both languages with their children, this strategy allowed these children to express themselves using all of their linguistic resources. Monolingual children do this when they overextend the meaning of common words, such as referring to all adult males as "daddy" until they learn more specific appropriate terms. The difference between bilingual and monolingual children is that bilingual children have two sets of resources to draw on, whereas monolingual children have only one.

We conducted a follow-up study to examine the limits of young bilingual children's ability to use their developing languages appropriately (Genesee, Boivin, & Nicoladis, 1996). Our initial study may have overestimated the ability of bilingual children to differentiate their languages because the children had had more than 2 years' experience with their parents, giving them ample time to learn to associate each language with each parent. If their languages are truly differentiated, then we should find evidence that the children can use their languages differentially and appropriately even with unfamiliar conversational partners. Our second study was intended to see if young bilingual children could do this.

In order to examine this question, we observed a number of additional French-English bilingual children during play sessions with monolingual strangers; the children were, on average, 26 months of age and their mean

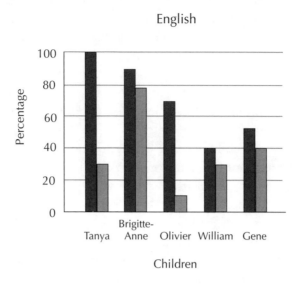

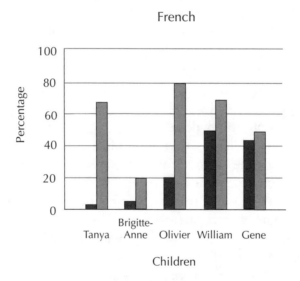

Figure 5.1. Children's use of French and English with parents together. *Note:* Mothers were English speakers, and fathers were French speakers. (Key = ■ mother; ▨ father)

length of utterances in French varied from 1.08 words to 1.59 words and in English from 1.33 words to 1.66 words. In other words, they were in the one-word or early two-word stage of development. Strangers were selected as conversational partners on the assumption that the children were not aware of each stranger's preferred language. Evidence that they could use the appropriate language with the strangers would attest to their ability to identify the stranger's preferred language and to make on-line adjustments to accommodate the stranger, a sign of true communicative competence.

Monolingual strangers were selected in order to ascertain the children's ability to stick to one language as much as possible because, unlike their parents who knew both languages, the stranger only knew one. Because the language spoken by the stranger was the less proficient language of three of the four children we examined in this study, this was a particularly rigorous test of their abilities to accommodate the stranger. The children had to draw on all of the resources of their less proficient language if they were to communicate with the interlocutor.

Three of the four children gave evidence of on-line adjustments to the stranger by using more of the stranger's language with the stranger than with their parents and, in particular, the parent who spoke the same language as the stranger, usually the father; we have presented the results for two of these children in Figure 5.2. The same three children also used less of the language that was not known by the stranger with the stranger than with either parent. One of the children did not modify her language use appropriately with the stranger. In short, these results indicate that three of these children were extending their use of the strangers' language as much as possible and minimizing their use of the language the stranger did not know as much as possible. Thus, despite the fact that these three children had had no prior experience with this adult and they were compelled to use their less-proficient language with the adult, they not only used the appropriate language, but they also used it more frequently with the monolingual stranger than with the parent who also spoke that language. Again, these findings do not support the confusion hypothesis.

Many bilingual children are more proficient in one of their languages in comparison with the other. Proficiency is defined in different ways by different researchers and can include mean length of utterance, relative number of **word types** and **word tokens,** number of **multimorphemic utterances** in each language, and parental reports. The more proficient language is often, although not always, associated with the amount of exposure to each language, with the more proficient language being the language of greater exposure. The fact that the children in our study used a great deal of the language not known by the stranger simply reflects their proficiency in that language, a pattern that is observed even when children talk with their parents. It is also noteworthy that the children in the stranger study did not all perform alike. One of the children did not appear to accommodate the stranger at all. This should not be surprising given the large individual differences that have been documented in a variety of other aspects of language acquisition. There is no reason to believe that the development of communicative competence (bilingual or monolingual) is not subject to the same individual variation among children that is demonstrated in other aspects of language acquisition.

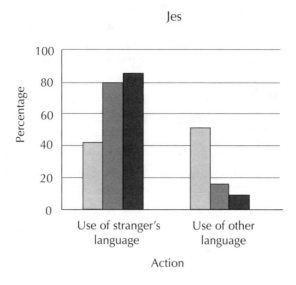

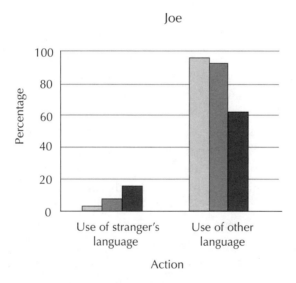

Figure 5.2. Children's use of their languages with parents and with a stranger. (Key = ▢ to mother; ▧ to father; ■ to stranger)

In summary, and contrary to many commonsense interpretations, child BCM does not reflect linguistic confusion or lack of differentiation in the child's developing languages. As noted in Chapter 4, researchers now agree that the Unitary Language System Hypothesis is not valid and, to the contrary, that bilingual children raised in communities where the two languages are used separately can and do differentiate their languages from the earliest stages of verbal production, perhaps even earlier. Many case studies of bilingual children indicate that these children, like the children in our research in Montreal, generally use the appropriate language with their conversational partners (De Houwer, 1990; Lanza, 1992; Meisel, 1990).

Gap-Filling Hypothesis

As shown previously, bilingual children do not code-mix because they are confused or cannot differentiate between their languages. In this and the following sections, we consider alternative explanations for code-mixing. BCM has multiple explanations, and more than one can apply to the same situation or conversation. In other words, no single explanation accounts for all BCM. Understanding why bilingual children code-mix provides some nonobvious insights into their linguistic and communicative competence.

One alternative explanation for child BCM is that it serves to fill gaps in the developing child's linguistic competence. The simplest illustration of this is the case of lexical (word) mixing. According to the **Lexical Gap Hypothesis,** bilingual children mix words from language X when using language Y because they do not know the appropriate word in language Y. Mixing syntactic patterns might also occur in order to fill syntactic gaps in the child's knowledge of the target language. There is considerable evidence in favor of this explanation. First, this explanation would account for the general observation, noted previously, that young bilingual children mix more when they use their less proficient language. By definition, their lexical and syntactic competence in their less proficient language is less developed than in their other language, and thus, they might be compelled to draw on the resources of their more proficient language in order to express themselves fully when using their less developed language. Second, there is direct evidence that bilingual children are much more likely to mix words for which they do not know the translation equivalent in the target language than for words for which they do, regardless of whether they are using their less or more proficient language.

We asked two sets of parents who were raising their children bilingually to keep detailed diary records of their sons' language use during a 3-week period (Genesee, Paradis, & Wolf, 1995). We asked them to focus especially on new words that the children used. Because the boys were 1 year, 8 months and 2 years of age, this task was feasible because the children were not producing many words. We did this so that we could identify how often the children code-mixed and whether they code-mixed words more often when they did not know the appropriate word in the language of their conversational partner. We then looked at the parents' diary entries carefully to see what kinds of words the boys code-mixed. We found that both boys were more likely to code-mix words for which they did not know the translation equivalent in the appropriate language. This was especially true of one boy for whom 100% of the words he code-mixed with his father were words the boy did not know in his father's language. For the other boy, as well, the majority of words that he code-mixed were words for which he did not know the translation equivalent; to be specific, he did not have translation equivalents for 65% of the words he code-mixed. Similar results have been reported in case studies of other children (Nicoladis & Secco, 2000).

In some cases of lexical mixing, it might not be a matter of the child not knowing the appropriate word, but an appropriate word might not exist in the target language. For example, the French word *dodo* is a word that is used primarily with children and means "nap" or "sleep" (from French *dormir,* "to sleep"). There is no exact equivalent in English because all such terms in English are equally appropriate with adults and children. It is not uncommon in bilingual families where French and English are spoken for parents to use *dodo* at all times, even when speaking English. There are many examples of bilingual adults who mix words because an exact equivalent does not exist in the target language; for example, *scholarity* ("years of school- ing"), *bourse* ("fellowship or grant"), *formation* ("training"), and *stage* ("intern- ship") are all French words that are commonly used by English speakers in Montreal because they have a particular meaning in Quebec.

In fact, borrowing is a well-documented phenomenon by which lan- guages acquire new vocabulary. English is a particularly good example. Many English words associated with food and eating are derived from French: *beef, mutton, ragout, veal,* and so on. We are witnessing a dramatic reversal in this pattern of borrowing. Words and expressions related to computers and electronic technology are being coined in English and then borrowed by many other languages (e.g., *fax, spam, the web, Internet, mouse*).

Mixing to fill gaps in children's lexical or syntactic knowledge in one or the other of their languages reflects bilingual children's flexibility in using all their linguistic resources in order to satisfy their communication needs; in other words, it reflects their communicative competence. Because many bilingual children grow up with other children who are also bilingual, this strategy can be effective and appropriate. When bilingual children use this strategy inappropriately with monolingual children, it is usually not because they have a language impairment that requires remediation. It is probably that they do not know the specific word in the target language. Some bilingual children may persist in code-mixing with monolingual people because they have failed to grasp that their interlocutor is monolingual; monolingual people may be rare in their day-to-day lives. A unique aspect of growing up bilingual is that children may encounter monolingual adults who are less linguistically competent than they are. As we saw in the stranger study, bilingual children must learn to accommodate the linguistic incompe- tence of monolingual adults. Given sufficient time, bilingual children make this adjustment.

Pragmatic Explanations

Yet another explanation of BCM concerns the pragmatics of communication. Bilingual children may code-mix for pragmatic effect—to emphasize what they are saying, to quote what someone else said, to protest, to narrate, and so forth. For example, when speaking English, Spanish-English bilingual children may interject expressions in Spanish in order to emphasize the importance of what they are saying in much the same way that monolingual children might repeat themselves, altering their wording slightly in order to emphasize an important detail (e.g., "I was terrified, scared to death!"). See Example 6 on page 92 for an instance from a French-English boy in Montreal.

For some bilingual children, one of their languages may have more affective load than the other, and they may use that language to express emotion when they speak. Mixing in order to quote what someone else said or when narrating events can be a way of rendering one's discourse more authentic if the event or material being quoted took place in the other language. For example, bilingual teenagers may use English and Spanish to describe a music video they saw in Spanish on television. They may use English and Spanish to describe what they did at school during the Spanish part of the day or during recess if they were playing with their Spanish-speaking friends. Bilingual children may use the language of schooling to talk about school when at home, even if the language of the home is different. Mixing speech or speaking styles is common in everyday discourse; it makes discourse colorful, authentic, and varied. Bilingual children have the advan- tage of being able to use two languages to enrich their discourse.

Social Norms

A third explanation of child BCM is related to social norms. We discuss social norms that are community based and family based and how they might influence child BCM. These different normative influences do not operate in isolation of one another. Children exposed to two languages are exposed to the normative patterns of BCM in their communities, and they learn these patterns at the same time as they learn the sounds, words, and grammati- cal patterns of the languages. Acquiring appropriate community-based pat- terns of code-mixing is an important part of bilingual children's language socialization, as we noted in Chapter 2.

Communities have different social norms with respect to appropriate kinds of mixing, when and where mixing occurs, and how often mixing is appropriate (e.g., see research by Poplack, 1987, and Myers–Scotton, 1993). In some communities, there is a great deal of tolerance and acceptance of mixing. Children raised in such communities learn to code-mix more than children in communities where mixing is frowned on or not tolerated. The specific forms of code-mixing children learn are also shaped by social norms in their community. For example, in an early seminal study on code-mixing, Shana Poplack (1980) examined code-mixing patterns in a Puerto Rican, Spanish-speaking community in New York City. She found that members of this community engaged in an especially fluent form of mixing where the same utterance could include several switches from Spanish to English and back again (see Example 9). BCM can be an important marker of social identity, and, in the Puerto Rican community that Poplack studied, rapid, fluent mixing served to identify the speaker as both Spanish- and English-speaking and, thus, as both Puerto Rican and American (see also Zentella, 1999). Establishing their dual identity/allegiance was important for members of this community.

9. Multiple code-switches (Poplack, 1980, p. 238)

"But I used to eat the *bofe* (brain), the brain. And then they stopped selling it because, *tenian, este, le encontraron que tenia* (they had, uh, they found out that it had) worms. I used to make some *bofe! Después yo hacía uno d'esos* (then I would make one of those) concoctions: the garlic *con cebolla, y hacía un moho, y yo dejaba que se curare eso* (with onion, and I'd make a sauce, and I'd let that sit) for a couple of hours. Then you be drinking and eating that shit. Wooh! It's like eating anchovies when they drinking. Delicious!"

In contrast, the norms regarding BCM are quite different among French-English bilingual people in the Ottawa region of Canada (Poplack, 1987). Generally speaking, bilingual people in this community, especially if they identify as French Canadian, use a different form of mixing. Their mixing tends to be less frequent and less fluent; it is often flagged to indicate that the discourse is bilingual (see Example 10) and is often restricted to private conversations or settings. The flagged mixing exhibited by this group was not due to lack of proficiency—as we saw in the case of second language learners—but rather to identity issues. More specifically, it is likely that this pattern of mixing reflects the desire among members of this community to identify with the French-speaking community in Canada and to set themselves apart from English Canadians. To use French and English as Puerto Ricans in New York City use Spanish and English would blur their identity. The somewhat hesitant form of mixing that Poplack noted in the Ottawa community, with its particular focus on keeping the languages separate, is also probably linked to their concerns about preserving French in the face of the dominating influence of English in North America. This was not a concern in the Puerto Rican community in New York City because members of that community could and often did return to Puerto Rico, where Spanish is the dominant language and is flourishing.

10.   Flagging (from Poplack, 1987, p. 61)

> *"Mais je te gage par exemple* . . . excuse my English, *mais les odds sont là."* (But I bet you that . . . but the odds are there.)

Children growing up bilingual in each of these areas learn distinct patterns of bilingual usage in order to fit into and to be fully functional members of the community. Children who have spent their whole childhood in their own communities may not be accustomed to patterns of language use in other communities and, thus, may need time to learn new patterns so that they can fit in to the new community. Some bilingual children may even have difficulty keeping their languages separate because they have grown up with other bilingual people; it may take them some time to accommodate for the monolingualism of others. Most children can learn new patterns easily, if they need to and if given appropriate time and encouragement. The challenges these children face when learning new patterns of language usage are not related to language impairment but rather to social adaptation.

Social norms in individual families can also influence child BCM. The pattern and frequency of code-mixing can vary from one family to another in the same community because some families and even individual parents within the same family are more tolerant of mixing than others. Lanza (1997), for example, described bilingual parents in Norway who were raising their child, Siri, bilingually. Although both parents were bilingual, Lanza observed that Siri code-mixed much less with her native English-speaking mother than with her native Norwegian-speaking father. Upon closer examination, Lanza noticed that Siri's mother discouraged Siri from code-mixing by avoiding mixing herself, by pretending that she did not understand Siri when she said something in Norwegian, or by indicating in her reply to Siri that she wanted Siri to express herself in English. By using these patterns of discourse with Siri, Siri's mother was sending the message that she preferred English and wanted Siri to use English as much as possible. One might imagine that Siri's mother sought to encourage Siri to use only English because this was one of the few opportunities Siri got to use English; elsewhere, everything took place in Norwegian. In contrast, her father indicated that using both English and Norwegian was acceptable. He did this by code-mixing himself and by indicating that he understood Siri even when she used his nonnative language, English. Consequently, Siri's language choice was not an issue with her father as it was with her mother.

Another example of the influence of family norms on child BCM comes from Suzanne Döpke in a study of German-English bilingual families in Australia. Döpke (1992) observed that some of the bilingual families she was studying were more successful than others in promoting the use of the minority language (German) in a community that was otherwise dominated by English. Döpke attributed this success, in part, to the use of child-centered discourse styles by the parent who spoke the minority language:

> The results of the present study indicate that there was a relationship between the parents' awareness of their roles as language teachers and the children's active acquisition of the minority language, in that those children whose minority language parent provided more structurally tailored input than did their majority language parent acquired an active command of the minority language. (1992, p. 191)

Lanza's and Döpke's findings illustrate that children differ in their style and frequency of BCM as well as in their preference to code-mix or stick to one language as a result of the different discourse styles of their parents.

Some bilingual children may overextend the mixing patterns they have learned in their family and neighborhood community to new settings in which they are not appropriate or effective. Most children can and will learn new patterns, given sufficient time and encouragement. Persistence in using inappropriate patterns of mixing even after some experience in a new setting might suggest that other factors are at play: 1) code-mixing fills gaps in the child's proficiency in the target language, 2) code-mixing is pragmatic, and 3) code-mixing asserts the child's identity as a bilingual person or a member of a different cultural group. Because these explanations are likely to account for the majority of patterns that one is likely to encounter, they should be examined and ruled out before issues linked to impairment are entertained seriously.

In summary, bilingual children, like all children, learn the social norms that pervade their lives. Their acquisition and adherence to these norms are essential to their fitting in with their family, community, and cultural group. Community and family-specific norms shape bilingual children's code-mixing behavior. Looking at the social context in which the children have learned their two languages can give a better understanding of why individual children are using their languages in certain ways. Professionals and clinicians who are concerned about a child's mixing should first seek to understand what BCM means to the child in the context of her family, the neighborhood community in which she lives, and the cultural group(s) of which she is a member. Looking to these sources of influence is especially important in the case of professionals who are not members of the child's community or cultural group and who are not themselves bilingual because the norms that are influencing the child are likely to be unfamiliar. Special effort is called for in such cases to ensure that the professional has a broader picture of the child's mixing.

IS CHILD BILINGUAL CODE-MIXING GRAMMATICALLY DEVIANT?

When two languages are used in the same utterance, grammatical incompatibilities can arise between them due to differences in word order or **inflectional morphology;** these, in turn, can result in patterns of language use that are awkward or illicit. Indeed, a commonly held perception of code-mixing is that it is a "bastardized" (ungrammatical) form of language. This is one of the reasons why parents and others are often concerned about child BCM and even avoid code-mixing with children. The stigma about the grammatical status of intrautterance code-mixing is evident in adult BCM as well. When questioned, many bilingual adults will say that they think code-mixing is not a proper form of language. As we noted previously in this chapter, however, it is clear from extensive research that adult BCM is constrained by the grammars of both languages and, contrary to some lay opinions, the most proficient bilingual adults engage in the most sophisticated forms of mixing.

But, what about child BCM? Is children's code-mixing grammatically constrained or deviant? An extensive body of research has examined the grammatical properties of intrautterance code-mixing by children acquiring a variety of language pairs, including English and French (Genesee & Sauve, 2000; Paradis, Nicoladis, & Genesee, 2000), French and German (Köppe, in press; Meisel, 1994), English and Inuktitut (Allen, Genesee, Fish, & Crago, 2002), English and Norwegian (Lanza, 1997), and English and Estonian (Vihman, 1998), among others. All of these studies indicate that the vast majority of bilingual children's code-mixing is systematic and, specifically, conforms to the grammatical constraints of the two participating languages. This is true for bilingual children as soon as they begin to use multiword utterances, when grammatical constraints become evident in their language use. Children who are in the one-word stage cannot engage in intrautterance mixing because, by definition, it entails the use of more than one word or morpheme. The finding that bilingual children code-mix grammatically as soon as they begin to organize their language according to grammatical principles is very important because it means that they learn how to code-mix grammatically at the same time as they learn their two languages. It is not something extra they have to learn; it comes automatically with being a bilingual learner. At the same time, they do learn the frequency or patterns of mixing that characterize their own families and communities.

A few examples follow to illustrate exactly what it means to say that children's code-mixing is grammatical. A common form of code-mixing by young bilingual children entails the mixing of single content words (e.g., nouns, verbs, adjectives) from one language into an utterance or sentence that is organized according to the grammar of the other language. This form of mixing is common in young children because they produce short, syntactically simple sentence that usually lack conjoined elements. When children mix single words, they usually treat the mixed word as if it were part of the host language and thereby produce grammatically correct constructions. Borrowing of single words is common in most modern languages, especially those in contact with other languages. The provenance of such borrowed words is often not recognized because they become full-fledged words in the host language; words such as *beef, teepee,* and *muffin* all originated from other languages but are accepted as bona fide English words.

Examples 11–14 illustrate this kind of mixing and are all taken from children younger than 4 years of age. Examples 11–13 were produced by French-English bilingual children in Montreal, and Example 14 is from a bilingual child learning English and Inuktitut in northern Quebec. In every case, the English word has been inserted in the correct place, assuming that the word is being treated as a member of the host language; the host language is considered to be the dominant language of the child's interlocutor, which was English, French, French, and Inuktitut for Examples 11–14, respectively. Example 13 is particularly interesting because in this case the child used the English subject pronoun (*I*) with a French verb (*aime,* "like"). There are other examples of this sort from his corpus. Subject pronouns in French are prohibited from appearing with certain verb forms, but in English they are not. This child obeyed this restriction when he mixed subject pronouns; he put English pronouns with a number of French verbs, but he only put French pronouns with English verb forms that followed the restricted category in French. In this way, he respected the distributional restrictions of English and French when he mixed pronouns.

11. **Mixing single content words into English
(from Paradis, Nicoladis, & Genesee, 2000, p. 255)**

    "big *bobo*" (bruise or cut)

12. **Mixing single content words
into French (from Paradis et al., 2000, p. 257)**

    "*je veux aller manger* tomato" (I want to go eat . . .)

13. **Mixing single content words
into French (from Paradis et al., 2000, p. 257)**

    "I *aime pas ça moi*" (. . . do not like that, me)

14. Mixing single content words into Inuktitut (from Allen, Genesee, Fish, & Crago, 2002)

"monkey-*uqquungimmat*" (it's probably not a . . .)

Example 14 is also interesting because it shows a young Inuktitut-English child inserting an English noun (*monkey*) in an otherwise Inuktitut utterance. This example is interesting because it is a case where the word order in English and Inuktitut are different, yet the child inserted the English word in the correct position for Inuktitut. It is also interesting because the English noun "monkey" is transformed into a verb by the Inuktitut morpheme *u* ("to be"); in effect, the noun *monkey* becomes "to be a monkey." Known as *noun incorporation,* this is a common construction in Inuktitut. This child demonstrated that he knew how to use this construction even with an English noun. In short, evidence from code-mixing in simultaneous bilingual people indicates that their mixing is constrained and reflects their grammatical competence in both languages.

As children get older, they mix larger fragments of language and use code-mixing for more sophisticated pragmatic functions. Examples 15–17 illustrate mixing of word combinations.

15. Child who is 3 years, 5 months old (from Paradis et al., 2000, p. 258)

"*Elle coupe* her hair" (she cuts . . .)

16. Child who is 12 years old (from Zentella, 1999, p. 100)

"*ello(h) te invitan a bailar,* so I GO, you know" (they invite you to go dancing . . .)

17. Child who is older than 8 years (from Zentella, 1999, p. 95)

"*Ella tiene*—shut up! Lemme tell you." (She has . . .)

Example 15 is from an English–French bilingual child, and Examples 16 and 17 are from English–Spanish bilingual children. All of these instances are grammatical insofar as the word order of the participating languages is respected; in other words, the switch from one language to the other occurs at a point in the utterance where there is grammatical equivalence in the two languages (e.g., in Example 15 between the verb and object; in Examples 16 and 17, the switches occur when the speaker makes an interjection). Example 17 is particularly interesting because it illustrates the use of switching to emphasize a point—in this case, the speaker's annoyance with the listener and his insistence that the listener pay attention. Thus, not only do the forms of code-mixing become more sophisticated with age, but also they serve pragmatic functions.

KEY POINTS AND CLINICAL IMPLICATIONS

What does BCM tell us about the language development of bilingual children, and what are the clinical implications of child BCM?

Key Point 1

BCM is a typical and ubiquitous pattern of language use among bilingual children and adults. Multiple sources of evidence indicate that, in most cases, child BCM is not a cause for clinical concern. Chief among these sources is the fact that most child BCM is grammatical. Thus, BCM is best viewed as a reflection of the child's developing linguistic competence. Indeed, in order to code-mix grammatically, bilingual children must be acquiring both grammars, and they must have access to both grammars on-line in order to integrate the languages in a single utterance.

Implications

- BCM should not be taken as evidence for language delay or impairment in bilingual children in most cases and without careful further examination.

- Children should not be reprimanded or explicitly discouraged from code-mixing. Nor should they be singled out in any way that would stigmatize them because they are bilingual children and code-mix.

- Language development specialists and other professionals should not recommend that children use only one language or that parents desist in using both languages on the assumption that this will rectify any problems associated with BCM.

Key Point 2

BCM is a communicative resource. Bilingual children are being resourceful in calling on both languages when they code-mix. They may be especially prone to draw on their dual language resources during stages of development when full proficiency in each language has not been achieved, but BCM is a resource even for fully proficient bilingual people who want to talk about ideas, events, or things that are part of their unique lives as bilingual individuals or that are best expressed in one or the other language.

Implications

- Most bilingual children will adapt to the communicative demands of monolingual social situations, given appropriate time and supportive encouragement.

- Efforts to get the child to express herself monolingually should not be punitive; they should always be positive; for example, provide the child with monolingual paraphrases of what she wants to say, while praising the child for making whatever efforts she makes.

- If individual bilingual children persist in code-mixing in settings or with individuals where it is inappropriate or ineffective, even after considerable time for adjustment is given, then the communicative demands of the situation should be examined for evidence of gaps in the child's communicative competence. If there are identifiable gaps in certain domains of the child's language proficiency, then language enrichment in the relevant areas should be provided, followed by careful monitoring of growth in the areas of concern.

- In most cases, it is recommended that the child continue in the situation or setting where concerns have arisen. Referring children to specialists or special classes is not likely to be effective in resolving the identified communication problems if the child is isolated from the positive incentives that are provided by contact with peers and mainstream language models.

Key Point 3

BCM is shaped by social norms in the families and communities in which bilingual children live. All children are socialized to the patterns of language use and social behaviors that are characteristic of their families and communities. Family and community norms guide their behavior in most settings they encounter, familiar and unfamiliar.

Implications

- Bilingual children who exhibit language or social behaviors that differ from mainstream monolingual/monocultural children should not automatically be singled out for special attention or referred for further examination because of suspicions of impaired or delay development.

- Most bilingual children will acquire the social norms appropriate to a new situation if they are given sufficient time and positive encouragement.

- Persistent inappropriate or ineffective language or social behavior by an individual bilingual child may result from overextended or rigid use of familiar patterns in environments that call for new patterns. The child should be provided with appropriate models that display appropriate behaviors and should be encouraged to adopt those behaviors.

- Professionals should familiarize themselves with the patterns of language and social behavior that characterize life in the child's family and community in order to better understand the child's language behavior. This may require interviews with caregivers or others in the community who are well informed about community norms; a home visit may even be called for.

- Where significant differences are found to exist between the home or community and the new situation, then steps must be taken in the new setting to help the child adjust.

Key Point 4

BCM may reflect the child's cultural identity. Language is an important marker of one's identity; this is why individuals and groups are willing to go to great lengths to defend their right to use their own language. For young language learners and school-age children, language is a fundamental part of who they are because it has been an inextricable part of the social world they have grown up in. To denigrate a child's language or refuse him the possibility of using his language(s) for self-expression is to diminish him as an individual. Many adults have personal resources for dealing with the complexities of being a member of a minority group or of having a dual identity. Most children lack these resources; this is particularly true for children from minority group backgrounds.

Implications

- It is incumbent on professionals, clinicians, and other adults caring for bilingual/bicultural children to nurture the children's unique identities, protect them from the challenges of being different, and provide them with strategies for coping with these challenges.

- Educators, professionals, and clinicians should provide positive recognition and support to bilingual children who express affinity to or identity with another culture, especially a minority culture.

- At the same time, if bilingual children are not fully socialized to the majority cultural group, they should be given assistance in acquiring the social skills and cultural understandings they need to make friends and function effectively in majority group settings.

- Steps should be taken to ensure that bilingual children from minority cultures do not become isolated from other children; for example, providing the child with a "buddy" who is bilingual and well integrated is one way of helping the child to socialize to a new group while minimizing the risks of isolation.

In sum, BCM can provide useful insights about the language competence of bilingual children, insights that can guide professionals and clinicians who are charged with caring for these children. It is important to remember that the prevalence of language impairment and delay will be the same among bilingual children and monolingual children. Thus, unusually high rates of diagnosed impairment or delay among a group of bilingual children should call into question the criteria that are being used to make such diagnoses. In particular, overestimation of impairment and delay may result from over-interpretation of BCM as evidence for impairment.

REFERENCES

Allen, S., Genesee, F., Fish, S., & Crago, M. (2002). Patterns of code-mixing in English-Inuktitut bilinguals. In M. Andronis, C. Ball, H. Elston, & S. Neuvel (Eds.), *Proceedings of the 37th Annual Meeting of the Chicago Linguisitics Society* (Vol. 2, pp. 171–188). Chicago: Chicago Linguistics Society.

De Houwer, A. (1990). *The acquisition of two languages from birth: A case study*. Cambridge, MA: Cambridge University Press.

Döpke, S. (1992). *One parent one language: An interactional approach*. Amsterdam: John Benjamins.

Genesee, F., Boivin, I., & Nicoladis, E. (1996). Talking with strangers: A study of bilingual children's communicative competence. *Applied Psycholinguistics, 17,* 427–442.

Genesee, F., Nicoladis, E., & Paradis, J. (1995). Language differentiation in early bilingual development. *Journal of Child Language, 22,* 611–631.

Genesee, F., Paradis, J., & Wolf, L. (1995). *The nature of the bilingual child's lexicon*. Unpublished research report, Psychology Department, McGill University, Montreal, Canada.

Genesee, F., & Sauve, D. (2000, March 12). *Grammatical constraints on child bilingual code-mixing*. Paper presented at the Annual Conference of the American Association for Applied Linguistics, Vancouver, Canada.

Köppe, R. (in press). Is codeswitching acquired? In Jeff MacSwan (Ed.), *Grammatical theory and bilingual codeswitching*. Cambridge, MA: MIT Press.

Lanza, E. (1992). Can bilingual two-year-olds code-switch? *Journal of Child Language, 19,* 633–658.

Lanza, E. (1997). *Language mixing in infant bilingualism: A sociolinguistic perspective*. Oxford, England: Clarendon Press.

Leopold, W. (1949). Speech development in a bilingual child: A linguist's record: Vol. III. Grammar and general problems. Evanston, IL: Northwestern University Press.

Meisel, J.M. (1990). *Two first languages: Early grammatical development in bilingual children*. Dordrecht, Germany: Foris Publications.

Meisel, J.M. (1994). Code-switching in young bilingual children: The acquisition of grammatical constraints. *Studies in Second Language Acquisition, 16,* 413–441.

Myers-Scotton, C. (1993). *Social motivation for codeswitching: Evidence from Africa.* Oxford: Oxford University Press.

Nicoladis, E., & Secco, G. (2000). The role of a child's productive vocabulary in the language choice of a bilingual family. *First Language, 58,* 3–28.

Paradis, J., Nicoladis, E., & Genesee, F. (2000). Early emergence of structural constraints on code-mixing: Evidence from French-English bilingual children. In F. Genesee (Ed.), *Bilingualism: Language and cognition* (pp. 245–261). Cambridge, MA: Cambridge University Press.

Poplack, S. (1980). "Sometimes I start a sentence in English y termino en español": Toward a typology of code-switching. *Linguistics, 18,* 581–618.

Poplack, S. (1987). Contrasting patterns of code-switching in two communities. In E. Wande, J. Anward, B. Nordberg, L. Steensland, & M. Thelander (Eds.), *Aspects of multilingualism: Proceedings from Fourth Nordic Symposium on Bilingualism, 1984* (pp. 51–77). Uppsala, Sweden: Ubsaliensis S. Academiae.

Vihman, M. (1998). A developmental perspective on codeswitching: Conversations between a pair of bilingual siblings. *International Journal of Bilingualism, 2,* 45–84.

Zentella, A.C. (1999). *Growing up bilingual.* Malden, MA: Blackwell Publishers.

CHAPTER 6

Second Language
Acquisition in Children

In Chapter 1, we presented profiles of eight different dual language children, five of whom—Samantha, Trevor, Bonnie, Carlos, and Pauloosie—were described as second language learners, as opposed to bilinguals, because they began to learn their second language after their first language had been established for at least 3 years. As with the bilingual children—James, Bistra, and Pasquala—one key difference between the language learning situations for Samantha and Trevor versus Bonnie, Carlos, and Pauloosie is the distinction between majority and minority languages. Samantha and Trevor are majority language speakers of English who are acquiring their second languages (L2) through the medium of schooling. Bonnie, Carlos, and Pauloosie have minority languages as their first languages (L1), Mandarin, Spanish, and Inuktitut, respectively, and began learning the majority language, English, as their second language through schooling and in contact with the majority ethnolinguistic community.

This minority/majority language distinction has an effect on both the ultimate proficiency a child acquires in her L2 and the maintenance of her L1. One can consider young L2 learners like Samantha to be privileged because they typically experience additive bilingualism, a concept discussed in Chapter 3, because they are bilingual by choice, and because, generally speaking, they do not have to cope with sociocultural integration and adaptation at the same time as they are learning a new language and beginning their schooling. The different language learning situations and outcomes for

L1 majority children like Samantha are covered in Chapter 7, and in this chapter we focus on L1 minority children like Bonnie, Carlos, and Pauloosie.

Children can come into contact with a second language at any age, but our focus in this chapter is limited to young children learning their second language in the preschool and early elementary school years because this is the time that children's development is most commonly assessed and concern over best practices in identifying children who would benefit from intervention and special education is most prevalent. It is important to keep in mind that many L1 minority children who become L2 learners during this time in their lives were born in the host society. Not all of these children are immigrant children like Bonnie. For instance, Carlos was born in the United States, and many Spanish L1 children in the United States who begin to learn English at school entry come from families who have lived in their region for generations.

We would also like to reiterate a point made in Chapter 1: Bonnie is a relatively fortunate immigrant child. Her parents have good jobs in their host country and high levels of education, and they could function in the majority language of their host country when they arrived. Many L2 children in both North America and Europe are not as fortunate in that their families are coping with severe financial hardships and sometimes with the stress of forced relocation. Often, parents do not speak the language of the host country very well and cannot communicate easily with educators and health practitioners, as is the case for Carlos's parents. It is worth remembering that these kinds of challenges can influence the extent to which parents can be involved in their child's schooling and can monitor and support their child's second language learning.

The purpose of this chapter is to familiarize readers with the oral language characteristics of L2 learners and what factors influence their rate of development toward becoming like native speakers in their spoken linguistic abilities. The literacy skills and school progress in general of L2 children will be discussed in Chapter 7. We emphasize research and current thinking about English as a second language (ESL) in particular. The information in this chapter is organized to address the following general questions:

1. What are the typical stages children go through in learning to speak their L2?

2. How long does it take, and what factors might make children acquire their L2 at different rates?

3. What happens to the L1 of language minority children in a majority L2 context?

4. What are the similarities and differences between the language of L2 learners and monolingual children with language impairment?

In this chapter, we give examples of ESL children's speech from an ongoing study with 23 immigrant children in a large urban center in Western Canada, Edmonton. These children were 4½ to 7 years of age at the onset and came from a variety of L1 backgrounds, including Spanish, Arabic, Ukrainian, Farsi (Persian), and Mandarin and Cantonese (two Chinese languages). At the beginning of the study, they had an average of 10 months of regular exposure to English through preschool or school. We have a variety of measures of these children's oral language proficiency over time, in both naturalistic and elicited contexts. We use the term *Edmonton ESL study* when we refer to the data from this study. *Round 1* means the data taken when the group had an average of 10 months' exposure to English, and *Round 2* means data taken 6 months later, when they had an average of 16 months' exposure to English.

WHAT ARE THE TYPICAL STAGES CHILDREN GO THROUGH IN LEARNING TO SPEAK A SECOND LANGUAGE?

Children's First Exposure to the Second Language

Tabors (1997) conducted an in-depth study of ESL children in a university nursery school in Massachusetts, in which she observed the children several mornings a week for 2 years. She witnessed several children experiencing their first contact with an English language milieu, and she noted the following early stages in their L2 development: 1) home-language use, 2) nonverbal period, 3) telegraphic and formulaic use, and 4) productive language use. Before we discuss what happens at each stage, we must emphasize the individual variation between children, so that some children might appear to skip Stage 2, and others might remain in Stage 2 for an entire year. Understanding these stages is useful to setting expectations, but they are not written in stone.

Stage 1, or the period of home language use, refers to the child using her L1 in the English environment, even though no one else speaks it. This period can be very brief, sometimes just a few days, because children try their home language in their new environment but rapidly realize that it doesn't work. Occasionally, ESL children persist in using their native language some of the time in an English-language classroom for longer, even 2–4 months, but this is not typical (Saville-Troike, 1987). The **nonverbal period**, Stage 2, follows the home language period, and during this time children are accumulating receptive knowledge of English, but they produce very few or no words in English. Tabors found that during this period, the ESL children developed a system of communication, heavily relying on gesture, to get some meaning across, and therefore, not talking during this period does not imply a complete lack of communication and interaction. The nonverbal period can last a few weeks to a few months, and, in general, younger children stay longer in this stage than older ones. During this nonverbal period, social interaction with peers is a crucial factor in enabling ESL children to get exposure to more English and to be motivated to begin speaking.

When children first begin to produce some English, they do not use full sentences right away. Instead, their utterances are imitative, with little original content. This is why Tabors has described this third stage as the period of **telegraphic** and **formulaic** use. The first English produced by the children she observed consisted of one-word utterances to label objects or count and identify colors, and thus the children were not using real sentences. Furthermore, the first sentence-like utterances were often memorized phrases that may not have consisted of separate words for the child, for example, "I don't know," "Excuse me," "So what?" and "What's happening?"

This period of formulaic and telegraphic use was also documented by Wong Fillmore in an observational study of naturalistic interactions between ESL and monolingual English-speaking children. Wong Fillmore (1979) characterized the ESL children's approach to learning English at this stage as including two key strategies: 1) give the impression—with a few well-chosen words—that you can speak the language; and 2) acquire some expressions you understand, and start talking. By doing so, the ESL children could engage and function in social interaction and therefore increase their exposure to English.

Gradually, ESL children start to construct sentences that are productive. A productive sentence is one that does not consist entirely of a memorized word sequence; the child uses some of her own repertoire of nouns, verbs, or adjectives and constructs an utterance that is wholly or partially original. Some beginner sentences in English appear to have a semiformulaic frame and slot construction, for example, "*I do* + noun" or "*I want* + noun," in which the child does not use another pronoun or form of the verb but just varies the thing (noun) that the child does or wants (e.g., "I do a ice cream," "I do letter B"). Wong Fillmore noted how one child, Nora, started with a formula she would use frequently across contexts, "How do you do dese?" Then, she expanded on it to say things such as "How do you do dese in English" and "How do you do dese little tortillas?" Next, she began to substitute words in the formula: "How do you make the flower?" and "How do you gonna do dese in English?" (1979, p. 214). Eventually, ESL children move beyond the frame and slot stage into a real productive period, Tabors's Stage 4, where they can vary what words they use to fill in all of the slots in a sentence. Then, they are well on their way toward developing some fluency in English.

When children have reached this fourth stage and can use their L2 productively, this does not mean that they sound like native speakers of the language. Even small children can have a foreign accent when they are learning their L2. They may mispronounce words and make errors in vocabulary choice and grammar. As we pointed out in Chapter 4, these errors are part of the typical process of learning a language, and therefore are not a sign that a child is struggling with language. In fact, in Chapter 4 we referred to errors in L1 such as "Me no want broccoli" for "I don't want broccoli" as target-deviant structures in order to move away from the mindset that the child is doing something wrong. On the contrary, through creatively constructing sentences in the language they are learning, whether L1 or L2, children are practicing and thus advancing their expressive and receptive linguistic abilities in that language and, with time, will converge on the correct or target-like structures.

The period in second language development between when the learner starts to use the language productively until when the learner achieves competence similar to a native speaker is referred to as **interlanguage.** Interlanguage is a systematic and rule-governed linguistic system, but it does not have the same characteristics as the target system, the L2. The reasons why interlanguage has different characteristics from the target system are 1) the L1 of the L2 learner can influence the pronunciation and grammar of their L2; and 2) developmental, target-deviant patterns are a typical part of language learning. In the next two sections, we discuss the developmental patterns in interlanguage, so-called **developmental errors,** as well as the L1 influences on interlanguage, so-called **transfer errors.** Our objective is to familiarize readers with the characteristics of ESL interlanguage in particular.

Developmental Errors in English as a Second Language

People who learn their L2 later in life usually have a noticeable foreign accent. What are the reasons for this accent? A foreign accent results partly from the influence of the L1, which we discuss later on, but other factors are responsible as well. Because some developmental errors in L2 interlanguage are common across learners regardless of the L1, transfer from the L1 cannot be the only source for interlanguage patterns. Most researchers agree that the majority of interlanguage patterns are developmental—just a natural part of the learning process—rather than influenced by the L1.

A prominent example of these developmental errors can be found in the English L2 acquisition of **grammatical morphology**, such as the past-tense marker *-ed* in *walked*. In a seminal study, Dulay and Burt (1973) found

---

BOX 6.1

What Are Grammatical Morphemes and
Why Are They Important to Learning a Language?

Grammatical morphemes are little words and inflectional affixes that are the "glue" that sticks the content words together in the sentence; they add subtle semantic meaning, and anchor the sentence in the discourse. Prototypical content words are nouns and verbs. Choosing two content words, such as *dog* and *run*, one can make several sentences with them. One can say, "A dog runs," "The dog runs," "The dogs are running," "The dog ran," and so forth. All of these sentences have different meanings based on whether they refer to any dog, a specific dog, or a group of dogs or whether the dog is running as a habit, running now, or running in the past. The grammatical morphemes (i.e., definite and indefinite articles *a* and *the*, plural *-s*, third person singular marker *-s*, progressive *-ing*, past irregular *run–ran*, auxiliary verb *to be*) generate these different meanings from the two base content words. Mastery of grammatical morphology is fundamental to being able to express a wide range of meanings in English, as well as in most other languages.

---

that 85% of the errors in spoken English by 145 Spanish-speaking ESL children were developmental in origin (i.e., not traceable to Spanish) and were errors with grammatical morphemes. They conducted a follow-up study with both Spanish and Chinese L1 children and found again that the major source of difficulty for both L1 groups was developmental errors with grammatical morphology, demonstrating that the learner's L1 was not the principal source of the errors in their interlanguage (Dulay & Burt 1974). In fact, grammatical morphemes are not only problematic for L2 learners of English, but also pose difficulties for English L1 children to acquire, both typically developing children and children with SLI. Because of this overlap between L2 and SLI, and because of the salience of errors with grammatical morphology in L2 English, we focus on this aspect of interlanguage in our discussion of developmental patterns, but we do not want to leave the impression that this is the only part of English interlanguage in which learners produce target-deviant structures. Developmental errors can also be observed in phonology, grammar, and pragmatics.

Table 6.1 contains a list of the grammatical morphemes that ESL children commonly have difficulty with, along with excerpts from conversations with children from the Edmonton ESL study, giving examples of correct use of these morphemes, as well as examples of typical errors ESL children make with them. In each case, the correct target morpheme, the error form, or the place the morpheme should have appeared in, is highlighted in the excerpts. The child's age as well as how much exposure to English he had had when the conversation took place is given. Data from the Edmonton

> **BOX 6.2**
>
> *Interlanguage*—"The term interlanguage was coined in 1972 by Selinker to refer to the language produced by learners, both as a system which can be described at any one point in time as resulting from systematic rules, and as the series of interlocking systems that characterize learner progression. In other words, the notion of interlanguage puts the emphasis on two fundamental notions: the language produced by the learner is a system in its own right, obeying its own rules, and it is a dynamic system, evolving over time" (Mitchell & Myles, 1998, p. 31).

ESL study as well as other research shows that ESL children make far more **errors of omission** than **errors of commission** with grammatical morphemes. Let us examine this distinction in more detail.

When ESL children do not use the appropriate grammatical morpheme required in the sentence, they often use no morpheme at all, and this is an error of omission. Quite simply, the children use a bare verb stem or bare noun instead of the correctly inflected form. Following are examples of omission errors in which what the child actually said is on the left, and the target-correct version is on the right. In Example 1, the child (CHI) is telling the experimenter (EXP) a story about something that happened in the past and uses bare verb stems instead of the correct irregular past forms. In Example 2, the child omits the third-person singular -*s*, plural -*s*, and the irregular past form of *give*. This same child also omits possessive -*s*, as shown in Example 3. Note that ages of the children in the examples are given as years; months (e.g., 1 year, 4 months is written as 1;4).

1. **Randall (exposure to English = 5 months; age = 7;9)**

    CHI: And then the boat *go* like that. [went] [Child tips the toy boat up.]

    EXP: The boat sank, huh?

    CHI: Yeah.

    EXP: And what happened to the people?

    CHI: They *get* some. [got]

2. **Oleg (exposure to English = 13 months; age = 6;7)**

    CHI: He like-Ø carrot-Ø [like-s, carrot-s]

    CHI: And one time I *give* to him carrot-Ø. [gave, carrot-s]

3. **Oleg (exposure to English = 13 months; age = 6;7)**

    EXP: T-Rex!

Table 6.1. Excerpts from conversations with ESL children from the Edmonton ESL study

Grammatical morpheme	Correct use	Omission errors	Commission errors
Be-copula	**Oleg (experience = 13 months; age = 6;7)**	**Felipe (experience = 10 months; age = 5;8)**	**Oleg (experience = 13 months; age = 6;7)**
	EXP: So tell me about the kids in your class. CHI: I have kid that**'s** really mad at me.	EXP: Is that your grandma? CHI: I dunno if she *Ø* my grandma. *Ø* = *is*	EXP: Do you like math? CHI: There**'s are** not maths. **-s are** = *there isn't*
Be-auxiliary	**Felipe (experience = 10 months; age = 5;8)**	**Reem (experience = 9 months; age = 4;2)**	
	CHI: That was my mom and my dad. CHI: When they **were** going in . . . boats. EXP: Mmhm. CHI: And look, they have two boats that **were** paddling.	EXP: What are you guys doing? CHI: We *Ø* playing hide and seek. *Ø* = *are*	
Past -*ed* and Past irregular	**Felipe (experience = 10 months; age = 5;8)**	**Cindi (experience = 5 months; age = 6;8)**	**Oleg (experience = 13 months; age = 6;7)**
	EXP: Yeah, what kind of good things happened in the Harry Potter movie? CHI: Um . . . the. CHI: Well, not so many. EXP: No? CHI: No, cause . . . cause. . . they **killed** his mom and dad.	EXP: What did you do this morning before you went to school? CHI: I open-*Ø* my eyes and **take** off my sleeping clothes. *Ø* = *ed* **take** = *took*	EXP: Oh Thumbelina! EXP: What happens in that? CHI: I didn't **sawed.** **sawed** = *see*

EXP = experimenter (adult interlocutor); CHI = child

Grammatical morpheme	Correct use	Omission errors	Commission errors
Past -*ed* and Past irregular (continued)	**Sebastián (experience = 16 months; age = 5;2)** EXP: So what did you do this weekend? CHI: I **went** on a fieldtrip.	**Oleg (experience = 13 months; age = 6;7)** CHI: I went one time, was in the line at first and then he ***come push*** outta the line and come stand beside me first. ***come*** = *came* ***push*** = *pushed*	
Prepositions	**Sebastián (experience = 16 months; age = 5;2)** EXP: So what did you do this weekend? CHI: I went ***on*** a fieldtrip. **Felipe (experience = 10 months; age = 5;8)** EXP: Is there any food that you know how to make? CHI: Uh . . . I know how to make waffles. EXP: How do you do that? CHI: You just put them ***in*** the toaster.	**Binofsha (experience = 10 months; age = 6;1)** CHI: . . . bus is going. EXP: You can't eat on the bus. CHI: No. EXP: No. CHI: They saying "no eating Ø bus." Ø = *on*	**Cindi (experience = 5 months; age = 6;8)** EXP: Who are the people you play with at school? CHI: Zach. CHI: I have two Zach ***on*** my classroom. ***on*** = *in*

(continued)

Table 6.1.   *continued*

Grammatical morpheme	Correct use	Omission errors	Commission errors
Plural -s	**Felipe (experience = 10 months; age = 5;8)**	**Cindi (experience = 5 months; age = 6;8)**	**Oleg (experience = 13 months; age = 6;7)**
	EXP: Is there any food that you know how to make?	EXP: Who are the people you play with at school?	EXP: Do you like math?
	CHI: Uh . . . I know how to make waffle**s**.	CHI: Zach.	CHI: There'**s** are not math**s**. *-s = ∅*
		CHI: I have two Zach-**∅** on my classroom. *-∅ = -s*	
Determiners	**Cindi (experience = 5 months; age = 6;8)**	**Felipe (experience = 10 months; age = 5;8)**	**Cindi (experience = 5 months; age = 6;8)**
	CHI: I am **a** girl and my ski pants is black color.	EXP: What's different about this house?	EXP: What's your favorite?
		CHI: Um . . . it's . . . bigger.	CHI: Summer.
	Felipe (experience = 10 months; age = 5;8)	CHI: And it gots **∅** basement. *∅ = a*	EXP: Because why?
	EXP: Is there any food that you know how to make?		CHI: I can eat . . . **the** ice cream.
	CHI: Uh . . . I know how to make waffles.		EXP: Oh, that's a good reason.
	EXP: How do you do that?		CHI: And I can put on **the** dress. *the = ∅*
	CHI: You just put them in **the** toaster.		

Grammatical morpheme	Correct use	Omission errors	Commission errors
Possessives	**Felipe (experience = 10 months; age = 5;8)** CHI: Harry Potter didn't want to shake that guy'**s** hand. CHI: The bad guy's hand.	**Reem (experience = 9 months; age = 4;2)** EXP: So what are you going to be when you grow up, Reem? CHI: I'm a be sleeping beauty. CHI: Because sleeping beauty **Ø** dress was so nice and pink or blue. **Ø** = -*s*	**Binofsha (experience = 10 months; age = 6;1)** EXP: And do you play Barbies with your sister? CHI: Yeah. EXP: Does she have one Barbie, too? CHI: Yeah. CHI: Just not like **my's**. **my's** = *mine (no -s)*
3rd person -*s*	**Sebastián (experience = 16 months; age = 5;2)** EXP: What's happening in these pictures? CHI: In this picture, that's where my mom work**s**.	**Cindi (experience = 5 months; age = 6;8)** CHI: And she is very hot. CHI: He want-**Ø** some ice cream. **Ø** = -*s*	**Felipe (experience = 10 months; age = 5;8)** EXP: What's different about this house? CHI: Um . . . it's . . . bigger. CHI: And it **gots** basement. **gots** = *got Ø (it's got)*
Do	**Cindi (experience = 5 months; age = 6;8)** EXP: You get to play Doctor ball or anything like that? CHI: I **don't** like play ball.	**Felipe (experience = 10 months; age = 5;8)** CHI: And then you eat them. EXP: With . . . what? CHI: With . . . um . . . how **Ø** you say that? CHI: Uh . . . honey. EXP: Honey. **Ø** = *do*	**Reem (experience = 9 months; age = 4;2)** EXP: He doesn't want to watch TV? CHI: My dad **do**n't wanna watch TV. **do** = *does*

BOX 6.3

Developmental and transfer errors—L2 learners, like L1 learners, produce sentences that have errors in them, from the perspective of the target language (i.e., the L2). These errors are a hallmark characteristic of inter-language and can have two sources. The most common form of error is developmental—these are target-deviant forms like those found in L1 acquisition that arise from the learning process itself and can be very similar across L2 learners with different L1s. In contrast, transfer errors are those target-deviant structures in interlanguage that are the result of influence from the L1 on the L2 phonology or grammar. In this case, L2 learners with different L1s make different errors.

EXP: Is that your favorite dinosaur?

CHI: Yes.

EXP: Umhum.

CHI: Not it's my friend-Ø favorite dinosaur. [*friend-'s*]

In contrast, commission errors appear when a grammatical morpheme is used incorrectly. In Example 4, the child uses the correct irregular past tense form *had* for *have*, but also adds a superfluous -*ed*, so he double-marks the past. In Example 5, the child adds a third person singular -*s* to the verb form *got*, which does not take an agreement morpheme. Double-marking, faulty agreement, and overregularization of the past, in which the -*ed* is added to a verb stem that typically has an irregular past-tense form (e.g., *comed* instead of *came*) are typical kinds of commission errors. Although these kinds of errors are often salient when ESL children make them, as we stated previously, they are far less frequent overall than errors of omission.

4.   **Felipe (exposure to English = 10 months; age = 5;8)**

EXP: Were there robbers in Columbia?

CHI: Yeah.

EXP: Mmhm?

CHI: That's why we *haded* to move. [had-Ø]

5.   **Felipe (exposure to English = 10 months; age = 5;8)**

EXP: What's different about this house?

CHI: Um, it's bigger.

CHI: And it *gots* basement. [(It's)got-Ø]

Although ESL children are in the process of acquiring grammatical morphemes, they often use a morpheme correctly and then make an error with it, even within the same conversation. Refer to Example 6, in which the child uses the past tense for the first two verbs in his story but then slips into using the bare verb stems for the rest. This kind of alternation between correct and incorrect usage is a typical part of the language learning process. In fact, even regression from a consistently correctly used form is possible.

In a case study of a Turkish-speaking ESL boy, Hadnezar (2001) noted that the boy used some irregular past-tense forms correctly and then switched to overregularization later on in his interlanguage development. Two examples of this are given in Example 7, and the dates show that the correct forms emerged earlier than the incorrect ones. Wong Fillmore (1979) suggested that this appearance of regression can happen in L2 acquisition because the correct structure represented more formulaic usage. When children really begin to become productive speakers of the L2, creative errors such as overregularization emerge.

One key implication of this back and forth use of grammatical morphemes by L2 children is that professionals don't know how to set their expectations appropriately. An L2 child's using a morpheme once or twice correctly does not necessarily mean that the child will use the morpheme correctly from then on. Children vacillate between correct and incorrect forms, and between supplying a form and not supplying it, before their use of the correct form is high and stable (steady at 90% or greater accuracy in obligatory context).

6. **Oleg (exposure to English = 13 months; age = 6;7)**

> CHI: I *went* one time, *was* in the line at first, and then he *come push* outta the line and *come stand* beside me first.

7. **Erdem (Turkish L1, English L2; from Hadnezar, 2001, p. 19)**

> CHI: My Daddy *brought* a toy. (February 14, 1995)

> CHI: She *bringed* me some new clothes. (May 19, 1995)

> CHI: Because it was not working, that's why I *broke* it. (February 22, 1995)

> CHI: Daddy open the window and the window *breaked*. (May 19, 1995)

Sometimes, an ESL child can make errors across several grammatical morphemes that are connected at the level of meaning. In the excerpt in Example 8, the girl makes several errors across different morphemes that have to do with singular versus plural. She uses the singular form of the *be*-copula with the word *skis pants*. Perhaps she thinks this is a singular noun because at the end of her story she says she wants *a purple one* instead of *a purple pair* or *purple ones,* but she also uses the singular copula when she says *they ski pants is,* meaning the boys' ski pants, which should be plural because there is more than one pair. She also misses the plural *-s* in *some boy*. Thus, the locus of her difficulty seems to be with expressing plurality in English grammar, and this is played out in both omission and commission errors with both verbs and nouns. Furthermore, her difficulty with plural cannot be attributed to an inability to pronounce *s* at the end of a word because she can say *ski pants*.

8.   Cindi (exposure to English = 5 months; age = 6;8)

> CHI: I am a girl and my *ski pants is* black color.
>
> EXP: And you don't like them?
>
> EXP: What color would you like?
>
> CHI: And I . . . I see some . . . *some boy.*
>
> CHI: And *they ski pants is* uh purple or green.
>
> CHI: But I . . . I want *a purple one.*

How many errors with grammatical morphology do child L2 learners make in their interlanguage throughout a conversation? Are they frequent, occasional, or rare? At the early stages, it is possible that ESL children will produce almost none of these morphemes correctly, so error rates can be very high, above 75%. Naturally, error rates decline as children become more proficient in English, but as we discuss in the next section, this decline does not happen very quickly.

We have taken a narrow focus in this section on grammatical morphology because it is such a salient problem area in ESL children's oral language, as well as in the language of monolingual children with SLI. As we mentioned at the beginning, however, it is important to keep in mind that the interlanguage of ESL children has many other developmental patterns. These children often overuse what are called *general-all-purpose* (GAP) words (and verbs in particular) when more specific words would be appropriate and characteristic of a native speaker; for example, they might say, "He *do* that to him," together with a gesture to mean "He *punched* him." Another salient characteristic of interlanguage has to do with pragmatics and having a limited range of vocabulary and grammar to express certain concepts. For instance, whereas a native speaker may be able to make requests in several ways, according to social context, second language users have limited pragmatic abilities. A native speaker would probably be able to use both informal (e.g., "shut the window") and polite forms (e.g., "would you please shut the window?"), but second language users might have only one such form.

It is fascinating that these children are able to get their general meaning across in an informal conversation, even with the limitations in accuracy and proficiency. This contrast between linguistic form and linguistic conversational ability sometimes leads teachers and other professionals working with L2 children to overestimate their overall proficiency in English. We return to this point in the section on rate of L2 development.

First Language Influence on Children's Second Language Development (Transfer)

Interlanguage patterns come, in part, from the L1 of L2 learners, which is why L2 learners of English who have the same L1 often have similar foreign accents. Both adults and children rely on their existing linguistic knowledge from their L1 when acquiring their L2, and this L1 influence on the L2 is often referred to as transfer from the L1. In the past, transfer was thought to be very detrimental to L2 learning, and there was a strong pedagogical orientation toward eliminating the effects of transfer; however, the L1 is now viewed as a valuable reservoir of linguistic resources for L2 learning. The phonology, vocabulary, and grammar of the L1 can provide essential scaffolding for building knowledge of the L2, and this reliance on the L1 is most prominent at the beginning of the productive language period in the L2, when learners' resources in the L2 are limited. When the L1 is different from the L2 with respect to, for example, word order in sentences or rules for pronunciation, this reliance on the L1 may result in target-deviant structures in L2 interlanguage that are commonly called *transfer errors*.

The phonological system is often a major source of transfer from the L1. For example, speakers of a language such as Japanese often have difficulty pronouncing consonant clusters and word final consonants in English because Japanese does not have consonant clusters, and only a nasal consonant can appear at the end of a word. Japanese speakers of English will often put vowels between the consonants to break up the clusters or at the end of a word ending in a consonant, which makes the English word sound more like Japanese. For example, *English* might be pronounced something like "engulisu." This kind of adaptation of the L2 phonology is a form of L1 transfer.

Even very small children can transfer phonological features from their L1 to their L2. In a case study of his son, Alvino Fantini (1985) noted that when Mario first began speaking English around the age of 2½, some of his first English words were pronounced using features of Spanish phonology. For example, English has tense and lax vowel pairs for the high vowels, /i/ (b*ea*t) /ɪ/ (b*i*t) and /u/ (b*oo*t) /ʊ/ (b*oo*k), whereas Spanish only has the tense vowels /i/ and /u/. Mario only used tense vowels in his first English words, and so said "bili" for /bɪli/ (i.e., Billy) and "luk luk" for /lʊklʊk/ (i.e., look look).

In the domain of grammar, when the L1 and L2 have a different word order, this is a common place for transfer. For instance, in Spanish and French, object pronouns come before the verb, but in English they come after the verb. So, the sentence "I see *it*" in French is "je *le* vois," in which the object pronouns are in italics to show the positional difference. English-speaking children learning French as an L2 will sometimes put a French object pronoun after the verb, thus transferring the syntactic structure from their native language.

Another distinction between Spanish and French versus English is the construction of possessives. In English, one can say "the dog's house" or "the house of the dog." In Spanish and French, only the second construction exists (e.g., "la casa del perro," "la maison du chien"). Spanish- and French-speaking learners of English have often been noted to prefer saying "the house of the dog" instead of "the dog's house" in English, even though most native speakers of English would agree that the latter is more natural. This preference on the part of the L2 learners is a subtler transfer effect from their L1 because the effect does not produce a target-deviant structure. Instead it influences the L2 learner to choose a less frequent construction that might sound odd, but is not, strictly speaking, a grammatical error (see quantitative crosslinguistic influence in Chapter 4, which is an analogous phenomenon in bilingual acquisition).

A third and even more subtle kind of transfer is avoidance of certain structures in the L2. Considering the example of pronouns used previously, it has been observed that English learners of French as an L2 avoid using direct object pronouns, presumably because of the contrast in word order between the two languages. So, instead of saying "je *le* vois," they might use the demonstrative pronoun in French, which comes after the verb, and say "je vois ça"/"I see *that*," or use a lexical object (e.g., "je vois *le chien*"/ "I see *the dog*"). Like the preference transfer example, avoidance does not lead L2 learners to produce, strictly speaking, target-deviant structures. All three kinds of L1 influence, 1) direct transfer of L1 structure into L2, 2) preference for a structure in the L2 that parallels the L1, and 3) avoidance of an L2 structure, can be observed in child L2 learners.

In sum, the period of productive language use in L2 acquisition involves creative construction of sentences in L2 interlanguage, sometimes resulting in target-deviant structures. The target-deviant structures arise due to influence from the L1 or, more often, as a result of the process of language learning, which is the same for children learning their L1. With respect to transfer from the L1, we want to reemphasize that it is a transitional and typical component of interlanguage, and it shows that children are using their L1 linguistic knowledge to draw them into L2 proficiency and to keep the conversational ball rolling, which is a positive and sensible learning strategy. L1 transfer is not a signal in and of itself that an L2 child is confused or impaired in any way. Overall, educators and health care practitioners who are working with L2 children should expect the children's language to contain errors in pronunciation, vocabulary choice, morphology, and grammar as they gradually become more proficient in the L2. A relevant question about this interlanguage period is, how long does it last? In other words, when do L2 children begin to sound like native speakers? This question is important because ESL children who may appear to learn the L2 very slowly can cause concern for parents and teachers alike.

HOW LONG DOES IT TAKE, AND WHAT FACTORS MIGHT MAKE CHILDREN ACQUIRE THEIR SECOND LANGUAGE AT DIFFERENT RATES?

Rate of Learning a Second Language

Adult L2 learners might always have a foreign accent, but L1 minority children are expected to eventually become like native speakers of the majority L2, and with respect to conversational oral competence, they can become indistinguishable from monolinguals. This ultimate outcome is relatively uncontroversial; however, how quickly L2 children reach this ultimate outcome is a topic of research. A popular belief is that young children can learn a language practically overnight. Some people think that when young children learn a new language they "soak it up like a sponge." There is considerable research evidence showing this popular belief to be false, and it is important for professionals working with L2 children to be aware of how long it can really take to acquire native-like competence in a second language, in order to have realistic expectations of children's performance.

At the early stages of ESL acquisition, children can function in an English conversation without using much English. To illustrate this point, let's examine a conversation that took place between Johanne Paradis and a 7-year-old boy. This child spoke Spanish as his L1 and had been exposed to English in elementary school in Canada for 4 months.

9.   **Samuel (exposure to English = 4 months; age = 7;3)**

    EXP: So, what grade are you in at school?

    CHI: Two.

EXP: Wow, grade 2 already. What's your teacher's name?

CHI: Mrs. Munro.

EXP: What's the name of your school?

CHI: Lendrum.

EXP: I've heard of that school. I think one of our other grad students sent their kids there. Do you like school here in Canada?

CHI: Yeah. Oh yeah.

EXP: What's your favorite subject? What do you like best at school?

CHI: Uhmm, math.

EXP: That's great. Not everybody likes math, but it's important. Do you take English second language classes?

CHI: Yeah . . . some days.

EXP: What do you think about all the snow? Does it snow like this in Chile?

CHI: I like it, the snow.

EXP: Do you go tobogganing with your friends?

CHI: Yeah, I like it.

EXP: The cold doesn't bother you?

CHI: [shrug] No.

At the end of this exchange, several people remarked on how good this child's English was, but can the child's English language skills really be judged from this exchange? The child's part of the conversation consisted mainly of one-word answers to questions on familiar topics, school and the weather. His comprehension may appear to be impeccable, but he could have used many kinds of nonlinguistic information to comprehend what was being asked (e.g., real-world knowledge about schools, experience with this line of questioning about school). More important, the expectations of the adult interlocutor and listeners were low. Many people don't expect children to initiate and elaborate much in conversation with an unfamiliar adult. Therefore, in terms of basic conversational skills and social expectations of a 7-year-old, this boy performed extremely well in an English language exchange, but actually, he might know very, very little English.

The point we want to make is that L2 children can often appear more linguistically advanced than they really are in casual conversation because their grammatical abilities are not being stretched in these situations. To put it differently, the ability to communicate and participate in an informal social interaction is not the same thing as producing accurate, target-like structures in the L2. In order to address the question of how long it takes for L2 children to achieve native-like proficiency, we need to take a closer look at their accuracy with some of the structural aspects of language, for example, phonology and grammatical morphology.

Regarding phonology, Catherine Snow and Marian Hoefnagel-Höhle (1977) studied the pronunciation of Dutch words by 47 English speakers (ages 3–60 years) learning Dutch as an L2 in the Netherlands. One interesting point they found was that the older, adult learners made more rapid progress toward native-like pronunciation initially, but after 1 year, the children eventually surpassed the adults in their abilities. Furthermore, even after 18 months of exposure, none of the children achieved perfect pronunciation of Dutch. These researchers conducted an additional study in which they asked English speakers, both adults and children, who had had no exposure to Dutch, to pronounce Dutch words in imitation, and measured how native-like their pronunciation was. The children did not perform better on this task than the adults. In the Edmonton ESL study, at Round 2, when the children had 16 months of exposure to English on average, all but one of the children still had a noticeable foreign accent. In sum, it is widely accepted that young children can eventually achieve native-speaker proficiency in the pronunciation of their second language, but they do not reach this outcome quickly.

The findings on acquisition rates for grammatical morphology are similar. In the Edmonton ESL study, we administered grammatical morpheme elicitation probes that have been standardized on monolingual native speakers of English. For ages 4–8 years, there is a minimum criterion accuracy score for the morphemes that all typically developing monolingual children reach in their oral production. One of our goals in this longitudinal study is to find out when ESL children meet the minimum criterion score of accuracy for their age, as set by monolinguals. At Round 1 (mean of 10 months exposure to English), 12% of the children met the criterion score, and at Round 2 (mean of 16 months of exposure), 42% met the criterion score. So, even after 1½ school years in English, less than 50% of these ESL children were as accurate as their native-speaking peers with these morphemes. We also found comparable results for ESL children's receptive vocabulary: At Round 1, 30% had a standard score within the low normal range (85–100) for a native speaker their age, and at Round 2, 50% were within the low normal range. Thus, for both grammar and vocabulary, for both expressive and receptive aspects of language, ESL children do not acquire the language as quickly as the "soak it up like a sponge" theory might suggest.

These results are in line with what other researchers of L2 children have found. Wong Fillmore (1983) observed 48 kindergarten children who spoke Spanish or Cantonese as their L1 for 2 years and found that only 5 of the 48 children observed at the end of the 2 years had reasonable fluency in oral English. When we consider the kinds of English language skills needed to perform academic tasks involving literacy, it can take much longer for ESL children to perform as their native-speaking peers. Jim Cummins, one of the foremost researchers on child bilingualism, stated that ESL children need about 5–7 years to obtain full proficiency in verbal academic skills (Cummins, 2000). This is difficult because the children are hitting a moving target; the native speakers are continually building their verbal academic skills, while L2 children are in the process of learning the language in addition to its applications to academic tasks.

One striking facet of children's acquisition rates in their L2 is the degree of variation among individuals. Substantial individual variation is noted by virtually all researchers of child L2, as evidenced in the Edmonton ESL study. At Round 1, the children's scores on the probes of grammatical morphemes were highly variable; the mean score was 27%, with a range from 0% to 94%. We found similar variation for raw scores on the receptive vocabulary test; the mean score was 45, with a range of 9–82. Furthermore, there was no statistical correlation between the individual children's months of exposure to English and their scores on either the elicitation probes or the vocabulary test at Round 1. This indicates that the children had a lot of heterogeneity in their rates of acquisition that were not directly linked to how much time they had spent in English preschool or school. In the next section, we discuss some other factors that may cause these large individual differences in children's rates of learning English. This point is also developed in Chapter 7 in the discussion of bilingual and L2-only school programs.

Not only is there variation between individual learners, but there is also variation between the acquisition rates for different aspects of language. Children may have mastered one linguistic structure but still be producing target-deviant structures or developmental errors for another structure. Dulay and Burt (1973, 1974) found that ESL children typically become 90% accurate with the copula *be* before they become 90% accurate with the third-person singular *-s* and the past tense. In the Edmonton ESL study, at Round 1, the mean score on the elicitation probe for *be* was 59%, and for past tense it was just 22%. Hadnezar (2001) noted that the Turkish L1 child she studied used the copula *be* accurately more than 90% of the time after 9 months' exposure to English in nursery school, but even after 19 months of exposure to English, he was using the past tense just 74% of the time. These findings indicate that different morphemes are acquired at different rates, and there appears to be an invariant acquisition order among the morphemes. Generally speaking, early-acquired morphemes in English L2 are progressive -*ing* and plural -*s*; late-acquired morphemes are past tense -*ed* and third person singular -*s*.

To return to the question at the beginning of this section, how quickly do children learn their L2? It varies a great deal between children and the aspects of language being considered. Above all, the research indicates that L2 children may achieve early success in communicating and interacting socially using English, but true native-like oral language competence in their L2 can take more than 1 school year, and possibly 2 or more, for some children.

Factors that Influence How Quickly Children Learn a Second Language

There is a lot of variation in speed of acquisition between children, and more research is needed to determine what causes this degree of individual variation. The research aimed at explaining individual differences in L2 learners often shows contradictory findings. One study might find a positive effect of a certain cognitive trait on language learning, but another study might find that this cognitive trait is not related to language learning success. Another reason has to with the "which came first, the chicken or the egg?" problem. For example, are children with outgoing personalities more advanced in their L2 because they seek out English-speaking playmates and thus get more practice, or are they able to be outgoing and seek out these playmates because they are competent in English and have achieved this competence for other reasons? Finally, even though researchers have examined numerous affective/attitudinal, personality/social, cognitive, and situational variables in an attempt to explain what causes some learners to be slower and less successful than others, only some of these variables pertain to L1 minority children because most research has been conducted with adult L2 learners.

For example, a great deal of attention has been paid to measuring and determining the effect of types and degree of motivation on success in L2 attainment. Although this may be an important variable for adult learners of a foreign language in a classroom, or for adult immigrants who, for various complex ethnic, religious, and cultural reasons, may not want to integrate with the host society, absence of motivation is not a common characteristic of L1 minority children. Wong Fillmore (1979) noted that some Spanish L1 children were initially reluctant to learn English, but this did not persist and, moreover, was most likely due to the fact that they had other Spanish-speaking children to play with and a vibrant minority community in their

L1. It is difficult to imagine a child whose L1 is not spoken by any other child in her class having low motivation for an extended period of time to learn the majority language.

One large-scale longitudinal project conducted in Berkeley, California, looked at the potential sources of individual differences in how quickly 48 minority Spanish L1 children acquired English (Wong Fillmore, 1983). The researchers divided the sources they looked at into two categories: 1) learner characteristics, and 2) situational characteristics. Learner characteristics consisted of the social style characteristics of the children, such as being outgoing and talkative versus shy and introverted, as well as language learning style, such as demonstrating strong analytic and other cognitive skills. Situational characteristics referred to the structure of the classroom and how this affected children's opportunities for exposure to English. Wong Fillmore reported on the relationship between learner and situational characteristics and success in L2 development after observing these children for 2 years.

The children who were considered "good English learners" numbered about 38% of the sample (18 of 48). The good learners seemed to come in two types. One type was highly social and outgoing; the children sought out opportunities to speak English through peer interaction, which followed the researchers' predictions about what social style would lead to L2 success. The other type was shy and not very sociable but very attentive in class and academically skilled enough to cope with the tasks of the classroom even when they did not speak the language well. In short, children in this second group had strong cognitive and analytic skills that permitted them to acquire English just as well as their highly social peers.

The situational characteristics examined interacted with these learner characteristics. Teacher-centered classroom settings helped shy and attentive learners to advance because they were exposed to a great deal of English through teacher talk and did not have to initiate social contact with their peers in order to get input. Children who were more outgoing and peer-oriented in their interactions, however, would get more out of a classroom structured around group activities in which they could interact with a diverse number of other children. The advantages of an outgoing social style would backfire in a classroom with lots of group activities where many of the children spoke the same L1 and there were few English native speakers. Some highly social minority children observed by Wong Fillmore spent an entire year in an English classroom and learned very little English because they spoke mainly Spanish with their peers during group activities. One important outcome of the Berkeley study is that there is no single package of learner and situational characteristics that can lead to rapid success in the

L2; even children who are shy can be, relatively speaking, quick to advance in their L2, and not every classroom setting suits every learner's style.

Among the research conducted with adult L2 learners, the variable that most consistently correlates with language learning success is **language aptitude.** Language aptitude is distinct from general intelligence and includes skills such as the ability to rapidly and accurately decode unfamiliar speech into phonetic (sound) units and parts of speech (e.g., nouns, verbs, adjectives). It is considered to be an intrinsic, not a learned, skill. Language aptitude is much more explanatory of individual differences in adult learners than personality and social style variables and may be a relevant factor in explaining why some L1 minority children acquire English faster than others.

Language aptitude tests are not easily administered to young children, and language aptitude effects on L2 acquisition have not been widely studied in L1 minority children. Ranta (2002) examined language aptitude and L2 attainment in 150 French-speaking children in grade 6 in Quebec, Canada, who were enrolled in an intensive, communicatively oriented English as a second language program. French is the majority language of this province, so these were not L1 minority children. The language aptitude tests were conducted in French so as not to confound L2 ability with this measure. Analyses showed that, for one group of children, high performance on language aptitude was associated with high attainment in their L2 after the 5-month program. For another group of children, poor performance on the language aptitude tasks was associated with poor performance on the measures of L2 proficiency. The children who fell in the middle on both L2 proficiency and language aptitude did not show these associations. These findings indicate that language aptitude could be as important in predicting individual differences in child L2 as it is in adult L2 and might be the relevant factor underlying the studious, attentive language learner style described in Wong Fillmore's Berkeley study.

One variable that has not been researched in depth to explain individual differences in child L2 learning is the distance between the L2 and L1 in terms of phonological or grammatical structure. In other words, when a child's L1 is very different from the L2, does this affect the child's rate of L2 development? For example, would it be harder for a Mandarin L1 child to learn English than a Dutch L1 child because Dutch is a related language with a large number of words that are close in form to their English translation equivalents? The results of Dulay and Burt's (1974) study on grammatical morphology may provide the hint of an answer. In this study, the Chinese L1 children showed the same acquisition sequence in terms of which morphemes they acquired early and late as the Spanish L1 children, but they

BOX 6.4

Language aptitude—"Foreign language learning aptitude has been defined by John Carroll, the most prominent scholar in this area as 'some characteristic of an individual which controls, at a given point of time, the rate of progress that he will make subsequently in learning a foreign language' (1974). Studies investigating L2 success in relation to language aptitude have generally yielded correlation coefficients in the .4 to .6 range (Carroll, 1981, p. 93). These are considered moderate to strong correlations, and although they imply that considerable learner variation remains to be explained by additional factors, they also demonstrate that language aptitude has consistently been the single best predictor of subsequent language learning achievement" (Sawyer & Ranta, 2002, p. 320).

had lower mean accuracy scores for use of the morphemes overall. More research needs to be undertaken to determine what effect L1 typology has on the rate of child L2 acquisition.

Another factor that may come to mind is how much absolute exposure to the majority language minority children receive. Wong Fillmore (1979, 1983) remarked that children who sought out social contact in English more often were faster learners presumably because they got more practice. Clearly, children do need consistent exposure to an L2 in order to learn it, but absolute quantity of L2 exposure, as measured by length of time in an English classroom, does not have a direct relationship to learner success, as shown in Wong Fillmore's research and in the results of the Edmonton ESL study. Research on acquisition of a majority language in school leads to the same conclusion; this research is discussed in Chapter 7. Quality, not quantity, of exposure is more likely related to rate of acquisition, but as yet, no easy way to measure quality of exposure exists. Moreover, sufficient exposure to the L2 to ensure adequate and successful L2 outcomes does not mean that time spent speaking the L1 interferes with this process. On the contrary, use of the L1 should be encouraged for a variety of reasons, including L2 advancement. We elaborate on this in the next section. In sum, the sources of individual differences in L2 learning are not well understood but most likely consist of a combination of interacting variables like social style, learning situation, and language aptitude.

WHAT HAPPENS TO THE FIRST LANGUAGE OF LANGUAGE MINORITY CHILDREN IN A MAJORITY SECOND LANGUAGE CONTEXT?

Immigrant parents often feel divided between their desire to have their children grow up speaking their native language and their desire to have their children become part of the host society. The truth is that immigrant parents need not worry about this issue because the goals of L1 maintenance and L2 acquisition are mutually supportive of each other, rather than being at odds with each other. On the face of it, it may seem contradictory to suggest that maintaining the L1 is important. We have just discussed how long it can take L2 children to get up to speed in English, and we reviewed the potential importance of social interaction in the L2 as a factor in development, but language learning is not a zero-sum game. As we pointed out in Chapter 3, the limited capacity hypothesis is not tenable. It is not the case that there is only so much space for language in the brains of young children and, therefore, the L1 must be dropped in favor of the L2. Nor is it true that increasing time on task is a prerequisite for rapid L2 advancement. Although it is commonly believed that children need to maximize exposure to the L2 and reduce exposure to other languages to maximize L2 development, akin to the "soak it up like a sponge" theory, there is little empirical support for these beliefs.

Minority language children learning a majority L2, such as immigrant children in North America, Western Europe, and Australia, are often in subtractive bilingual environments because their ultimate bilingual proficiency might be low due to lack of proficiency in their L1, and they may not experience the cognitive advantages conferred by dual language learning that are found in additive bilingual environments. A subtractive environment can create ambivalence toward the heritage language on the part of young language learners and their caregivers. The heritage language comes to be seen as an impediment to acquisition of the majority language and a marker of minority group inferiority, with the result that the L1 is abandoned. A corollary effect is that parents and others who speak the heritage language no longer provide rich linguistic input to the child as they strive to interact with their children in a language that they themselves have usually not mastered. In effect, the bilingualism of the child is devalued, and the rich linguistic input that is critical to full acquisition is compromised. The academic benefits to second language learning that come from full competence in one's native language, which we discuss next, are also compromised. Thus, there are significant psychological and sociocultural reasons to promote the maintenance of the L1 as beneficial for minority language children. Wong Fillmore passionately expressed why loss of the L1 can be detrimental to such children:

> What is lost when children and parents cannot communicate easily with one another? What is lost is no less than the means by which parents socialize their children: When parents are unable to talk to their children, they cannot easily convey to them their values, beliefs, understandings, or wisdom about how to cope with their experiences. They cannot

teach them about the meaning of work, or about personal responsibility, or what it means to be a moral or ethical person in a world with too many choices and too few guideposts to follow. . . . Talk is a crucial link between parents and children: It is how parents impart their cultures to their children and enable them to become the kind of men and women they want them to be. When parents lose the means for socializing and influencing their children, rifts develop and families lose the intimacy that comes from shared beliefs and understandings. (1991, p. 343)

Not only can loss of L1 have pernicious effects on a child's social and psychological well-being, but it can also have negative cognitive consequences for a bilingual child academically. There is extensive research evidence pointing to the interdependent development of L1 and L2 verbal skills for academic purposes, indicating that children who have highly developed language skills in domains that are relevant to schooling reap the benefits of this knowledge in their L2 performance in school (Cummins, 1991, 2000). The clearest example of this is L2 reading. Minority language children who have acquired emergent literacy skills in their L1 prior to coming to school make faster progress in L2 literacy than children who lack such preliteracy skills. The link between L1 and L2 literacy is even more evident when considering the case of language minority students who have already acquired reading skills in the L1. For these children, acquisition of literacy skills in an L2 is straightforward. Further elaboration on the advantages of maintaining the L1 for enhanced performance in L2 school settings is covered in Chapter 7.

In spite of the importance of L1 maintenance for the minority language child's personal well-being and academic success, many minority language children gradually lose their L1 abilities over time. This process of language loss is referred to as **L1 attrition.** Some kind of attrition can occur even in children whose L1 is supported in their surrounding community, such as Spanish in some regions of the United States. It is important for professionals working with children to expect that the L1 abilities of most minority language children will not remain stable. Gradual shift from the heritage language to the majority language, even in the home, is inevitable for most immigrant families in the United States, Canada, Western Europe, and Australia.

Many researchers and practitioners working with L2 children have noticed that some of these children can go through a transitional period when their L1 ability has declined considerably and rapidly, but their L2 ability is nowhere near complete or native-like. This transitional period has often been labeled **semilingualism.** Children in this transitional stage are also referred to as "non-nons," nonspeakers of either English or the heritage language. These terms are very controversial because they imply that the child is in a kind of linguistic vacuum from which there may be no escape.

BOX 6.5

First language (L1) attrition—process whereby the proficiency in the primary language declines as the second language (L2) becomes dominant. This can result in restricted communicative competence in the L1 compared with the L2, and/or eventual complete loss of the L1. Attrition can take many forms: decay or stagnation in size of L1 vocabulary, reduction in fluency/spontaneity in the L1, transfer of grammatical rules from the L2 into the L1, or borrowing vocabulary from the L2 into the L1. When the L1 is a minority language, there is a risk of L1 attrition.

We believe these terms should be avoided for many reasons. First of all, there is much doubt about how linguistically deficient children are in this transitional phase. Children always have some level of proficiency in their L1 and L2 during this kind of transitional period, and their L2 interlanguage during this phase is a language: It is systematic; it has a grammar; and it is a functional system for communication. The idea that a minority language child could be a speaker of no language (a non-non) is too categorical to be useful because, as we pointed out, the appearance of "semilingualism" is a result of a dynamic process of changing language competencies. In addition, the concept of semilingualism is also misleading because it is often taken as a description of a *state* that all early bilinguals are in, possibly forever. This is usually not the case. The apparently limited proficiency of language minority students who are acquiring an L2 is usually transitional, not permanent. The belief that semilingualism might be a permanent state is based on the Limited Capacity Hypothesis, which we know to be false. In our experience, most minority language L2 children do not go through the transitional stage so quickly that they could be deemed semilingual in any real sense. Their L1 abilities do not decline so precipitously that they could validly be deemed to lack functional competence in that language, and their L2 abilities usually increase sufficiently during the transition period that they are proficient enough in the L2 to satisfy their interpersonal communication needs.

This transitional phase between descending L1 abilities and ascending L2 abilities has been examined by Kathryn Kohnert and her colleagues in Spanish L1/English L2 children and adolescents of Mexican American descent in California (Kohnert, Bates, & Hernandez, 1999; Kohnert & Bates, 2002). These researchers examined the speed and accuracy with which these students recognized and named words in both Spanish and English at different ages, from 5 to 16 years of age. The students' word processing skills were stronger in Spanish production initially until they had approximately 10 years' experience with English, at which point their dominance shifted from Spanish to English. In terms of comprehension, this shift occurred earlier, at about 6 years and

9 months of exposure to English. Thus, even for L2 children who live in a community in which they have many opportunities to use their L1 and maintain it, their language abilities show dynamic shifts, with many children eventually becoming stronger in the majority language, especially if it is the language of schooling.

A final flaw in the use of the term *semilingualism* is linked to testing issues. Many minority language children are labeled semilinguals (or non-nons) because they have scored poorly on a test of language ability that was designed for native, monolingual speakers of the test language. Using test norms based on monolingual, native speakers to interpret the performance of minority language children is clearly an invalid use of test norms. Moreover, minority language children can perform poorly on a test of L2 ability if they are too shy to speak as volubly as the test requires (see also Chapter 2) or if they don't know how to respond to unfamiliar protocols (e.g., answering in a complete sentence). The demands of taking a test in the L2 can depress the real language abilities of L2 children and give an overly simplified and false indication of their actual abilities. For all of these reasons, we strongly urge avoidance of terms such as *semilingual* and *non-non*.

What Causes First Language Attrition?

Many immigrant families we have dealt with complain that their children refuse to speak the L1; they can understand it, but they answer back in the L2. This refusal can turn into language loss over time or may be the result of it. Why are some language minority children reluctant to use their L1? The reasons include factors such as 1) a desire for assimilation to the majority society, 2) the absence of academic support for the L1, 3) dominance of the majority culture, and 4) language shift in the home (which can be both cause and effect). When minority language children arrive in English-only schools, they are confronted with the majority culture and language head on. Their heritage language and culture may not be represented at all, or very little, and they quickly come to realize that being accepted into the social fabric of the school and developing a sense of belonging depends on learning the majority language and assimilating to the majority culture. As mentioned in the previous section, this drive for assimilation can come at the price of feelings of inferiority for being a minority. In addition, because there is no academic support for the children's L1, they may gradually feel restricted in the range of topics they can express in their L1, as compared to their L2.

One example is discussing the topic of school itself. Because school instruction is in English, children often prefer to talk about school in English and may even lack the vocabulary to talk about it in their L1. In addition, the dominance and prestige of the majority culture can lead minority language children to lose interest in speaking the L1 or using L1 books and videos. Finally, children's reluctance to use their L1 can be a response to language shift in the home. Over time, many minority language parents become bilingual, and they might begin to use the majority language at home. However, not all minority language parents become balanced bilinguals; they do not become very proficient in the majority language but use it anyway with their children because they are persuaded that this is the best tactic for enhancing their child's L2 development.

A large-scale survey carried out by Wong Fillmore (1991) in the United States showed that early introduction of English through preschool programs was a major factor in L1 erosion and loss among minority language children. The study consisted of interviews with 1,001 minority language families (Native Americans, Latinos, Arabs, and East and Southeast Asians). The respondents were categorized into two groups. Group 1 consisted of families with children in English-only or bilingual preschools, and Group 2 consisted of families with children in heritage language–only preschools (in this case, Spanish-only). Comparisons between Group 1 and Group 2 showed that 73% of the children in English-only and bilingual programs used English only or a mix of English and the heritage language in the home, although this was true for only 48% of the children in Spanish-only preschool programs. Parents of the Group 1 children were six to eight times more likely to describe their children's abilities in the heritage language as deficient or nonexistent.

Furthermore, the language shift that the Group 1 children were introducing into the household forced parents to use more English, even in cases where they admitted that their English was poor and they could not express themselves fully in that language. Even though the results of this survey clearly indicate that early exposure to English for minority language children is a factor in L1 attrition, we want to emphasize that bilingualism in the preschool years does not have a negative impact on children in and of itself; more specifically, it does not lead to erosion or loss of children's primary language per se. Samantha (profiled in Chapter 1) is in no danger of losing her first language, English, by attending a preschool and elementary school in Spanish in Arizona. We have already stressed in Chapters 3 and 4 how early simultaneous bilingualism is not a risk factor for language development. Our concern here about when it is best to introduce an L2 pertains to L1 maintenance for *minority language children* in subtractive bilingual environments. The results of Wong Fillmore's study suggested that for some minority language children, particularly those whose L1 is not widely used outside their homes, maintenance of the L1 can be compromised by early exposure to English.

Another large-scale study was conducted with Mexican American adolescents in California (Hakuta & D'Andrea, 1992). Although the participants in this study were not young children themselves, they can shed light on the expected outcomes for dual language children. The researchers interviewed and tested the language proficiency of 308 teenagers of Mexican descent. The interviewers gathered information about the adolescents' family backgrounds, language use in various settings, and attitudes about Spanish. The key finding from this study was that proficiency in Spanish was much more related to parental use of the language in the home than to the teenagers' attitudes about Spanish or settings of language use. Proficiency in Spanish was lowest among participants whose parents spoke English in the home. More important, English language proficiency was high and relatively stable among the teenagers who had resided in the United States for about 8 years, regardless of how well they spoke Spanish. This study indicated that if parents want their children to maintain their abilities in their L1, they must use that language in the home as much as possible, and this practice does not take away from minority language children's chances at success in acquiring English.

In sum, L1 attrition is a normal and expected outcome that most minority language children face. It can take various forms, from complete loss to a gradual shift in dominance to the majority language; however, maintenance of the L1 has many psychosocial and educational advantages for minority language children. Taking steps such as delaying the introduction of English until school age for some children and speaking the minority language as much as possible at home can help in the development of bilingual proficiency.

HOW ARE SECOND LANGUAGE LEARNERS AND MONOLINGUALS WITH LANGUAGE IMPAIRMENT SIMILAR AND DIFFERENT?

In Chapter 4, we discussed the case of children who are raised bilingually and also have specific language impairment (SLI). In this section, we highlight a different relationship between dual language and disorder that parallels monolingual children with SLI and typically developing children who are learning a second language. Minority language children are overrepresented in special education and are considered more likely at risk for educational failure (see Chapter 3), as are children with language disorders (see Chapter 1). Some L2 minority language children are inappropriately placed in special education simply because their English language abilities are not strong enough for them to perform well academically. A poor understanding of how long it takes to learn a second language can influence these kinds of decisions (we discuss this issue further in Chapter 7). We refer to this type of misplacement of L2 children as cases of "mistaken identity." Decisions of mistaken identity can have long-lasting negative consequences for children with respect to their self-esteem, their attitudes about schooling, and even their future educational opportunities.

The flip side of the diagnosis problem is "missed identity," in which an L2 child with SLI is overlooked and does not receive the intervention he needs. Missed identity can occur because teachers' and clinicians' expectations of the language and learning abilities of minority language students are too low. To be more specific, if professionals expect minority language children to struggle with language and to attain low levels of achievement, then they may not be able to distinguish the signs of impairment from the usual interlanguage characteristics that are also likely to mark these children's language development. In cases of missed identity, everything the child does is simply interpreted as a reflection of his language minority status. In order to reduce instances of mistaken and missed identity, it is vital to be aware of the similarities between impaired language and interlanguage and to know how to spot the differences.

Not much research has directly compared children with SLI and typically developing children who are learning a second language; however, there has been some comparative research of this type in French, Swedish, and English (Crago & Paradis, 2003; Håkansson & Nettelbladt, 1993; Paradis, in press, under review; Paradis & Crago, 2000, in press). The findings from this research can be summarized as follows:

- Children with SLI and typically developing L2 children often have difficulties with the same domains of language. For example, both populations of children make errors with grammatical morphemes in French and English and make word order errors in Swedish. Also, children with SLI and their L2 peers have similar limitations in vocabulary, their verb vocabulary in particular, when compared with monolingual, typically developing same-age peers in French and English. Isolating a problematic language domain that is unique to typically developing children who are acquiring a second language and children with SLI is a challenge.

- Although the domains of vulnerability appear to be shared between children with SLI and L2 children (as far as we know to date), a close examination of the error types that these two kinds of learners make in these domains is a promising area for detecting differences. The most common errors overall in oral language for both L2 children and children with SLI are omission errors, but preliminary analyses indicate that the L2 children from the Edmonton ESL study had a wider variety and greater proportion of commission errors with grammatical morphemes than has been reported for children with SLI. This may be an important area to focus on in the search for distinguishing characteristics between SLI and L2 children.

- Magnitude of difficulty with certain aspects of language could also be a promising area for detecting differences. For example, in the Edmonton ESL study, the children had more difficulties with grammatical morphemes such as progressive -*ing* and plural -*s* than has been reported for children with SLI at a similar level of English proficiency. Thus, even if a domain of language, like grammatical morphology, is problematic for both groups, the profile of difficulty within that domain could be distinct for each group.

- Both children with SLI and L2 children are very heterogeneous populations with respect to their performance on language tasks. This makes it difficult to distinguish a slow L2 learner with SLI from a typically developing but slow L2 learner. The root of this problem lies in the fact that the typical range for L2 learning in children is unknown.

In sum, present knowledge about the parallels between children with SLI and typically developing L2 children is insufficient to permit us to propose a set of unique criteria for differential diagnosis; however, we believe that the instances of mistaken and missed identity could be minimized if professionals dealing with dual language children have a good understanding of the process of typical L2 acquisition in children and an awareness of the potential overlap between children with SLI and L2 children in oral language. This could enhance policy and practice to the benefit of dual language children.

KEY POINTS AND CLINICAL IMPLICATIONS

Key Point 1

Children acquire grammatical proficiency and build their vocabularies slowly in their L2; they do not soak language up like a sponge. They may even go through a silent period when they first come into contact with the new language. When they start producing their second language, their first utterances are usually short and formulaic. L2 children may become good communicators with their peers and with adults within a few months of exposure to English, but this does not mean that their accuracy with grammar, their vocabulary size and diversity, and their pronunciation is in the range of their native-speaking peers. Even after 2 years of full-time English exposure at school, L2 children may not sound like native speakers, and it could take them 5–7 years to master those aspects of the target language that are relevant to schooling.

Implications

- If an L2 child seems reluctant to speak at all or responds to questions with one-word answers, it is important to determine how long she has had *consistent* exposure to the L2 before considering whether the child appears to have language delay or disorder. Consistent exposure to the L2 would mean schooling or full-time preschool in the L2. If the child has had less than a year of exposure, it is possible that she is in the early stages of L2 acquisition when this kind of behavior is typical. It may also be the case that the child's seemingly uncommunicative behavior is culturally determined (i.e., in the child's culture, being talkative with adults is not encouraged). Another factor may be that the child has recently experienced some emotional trauma due to recent relocation, time spent in a refugee camp, or forced separation from one or both parents. These kinds of experiences can be sources of uncommunicative behavior in young L2 children.

- Be careful using standardized tests of language development with ESL children. Research has yet to tell when such tests would be appropriate for ESL children, but they are most likely not appropriate for L2 children within the first 2 years of exposure. Recall that only about half of the children in the Edmonton ESL study scored within the typical range for native speakers on tests of receptive vocabulary and grammar production in English after 16 months of exposure.

- Translations of language tests are not useful because 1) cultural differences make what is considered age-appropriate vocabulary different between languages; 2) typological differences between languages mean that certain target grammatical structures that are typical of children at a certain level of development in one language are not the same in other languages; and 3) above all, a translation is not normed. Use of a translated version of a test can give invalid assessments of L2 children.

Key Point 2

There is a great deal of individual variation between children in how quickly they learn a second language. Amount of exposure to the second language does not always clearly determine how advanced a child will be. Some children can carry on a conversation easily after 1 school year in English, but others may be just beginning to speak the language productively after the same amount of time. Factors distinct from amount of exposure that might determine how quickly a child learns the L2 include personality/social style and language aptitude. Language aptitude is not the same as general intelligence, which is more highly correlated with literacy skills than with oral skills in a second language.

Implications

- Range of individual variation is another reason for exercising caution when using standardized tests with L2 children. To give one example of how extreme differences can be, two children in the Edmonton ESL study did not reach native-speaker criterion on grammar probes after 21 months of exposure, yet one child did after 10 months. It is important not to set expectations for all L2 children on experiences with a small number of children. What if a professional's expectations were based on the experience of the child in the Edmonton ESL study who met criterion after 10 months?

- Acquiring an L2 under difficult personal circumstances can affect children's interpersonal style with teachers and other children, as well as their desire to socialize with other children. This may, in turn, affect their ability to get input in the L2 and so should be taken into account when judging their progress in their L2 development.

Key Point 3

The interlanguage of L2 children is characterized by some phonological, lexical, and grammatical differences from the target language. One salient domain for errors is grammatical morphology. L2 children can take more than 2 years to accurately produce grammatical morphemes on a consistent basis. During this time, they may become more accurate with one morpheme before another, and they may alternate between accurate and inaccurate uses of the same morpheme. It is important to keep in mind that grammatical morphology is also a major area of weakness for children with SLI. It could be very easy for an ESL child who is a slow learner to be mistaken as a child with SLI, or for an ESL child with SLI to be missed as having a language disorder because it is difficult to discern the difference between slow L2 acquisition and the acquisition of an L2 under conditions of impairment.

Implications

- If an L2 child seems to vacillate between using correct and incorrect sounding sentences, realize that this behavior is a typical part of L2 acquisition and should not be considered to be a sign of impairment when it is the only sign of impairment. Such back and forth behavior is expected in L2 learner language.

- Because we have found that bilingual children with SLI are impaired in both of their languages, we expect this to be true for L2 children as well. Thus, if an L2 child is suspected of having language impairment, it is essential to find out whether she shows evidence for impairment in her L1 as well. This might be the surest way of determining whether the child really has language impairment. For example, parents could be asked if the child was a late talker.

Key Point 4

L1 attrition (shift in dominance, erosion, or complete loss of the L1) is a common phenomenon in minority language children; however, maintaining proficiency in the L1 is beneficial for both psychosocial and cognitive/educational reasons, in particular for L2 children in subtractive bilingual environments. Maintenance of the L1 is more difficult if the child is being educated entirely through the medium of the second language.

Implications

- The L1 abilities of children who have no schooling in the L1 and who grow up in an L2 majority language environment may be limited. Such children often do not sound like their monolingual L1 peers. This does not mean that they cannot speak the L1, only that they have a different variety of the language, a variety that is influenced by contact with the L2. This is a natural process and should not be cause for concern about the child's language learning capacity. If parents are worried about how their child speaks the L1, that he sounds funny or doesn't speak it well, this may not be a sign of impairment, but instead, a sign of L1 attrition.

- Dual language children should be given full support, affective and linguistic, to learn both languages fully. Continuous, consistent, and rich exposure to both languages is important for full dual language development. Decisions that interrupt the child's exposure to one or both languages should be avoided. Continuity is important for successful dual language development. Thus, decisions that create discontinuity in the child's language experiences should be avoided, all other factors being equal.

- The child's dual language skills should be viewed positively and reinforced as much as possible. Others who work with or care for dual language children (e.g., teachers, child care workers) should be taught to view the child's dual language skills as a positive personal and social asset without detrimental consequences. It is important that they, in turn, support the child's language learning and nurture the child's self-esteem as a dual language learner.

- Educators and clinicians should be very cautious about considering a child to be semilingual. This is a controversial concept and serves mainly to cast dual language children in a negative light.

REFERENCES

Carroll, J. (1974). The aptitude-achievement distinction: The case of foreign language aptitude and proficiency. In D. Green (Ed.), *The aptitude-achievement distinction* (pp. 289–303). Monterey, CA: McGraw-Hill.

Crago, M., & Paradis, J. (2003). Two of a kind? Commonalities and variation in languages and language learners. In Y. Levy & J. Schaeffer (Eds.), *Language competence across populations: Towards a definition of specific language impairment* (pp. 97–110). Mahwah, NJ: Lawrence Erlbaum Associates.

Cummins, J. (1991). Interdependence of first and second language proficiency in bilingual children. In E. Bialystok (Ed.), *Language processing in bilingual children* (pp. 70–89). New York: Cambridge University Press.

Cummins, J. (2000). *Language, power and pedagogy: Bilingual children in the crossfire.* Clevedon, England: Multilingual Matters.

Dulay, H., & Burt, M. (1973). Should we teach children syntax? *Language Learning, 24,* 245–258.

Dulay, H., & Burt, M. (1974). Natural sequences in child second language acquisition. *Language Learning, 24,* 37–53.

Fantini, A. (1985). *Language acquisition of a bilingual child: A sociolinguistic perspective.* San Diego: College-Hill Press.

Hadnezar, B. (2001). The acquisition of the IP system in child L2 English. *Studies in Second Language Acquisition, 23,* 1–39.

Håkansson, G., & Nettelbladt, U. (1993). Developmental sequences in L1 (normal and impaired) and L2 acquisition of Swedish syntax. *International Journal of Applied Linguistics, 3*(2), 3–29.

Hakuta, K., & D'Andrea, D. (1992). Some properties of bilingual maintenance and loss in Mexican background high-school students. *Applied Linguistics, 13*(1), 72–99.

Kohnert, K., & Bates, E. (2002). Balancing bilinguals, II: Lexical comprehension and cognitive processing in children learning Spanish and English. *Journal of Speech, Language, and Hearing Research, 45,* 347–359.

Kohnert, K., Bates, E., & Hernandez, A. (1999). Balancing bilinguals: Lexical-semantic production and cognitive processing in children learning Spanish and English. *Journal of Speech, Language, and Hearing Research, 42,* 1400–1413.

Mitchell, R., & Myles, F. (1998). *Second language learning theories.* London: Arnold.

Paradis, J. (in press). On the relevance of specific language impairment to understanding the role of transfer in second language acquisition. *Applied Psycholinguistics.*

Paradis, J. (under review). *Grammatical morphology in children learning English as a second language: Implications of similarities with specific language impairment.*

Paradis, J., & Crago, M. (2000). Tense and temporality: Similarities and differences between language-impaired and second-language children. *Journal of Speech, Language, and Hearing Research, 43*(4), 834–848.

Paradis, J., & Crago, M. (in press). Comparing L2 and SLI grammars in French: Focus on DP. In J. Paradis & P. Prévost (Eds.), *The acquisition of French in different contexts: Focus on functional categories* (pp. 89–108). Amsterdam: John Benjamins.

Ranta, L. (2002). The role of learners' language analytic ability in the communicative classroom. In P. Robinson (Ed.), *Individual differences and instructed language learning* (pp. 159–181). Amsterdam: John Benjamins.

Saville–Troike, M. (1987). Bilingual discourse: The negotiation of meaning without a common code. *Linguistics, 25,* 81–106.

Sawyer, M., & Ranta, L. (2002). Aptitude, individual differences, and instructional design. In P. Robinson (Ed.), *Cognition and second language instruction* (pp. 319–353). New York: Cambridge University Press.

Snow, C., & Hoefnagel-Höhle, M. (1977). Age differences in the pronunciation of foreign sounds. *Language and Speech, 20*(4), 357–365.

Tabors, P.O. (1997). *One child, two languages: A guide for preschool educators of children learning English as a second language.* Baltimore: Paul H. Brookes Publishing Co.

Wong Fillmore, L. (1979). Individual differences in second language acquisition. In C. Fillmore, D. Kempler, & W.S.-Y. Wang (Eds.), *Individual differences in language ability and language behavior* (pp. 203–227). San Diego: Academic Press.

Wong Fillmore, L. (1983). The language learner as an individual: Implications of research on individual differences for the ESL teacher. In M. Clarke & J. Handscombe (Eds.), *On TESOL '82: Pacific perspectives on language learning and teaching* (pp. 157–173). Washington, DC: Teachers of English to Speakers of Other Languages.

Wong Fillmore, L. (1991). When learning a second language means losing the first. *Early Childhood Research Quarterly, 6,* 323–346.

CHAPTER 7

Schooling in
a Second Language

This chapter discusses children who are educated in part or entirely through the medium of a second language (L2). These children are linguistically diverse. For example, many immigrant children begin to learn English when they start school in Canada, the United States, Australia, and other English-dominant countries. In many regions of the world, there are children who grow up speaking a language other than the majority language of the community in which they have been born and raised—for example, children, such as Carlos, born of Spanish-speaking parents, who live in some regions of the United States, and Canadian children from an indigenous language group, such as Pauloosie, who grow up speaking a non-English heritage language. If these children live in neighborhoods in which their heritage language predominates, their first significant experience with the majority group language is often when they begin schooling.

Children from minority language backgrounds are not the only ones who are educated in their L2. An increasing number of children speak the majority group language, such as English in Canada, but attend schools where a substantial proportion of their school subjects are taught through the medium of a second or foreign language—Samantha from Tucson is an example of such a child. These programs are often referred to as **immersion programs**, after the St. Lambert French immersion program that was established in Quebec in 1965 (Lambert & Tucker, 1972). In addition, the children

155

BOX 7.1

Minority language students—students whose first language or dominant language is different from that spoken by the majority of speakers within the political entity in which they live, for example, Spanish speakers in the United States or Chinese speakers in Canada and the United States. Minority language students may constitute a majority within their neighborhood community but are a demographic and social minority in the larger community of which they are citizens or members (e.g., Spanish speakers in Miami or sections of Los Angeles may be a majority in those urban areas, but are a minority in their respective states and in the United States as a whole). Minority language students are usually members of cultural minorities as well.

Majority language students—students whose first language is the same as that spoken by the majority of speakers in their state/province or country. The majority language usually has legal and social status that is lacking in the case of minority languages; the same is true of the majority culture.

---

of parents who work in foreign countries often attend schools where the national language is used (e.g., Trevor).

We refer to children who come to school speaking a language other than the one spoken by the majority of the larger community in which they live as **minority language students.** Spanish-speaking students in U.S. schools in which English is used for instruction are an example. We refer to children who speak a majority group language but are educated partially or entirely in another language as **majority language students.** As noted in Chapter 3, children who speak a minority group language are likely to experience subtractive bilingual learning environments unless special care is taken, whereas children who speak a majority group language usually experience additive bilingual learning environments. This chapter focuses on children from each language background and their language and academic development in school. We exclude from this discussion majority language students whose only exposure to a second or foreign language in school is limited to conventional foreign or L2 instruction. These children are excluded because their L2 learning experience is so limited as to be inconsequential from a clinical point of view.

MINORITY LANGUAGE STUDENTS

As already noted, in many regions of the world, children learn a language at home that differs from that which is used for instructional and social communication in school. When they begin school, they must learn the majority group language in order to fit in socially and to succeed academically. Although we highlighted the situation in industrialized countries in our introduction, such children can be found in countries in virtually all corners of the world, regardless of their economic and political status. Immigration resulting from voluntary movement of people for social or economic reasons or from involuntary movement due to war, political oppression, or economic plight have resulted in unprecedented levels of international migration and, as a result, increased numbers of minority language students being schooled in their L2. These diverse patterns of migration also mean that children can begin schooling in another language at any age, ranging from typical school entry (around 5 years of age) all the way to the secondary school level.

Most such children are educated exclusively through the medium of the L2, with little formal attention paid to their native language. In some regions of the world, most notably the United States, some minority language children have the possibility of being educated partially through the native language along with the majority language of the dominant society. These are often referred to as **bilingual programs** or **bilingual education.** There are alternative forms of bilingual education, which we describe shortly.

In this chapter, we examine a number of issues concerning the language and academic development of minority language students who participate in bilingual programs as well as those in programs in which only the L2 is used. The development of these two groups has important clinical implications associated with each form of education. We treat each form of education (i.e., L2-only or bilingual) on par with one another because there are minority language students in each type of program. At the same time, and for philosophical and educational reasons, we support bilingual forms of education for all children where resources are available and parental support is strong.

In contrast, some have argued against bilingual education for minority language students on the grounds that education in part or in total through their native language delays or even retards their acquisition of the majority language (see, e.g., Porter, 1990; Rossell & Baker, 1996). In fact, there is no evidence for these claims. To the contrary, a review of evaluations of bilingual programs for minority language students in the United States found that students tend to perform as well as, and often better than, similar students in programs in which only English is used for instructional purposes. We review evidence about the effectiveness of bilingual education for minority language students in more detail later in this chapter. To argue for educational programs that result in loss of any child's native language is wasteful, squandering a language resource that these children bring to school. It is also disrespectful of these children's cultural skills and backgrounds, in some cases to their educational detriment. The purpose of the following discussion is

---

BOX 7.2

Bilingual education/programs—kindergarten through grade 12 programs for minority language students in the United States in which both English and the students' native language are used for instruction during several grades.

Developmental bilingual programs—bilingual programs for minority language students that aim for full bilingual proficiency and grade-appropriate standards in academic subjects. English and the students' native language are both used to teach literacy and academic subjects throughout the elementary grades and sometimes through the secondary grades.

Two-way immersion/bilingual programs—bilingual programs in which half the students are from a minority language group (e.g., Spanish) and half are from the majority language group (i.e., English). Both English and the minority language are used to teach literacy and academic subjects throughout the elementary grades and sometimes through the secondary grades. They aim for full bilingual proficiency and grade-appropriate standards in academic subjects.

Transitional bilingual programs—programs for minority language students that use the students' native language to teach literacy and some academic subjects during the primary grades for up to 3 years, at which time the students are transitioned into mainstream classes, in which all instruction is provided in English. These programs aim for full proficiency in English only and grade-appropriate academic standards.

Second language (L2)–only/English-only programs—programs for kindergarten through grade 12 minority language students in the United States in which all instruction is provided in English. Language minorities students may be provided with some English as a second language instruction by trained specialists; otherwise, all instruction is provided by general classroom teachers.

---

not to engage in this debate, but rather to consider the educational outcomes, especially with respect to language development, and the clinical implications of each form of education for minority language students.

Minority Language Students in Second Language–Only School Programs

Educating minority language students through the medium of the majority language is by far the most common form of education for minority language students, even in the United States, where some forms of bilingual education are offered (see Genesee, 1999, for a summary of bilingual forms of education for minority language students). Programs in which only the L2 is used are sometimes referred to as **submersion** or **sink-or-swim programs** on the grounds that they do not take into account the students' special language learning needs and their particular cultural backgrounds. We use the more neutral term **L2-only programs.**

We discuss these programs and factors that influence student performance so that clinicians will be better able to consider educational factors that might account for minority language students who have difficulty in their language development. We do not provide evidence for the effectiveness of L2-only programs for minority language students because there is wide variation in how effective L2-only education is; some minority language students do well in L2-only programs, but many do not. It is difficult to ascertain with precision how successful minority language students in L2-only programs are because we are aware of no statistics that disaggregate minority language students who know the majority language from those who do not. We do know, however, that in most industrialized countries, immigrant and other ethnic minority students are generally overrepresented in the underachieving categories and in special education classes. This would imply that, notwithstanding some successes, minority language students face a higher than average risk of failure or difficulty in L2-only programs. This should not be surprising given the challenges that such students must face in an L2-only program: They must acquire a new language; they must integrate socially and culturally into a new peer group; and they must learn new academic skills and knowledge.

In the following sections, we present a number of factors to consider when examining the performance of minority language students in L2-only programs in order to ascertain the causes of their difficulty and, in particular, if the difficulty is due to language impairment. The factors we consider are related to language, culture, and family background.

Language Factors   One of the truly useful insights about language to emerge since the 1980s is the distinction between language for academic purposes and language for conversational purposes. This distinction goes by several names, including Vygotsky's spontaneous and scientific competence, Bruner's communicative and analytic competence, and Donaldson's embedded and disembedded thought and language. For our purposes, we draw on Cummins' notions of language proficiency, developed to help understand the linguistic challenges that minority language students face in L2-only classrooms (Cummins, 2000). Cummins's language proficiency framework consists of two intersecting continua, one that describes the extent of contextual support for language use and one that describes the cognitive demands that are implicated during verbal communication (see Figure 7.1).

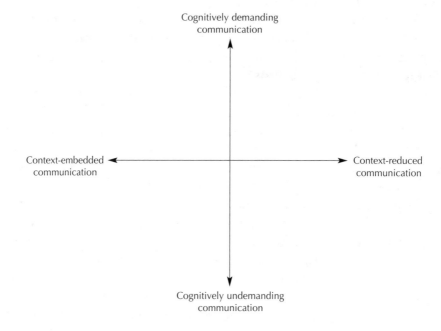

Figure 7.1. Cummins's Language Proficiency Framework.

With respect to the horizontal axis in Figure 7.1, the extremes of this continuum refer to the amount of contextual support available during communication. **Context-embedded communication** is characteristic of day-to-day social language use. During context-embedded communication, the meanings participants seek to convey are supported by shared context, and, moreover, the participants are able to actively negotiate meaning directly through feedback to one another. Context may be shared by virtue of common past experiences or by the immediate setting in which communication is taking place. A face-to-face conversation about a movie that two people have seen is an example of context-embedded communication. The speakers have the shared experience of seeing the movie that they can draw on when discussing it. Talking about a football game that both speakers are watching is another example of context-embedded communication.

In contrast, discussing a movie with someone who has not seen it is a form of **context-reduced communication.** In this case, careful use of language is required to provide details about the movie to make sure that one's meaning is clear and to explicate one's views about the movie because the participants have little recourse to immediate contextual cues or shared experiences to draw on. As Cummins noted, "The essential aspect of *academic language proficiency* is the ability to make complex meanings explicit . . . by means of language itself rather than by means of contextual support or paralinguistic cues (e.g., gestures, intonation etc.)" (2000, pp. 68–69; italics added). Indeed, long-term success in school ultimately depends on students' ability to read about or express abstract, complex ideas without the benefit of past experience or concurrent contextual cues.

Each form of communication can occur in oral or written mode; in other words, context-embedded communication could be oral or written (e.g., note to one's partner to pick up the bread on the way home), and similarly for context-reduced communication (e.g., lecture about homeostasis). Academic language proficiency is not the same thing as literacy; it includes literacy, but it also includes oral uses of language for academic purposes, such as understanding the teacher's explication of an experiment or writing up a report of a science project. These different forms of communication are often referred to in binary form as BICS (basic, interpersonal communication skills) and CALP (cognitive/academic language proficiency); however, these terms should be avoided because, as Cummins emphasized, these forms of communication are not discrete, but, rather, differ continuously from one another along the dimensions proposed in his framework.

The vertical axis in Figure 7.1 represents the cognitive demands required of communication. **Cognitively undemanding communication** requires language skills that have been overlearned and, thus, call for little cognitive involvement on the part of the participants. For example, talking about a favorite sport while watching it makes few cognitive demands, and whatever cognitive demands might be entailed are probably well practiced and overlearned. **Cognitively demanding communication** calls for language skills that have not been fully automatized and, thus, demand active cognitive involvement. For example, explication of the methods and results of a scientific experiment or arguments for and against nuclear disarmament are cognitively demanding, relatively speaking, and require careful use of language to explicate one's intended meaning or point of view. The task of writing this chapter so that it is coherent and meaningful to readers around the world was also cognitively demanding and required careful use of language, with innumerable revisions. Each writer had to think carefully and in great detail how specific ideas would be presented so that readers who are unfamiliar with this material could comprehend it. The fact that the ideas presented are complex and abstract added further cognitive demands to the task.

Cummins's framework includes a developmental component that reflects the time required to acquire proficiency in academic versus conversational language skills in typical learners. More specifically, conversational skills are acquired relatively quickly because their acquisition is supported by contextual and interpersonal cues, and they make relatively few cognitive demands on the learner. Indeed, virtually all typically developing children acquire proficiency in these forms of communication in their first language (L1) during the first 3 or 4 years of life, without formal instruction. In contrast, proficiency in language for academic purposes can take considerably longer to master. It is primarily, and often only, through schooling that children gain competence in academic language use. Moreover, as students progress from the lower to higher grades in school, they are called on more and more to use language in cognitively demanding and context-reduced situations as the subject matter of teaching and learning becomes more abstract and complex. It has been estimated, based on research of student performance in school settings, that minority language students can take 5–7 years to achieve proficiency in English for academic purposes that is at par with that of native speakers (Cummins, 2000; Lindholm-Leary & Borsato, in press; Thomas & Collier, 1997).

The protracted time frame needed to acquire language for academic purposes can be useful in understanding the school performance of minority language students. Minority language students who come to English-speaking schools with no or limited proficiency in English often acquire conversational skills in that language relatively quickly; they learn it from their peers, from television, and on the street. Although these kinds of language skills may be acquired quickly relative to language for academic purposes, they are not acquired in 1 or even 2 years of exposure to the target language. Nevertheless, it takes longer for minority language students to acquire proficiency in language for academic purposes, both oral and written forms. Thus, minority language students can experience a significant gap in the their ability to communicate effectively in English in social contexts in contrast to academic contexts. They may be proficient in forms of the L2 that are useful in social interactions with their peers on the playground, but they may lack sufficient proficiency in forms of the L2 that are needed to perform academic tasks and, thus, may be silent or even withdrawn during classroom activities and discussions.

An important caveat is called for here. The fact that minority language students may require some time to master language for academic purposes does not mean that they cannot or should not be taught age-appropriate, challenging academic content. Linguistic modifications are called for to make such content comprehensible (see, e.g., Echevarria, Vogt, & Short, 2000). Moreover, the best way to teach academic language skills is to teach them in meaningful academic contexts.

Professionals need to be sensitive to the possibility that minority language students may be nonresponsive or even inept in the classroom, not because they have a learning disability or language impairment, but simply because they have not yet acquired sufficient proficiency in the L2 to interact actively and appropriately. Cummins (1984) argued further that the failure of teachers and other professionals working with minority language students to make this distinction can lead to misleading or invalid assessments. They might be prone to interpret the child's behavior in class or during testing situations as signs of a learning disability on the grounds that the child appears to know the language and, therefore, his behavior in class must be due to more general learning or behavioral problems. Indeed, minority language students are often overrepresented in special education classes, arguably because their incomplete acquisition of the language of instruction has been misinterpreted as a learning problem.

Cultural Factors   Cultural factors should also be considered when trying to understand individual minority language children's patterns of L2 use, especially if language impairment is suspected. Different cultures have different sets of expectations concerning appropriate patterns of language use and social interaction on the part of children and adolescents (see Roseberry-McKibbin, 2002, for descriptions of some of the differences that distinguish various cultures). In our discussion, we refer primarily to English as the majority or societal language and **Anglo-Western** culture as the dominant culture because we are most familiar with this language and culture and because we assume our readers are familiar with English and share some knowledge of the cultures that underlie English-speaking communities.

In Chapter 2, we noted that most English-dominant cultures and other European cultures treat children as legitimate and important conversational partners and expect them to actively engage in, initiate, and maintain talk with adults. Such cultures also expect school children to show off what they have learned in school by responding actively and verbally to teachers' probes and encouragements. Eye contact between students and teachers is considered appropriate and is taken as a sign that the student is attending to the teacher and is engaged in learning. Boys and girls are generally held to the same general expectations and work and learn together. Not all cultures share these norms and expectations. In some cultures, students are not regarded as appropriate conversational partners for adults, and as a result, they are expected to be seen and not heard and to show deference to adults during verbal encounters by averting their gaze. In such cultures, students are not expected, nor appreciated, when they initiate verbal exchanges or actively assert themselves verbally. Students in such cultures often learn primarily by watching others, and they demonstrate what they have learned in groups or discreetly on their own. Students from certain cultures may be uncomfortable in mixed gender groups in school.

Minority language children bring the socialization patterns that they have learned at home to school. The same is true for children educated in schools in which English is not the dominant societal language. For example, even children raised in Anglo-Western homes would face cultural challenges if schooled by Inuit or Arabic teachers in those cultures' schools. As a result of differences in the cultures of the home and school, some children will avoid initiating talk with their teachers or other adults; they will be uncomfortable or even unwilling to give an individual response to a direct question or request from their teachers; they will avoid eye contact or physical proximity with adult interlocutors; and they may be uncomfortable and even resist working in groups with students of the other sex. Such cultural norms can influence learners' social interactions with others long after they have acquired competence in the language of schooling because these norms constitute part of their personal identity. Minority language children from cultures with language socialization patterns that differ from Anglo-Western cultures could give the impression that they are language delayed or impaired or even that they have learning disabilities because they do not respond actively, the way teachers from the Anglo-Western cultures expect.

An example of this comes from research in Inuit schools. When a speech-language pathologist asked for a list of children who the southern Canadian non-Inuit teachers thought had speech-language problems, she was presented with a list of the names of one third of the children in the school. Next to each name was written "Does not talk in class." Because the numbers of children listed far exceeded the typical incidence rate of 5% for speech-language problems in the childhood population, the speech-language pathologist asked for help from a local Inuk special education teacher. This experienced Inuk educator looked at the list and said with a discouraged tone, "These Qallunaat (non-Inuit) teachers never seem to learn that well-raised Inuit children should not talk in class. They should be learning by looking and listening" (Crago, 1988, p. 212). In instances where there is no cultural expert to interpret such information for Anglo-Western professionals, this kind of misunderstanding could place minority children at a severe educational disadvantage.

Cultural effects can influence children's language use in yet other ways— through the sheer nature of the experiences children have when growing up. For example, children from cultural minority groups may not have had the same experiences with doctors, dentists, or other professionals as children from the mainstream culture. Their experiences with food, music, toys, and religious customs are often different as well. As a result, they may find it difficult to engage in classroom discussions or activities that involve experiences that are foreign or novel to them. This may, in turn, dampen their language use because they are simply unfamiliar with the subject of the activity.

Professionals working with minority language students from different cultural backgrounds must consider the role of cultural factors in their language use and development when seeking to identify children suspected of having specific language impairment. In particular, they must take care to avoid misattributing culturally conditioned patterns of language use to underlying impairments of a linguistic or general learning nature. Such misattributions must be minimized to achieve valid diagnoses of dual language learners suspected of having specific language impairment. It can be a real challenge for professionals who are monolingual and monocultural, and even for those with diverse cultural experiences, to know all of the cultures of the minority language children they are dealing with when students come from multiple and diverse cultural backgrounds. When educators and speech-language professionals encounter a case of a child from a culture with which they are unfamiliar, they should seek input from members of those cultural groups or other professionals who have more experience with the culture in question. In addition to being responsible for the education or professional care of children from diverse language backgrounds and identifying cultural influences in the lives of their young charges, professionals must also work to help minority language students expand their cultural repertoires to include the norms of the majority group. After all, their successful integration into the broader community will depend on their becoming bicultural as well as bilingual.

Family Background Factors   The school performance of L2 learners, including their language use, can also be influenced by a host of factors that are linked to family background. Performance in school, including grades and other formal indicators of progress, is correlated with socioeconomic status (SES). For example, in a review of research on the literacy development of **English language learners** in the United States since the 1980s, Genesee and Riches (in press) found that SES was correlated with performance on a variety of literacy measures so that students from low SES backgrounds scored significantly lower than students from higher SES backgrounds. SES, however, is not a causal factor in and of itself, but it is associated with a variety of other factors that can mediate the effects of low SES, factors such as knowledge of letters, experience with books at home, writing at home, learning and reciting rhymes, and getting assistance from parents or other siblings in doing homework (Goldenberg, 2003). Research indicates that many family-related variables promote literacy development in school. Students from relatively advantaged SES backgrounds enjoy the benefits of these influences more than students from less advantaged homes. We know that minority language students are overrepresented in low SES categories, and thus, minority language students may experience less rapid progress or even retarded progress in language and literacy development in school because of such influences.

These kinds of factors should be considered when assessing the source of individual minority language students' difficulty with language and learning in school. It is important not to overgeneralize these patterns to individual children and assume that all minority language students lack the benefits of literacy and enriched language experiences in the home. The general patterns that have emerged from research on students from low SES backgrounds are just general patterns and do not necessarily pertain to all minority language students in mainstream classrooms. Research, however, indicates that the effects of low SES on school performance are particularly likely for minority language children who live in communities and attend schools that are populated by large numbers of families and children from low SES backgrounds (Goldenberg, 2003). It is important for clinicians to look at the language and literacy practices of the families and communities of dual language children suspected of language impairment as possible explanations of their difficulties.

Minority Language Students in Bilingual Programs

We focus our discussion of minority language students who are educated in bilingual programs on programs in the United States because bilingual programs for minority language students have been well documented there. There has been a strong civil rights influence on the development of educational alternatives for students from such backgrounds in the United States. Providing minority language students access to education through their native language has been a major outcome of this initiative. In bilingual programs, the students' native language, along with the majority language (English in the case of the United States), is used for instructional purposes.

There are alternative models of bilingual programs; the main ones are **transitional bilingual, developmental bilingual,** and **two-way bilingual/immersion** (see Genesee, 1999, for detailed descriptions of these programs). In developmental bilingual and two-way bilingual programs, academic and literacy instruction are provided through the medium of both the students' native language and English, starting in kindergarten. The portion of the school day that is taught through English and the native language differs in different program models, the most common patterns being 90% L1 and 10% English, or 50% L1 and 50% English. These are the so-called **90/10** and **50/50 models,** respectively. Use of both languages for instruction is continued throughout the elementary grades and, ideally, during secondary school as well.

Developmental bilingual programs differ from two-way immersion programs in that all of the students in the former are minority language students, whereas half of the students in two-way programs are members of the majority language group. Two-way programs aim to promote bilingualism among both minority language and majority language students, and they seek to do this by using each group's language for academic instruction to teach a portion of the curriculum. Both developmental and two-way bilingual models are considered additive forms of bilingual education because they both aim to maintain the students' native languages at the same time as they promote competence in the other language. These two forms of bilingual education see the minority language students' native language as an important personal asset and resource and as an essential foundation on which to build their competence in the L2 and in academic domains. Two-way programs see bilingualism as an asset for all students, including majority language students.

Transitional programs are the most limited form of bilingual education but have been the most prevalent in the United States. All students in transitional bilingual programs are from minority language backgrounds. The typical transitional program provides initial instruction in literacy and some academic domains through the medium of the students' native language, along with instruction in English oral language development; nonacademic subjects, such as music and physical education, are also often taught through English. The most common minority language used in transitional bilingual programs is Spanish, followed by Vietnamese, Hmong, Cantonese, and Korean (Kindler, 2000). As students acquire proficiency in English, there is a shift toward greater use of English to teach academic subjects and a commensurate decrease in the use of the students' native language. The shift is often completed by grade 3, at which point the native language ceases to be used at all. Transitional bilingual programs are considered subtractive forms of bilingual education insofar as the students' native language is used only until such time as they can make a transition to L2-only instruction. Consequently, the goal of this program is not bilingual proficiency but proficiency in English only. Socioculturally, transitional programs can convey to students the impression that their native language is not useful or viable in the long run, but is a crutch to be used until they learn sufficient English to be schooled exclusively through English. In fact, participation in such programs often results in loss of the native language, especially in literacy, as English takes a stronger hold in their daily lives.

A number of important questions arise concerning the language development of minority language students in bilingual programs that are relevant to our concerns in this book. We address the following two: 1) Does schooling in bilingual programs enhance or retard students' acquisition of the majority language? and 2) What is the relationship between amount of exposure to the minority language in school and acquisition of that language? An ancillary question is: Which program models are most effective in building bilingual proficiency? The answers to these questions are important because they help to formulate reasonable expectations about outcomes for typically developing minority language students in bilingual education and, by implication, provide valuable information that can be used to distinguish atypical from typical patterns of development. To answer these questions, we turn to research on bilingual programs in the United States because much of the systematic research on these issues was conducted there.

Does Schooling in Bilingual Programs Enhance or Retard Students' Acquisition of the Majority Language? Diametrically opposite

predictions have been made about the impact of bilingual education on minority language students' acquisition of English. On the one hand, critics of bilingual education (see, e.g., Baker & de Kanter, 1981; Porter, 1990; Rossell & Baker, 1996) argued that use of minority language students' native language for significant portions of their schooling detracts from their acquisition of English because it reduces their exposure to English. This is what is referred to as the time-on-task argument. On the other hand, others have argued that the language capacity of children is not limited to the acquisition of one language (Genesee, 2002) and, moreover, that development of the native language in the case of minority language students is a useful scaffold for developing competency, especially literacy, in the L2 (Cummins, 2000; Thomas & Collier, 1997). According to these latter points of view, additive forms of bilingual education should either enhance or have no detrimental effect on the development of the L2 of minority language students. What does the research evidence say about these possibilities?

Two patterns of results have emerged from evaluations of bilingual education. In some cases, there is evidence of an advantage to students in developmental and two-way bilingual programs over students in English-only or transitional bilingual programs (see, e.g., Lindholm, 2001; Lindholm-Leary & Borsato, in press; Ramirez, Yuen, & Ramey, 1991; Thomas & Collier, 2002). In particular, minority language students in developmental bilingual alternatives, especially those that continue use of the native language into secondary school, demonstrate higher levels of proficiency in English in comparison to students in nonbilingual or transitional bilingual programs. In other cases, there has been no evident advantage or disadvantage for minority language students in developmental and two-way bilingual programs. In these cases, minority language students were shown to perform at the same level as minority language students in English-only programs or on par with district- or state-level standardized achievement test results (see Lindholm-Leary & Borsato, in press, for a review of these studies). In sum, research has shown that schooling through and maintenance of the native language of minority language students does not appear to hamper these students' development of English in comparison to minority language students in all-English programs.

A related question concerning bilingual education—What is the relationship between amount of instruction in or exposure to the majority language and level of proficiency attained in that language?—focuses on the more specific question of whether there is a linear relationship between amount of exposure to the majority language and level of proficiency attained in that language. It is widely believed that there is a correlation between students' exposure to language in school and their acquired competence in that language. Clearly, in the extreme, such a relationship is bound to occur.

Students with very little exposure and those with a great deal of exposure are likely to differ, obviously, to the advantage of the latter; however, research does not support this expectation within the limits of current models of bilingual education. To be more specific, minority language students with more exposure to English in school (e.g., those in 50/50 bilingual programs) show an initial advantage in English over students with less exposure to English (i.e., those in 90/10 programs), but this advantage is marginal and short lived.

By the end of grade 3, minority language students in 50/50 two-way bilingual programs no longer show this advantage despite their considerably greater exposure to English in the beginning, in comparison with 90/10 students. This is also true when comparisons are made between minority language students in English-only programs and those in developmental bilingual programs. The former often show an initial advantage in English, but there is usually no difference or a difference in favor of bilingual program participants by the later elementary or middle school grades (Lindholm-Leary & Borsato, in press). These findings mirror a pattern that has been reported for majority language students in L2 immersion programs, to be discussed in the next section.

Arguably, the relationship between amount of exposure to the majority language in school and students' acquired level of proficiency in that language is mitigated by students' exposure to the majority language outside school. The considerably extended exposure that most students, even minority language students, have to English in an English-dominant community offsets differences in exposure between groups of students in different programs in school. Arguably, differences in exposure to English in school is also offset in the case of bilingual program participants by transfer from the L1 to English; transfer is more likely and more extensive the more developed the students' L1 literacy skills and this, in turn, is more likely in developmental and two-way bilingual programs than in transitional and English-only programs.

These results do not indicate that minority language students in additive bilingual programs always achieve the same level of competence in English literacy as native speakers of English. In fact, they often do not, but often these residual differences can be traced to other factors, such as the quality of the program itself or socioeconomic differences. Lindholm-Leary and Borsato (in press) found that minority language students who had consistent exposure to coherent bilingual programs demonstrated higher levels of language and academic achievement than students whose program of instruction varied from year to year.

Relevant to SES, minority language students, as a whole, generally experience lower SES than majority language students, as a whole, and we know that students from low SES backgrounds, whether they are minority language or majority language, generally do worse on tests of literacy and academic achievement than students from advantaged SES backgrounds. These results indicate that bilingual education can be effective at promoting proficiency in minority language students' native language and English at the same time as they promote grade-appropriate levels of academic achievement.

What Is the Relationship Between Amount of Exposure to the Minority Language in School and Acquisition of that Language?   The significance of this question is linked to students' development of bilingual proficiency. If amount of exposure to the minority language has a positive impact on the development of proficiency in that language, then this will contribute to the development of bilingual proficiency, given that minority language students seem to develop the same levels of proficiency in the majority language despite variations in exposure to that language in school. Interestingly, and contrary to the pattern we just noted for the majority language, amount of exposure to the minority language does make a difference to proficiency. Minority language students who have more exposure to the minority language in school acquire greater proficiency in that language than students with less exposure (Lindholm-Leary & Borsato, in press). This stands to reason, given the relative lack of exposure to the minority language in the broader community, especially when it comes to forms of the language linked to literacy.

These findings are important because they indicate that extending exposure to the minority language in school provides minority language students with greater opportunities to develop high levels of bilingual proficiency in that extending exposure to the minority language does not detract from their development of the majority language. These findings are also significant because Lindholm and Aclan (1991) have found that higher levels of bilingual proficiency among minority language students are associated with higher levels of academic language proficiency. In short, and contrary to some people's expectations, the evidence indicates that additive bilingual education that includes significant portions of instruction through the native language of minority language students contributes to their bilingual proficiency and their academic development. It also follows that minority language students with higher levels of bilingual proficiency are likely to experience the cognitive benefits discussed by Bialystok (2001) and Cummins (2000).

In summary, the available evidence indicates that minority language students in additive forms of bilingual education—two-way immersion and developmental bilingual programs—attain the same or higher levels of proficiency in English as minority language students in L2-only or transitional bilingual programs. There is no simple correlation between amount of exposure to the majority language in school and the level of proficiency that students attain in that language. In contrast, proficiency in the minority language is often associated with amount of exposure to that language in school, especially in domains of proficiency related to reading and writing. Lindholm and Aclan (1991) found further that academic achievement is positively correlated with bilingual proficiency, providing additional evidence that bilingual education for minority language students can be beneficial.

MAJORITY LANGUAGE STUDENTS

Although we probably associate schooling in an L2 with immigrants, indigenous language groups, and others who grow up speaking a minority language, there is a growing number of children who acquire a majority language as their L1 but are nevertheless educated through the medium of a second, or even third, language—children like Samantha, from Chapter 1. A common form of L2 education for majority language students is immersion. Immersion programs were first developed in Quebec in order to provide English-speaking Quebec students with opportunities to learn French along with English. French is the official language of Quebec and one of the two official languages of Canada (see Genesee, 1987, for an historical review). We focus our discussion in this chapter on immersion forms of bilingual education for majority language students because of the extensive body of descriptive and empirical literature on them. This research is a very useful source of information about the development of majority language students who are schooled in an L2.

Students in immersion programs receive all or a significant portion (usually a minimum of 50%) of their academic instruction, including language arts instruction, through the medium of an L2. The rationale behind immersion is that students can learn a language effectively if it is used for significant periods of time and for substantive communication in school, much as children learn their native language in the home (see Genesee, 2004, for a detailed description). Since their inception in 1965, immersion forms of education have been implemented in other regions of Canada, the United States, and worldwide (see Christian & Genesee, 2001, and Johnson & Swain, 1997, for case studies of immersion around the world). Immersion students also receive instruction through the medium of their native language, and thus, these programs are bilingual forms of education. In addition to the general goal of bilingualism, immersion programs serve a variety of linguistic and cultural objectives that differ from community to community:

• To promote national policies of bilingualism (e.g., French immersion for English-speaking students in Canada)

- To promote national languages in countries with students who do not speak the dominant language of the community (e.g., Estonian immersion for Russian-speaking students in Estonia)

- To promote proficiency in important regional and/or world languages (e.g., English immersion in Japan)

- To promote proficiency in heritage languages (e.g., Hungarian immersion in Slovakia)

- To promote indigenous languages that are at risk (e.g., Mohawk immersion in Canada, Hawaiian immersion in Hawaii)

There are a variety of alternative forms of immersion. They differ with respect to the grade/age level when the L2 is used for intensive academic instruction and the amount of instruction provided through the medium of the second and native languages. One can distinguish **early immersion** (beginning in kindergarten or grade 1) from **delayed** or **middle immersion** (beginning in grade 4 or 5) and **late immersion** (beginning in grade 7 or the initial grades of secondary school). Programs that provide a delayed or late start provide core L2 instruction to students in those grades that precede the beginning of immersion (e.g., from kindergarten to grade 6 in the case of a grade 7 late immersion program). This means that students do not begin academic instruction through the L2 without having had some prior instruction in the target language. Schematic representations of early, delayed, and late immersion program models are presented in Figure 7.2. Programs also differ with respect to the extent of instruction through the L2. In **partial immersion programs,** 50% of instruction in a given year is presented in the L2 and 50% in the native language of the students. In **total immersion programs,** all instruction for 1 or more years is presented through the medium of the L2.

Notwithstanding their different programmatic characteristics and goals, these programs share a number of core objectives:

1. Development of full, native-like proficiency in the students' native language

2. Development of advanced functional proficiency in all domains of the L2: reading, writing, speaking, and listening

3. High levels of academic achievement in core school subjects, such as mathematics, science, and history

4. Understanding and appreciation of the culture of the target language group, along with understanding and appreciation of the culture of the student's own group

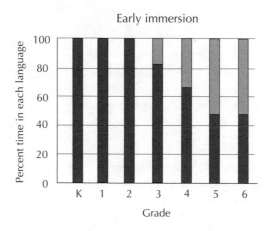

Early immersion

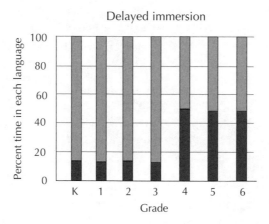

Delayed immersion

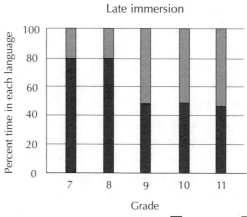

Late immersion

Figure 7.2. Models of second language immersion programs. (Key = ■ first language; ▨ second language)

BOX 7.3

Immersion programs—educational programs for kindergarten through grade 12 majority language students in which at least 50% of instruction, including reading, writing, and other academic subjects, is given through the medium of a second/foreign language. Immersion programs aim for advanced levels of second language proficiency, typical levels of native language proficiency, and grade-appropriate academic achievement.

Early total immersion—immersion programs that begin in kindergarten and provide 100% of instruction through the medium of a second/foreign language for a minimum of 2 years. Instruction through the native language of the students is introduced in grade 2 or higher. The percentage of instruction in English varies among programs.

Early partial immersion—immersion programs that begin in the elementary grades and provide up to 50% of instruction through the medium of a second/foreign language. The number of years of partial immersion and the initial grade level in which immersion begins varies among programs.

Late immersion—immersion programs for majority language students that provide at least 50% of instruction, including reading, writing and academic subjects, through the medium of a second/foreign language beginning in middle or high school.

In effect, these programs aim for the same native language and academic goals as monolingual school programs while also aiming for bilingual competence and cultural tolerance.

It is important to differentiate these programs from programs in which minority language students are educated through the majority language. In the United States, English-only programs for minority language students are often referred to as *English immersion* by some educators, but they are more aptly referred to as *submersion,* as noted earlier, because there is little accommodation made to these students' particular linguistic and cultural needs most of the time. Minority language students may be pulled out for English as a second language instruction while receiving most of their other academic instruction along with native English-speaking students. Students in these kinds of submersion programs are often expected to give up their native language and culture for the sake of acquiring English. In direct contrast, immersion programs for majority language students are additive forms of bilingual education that aim to promote full bilingual proficiency. Most important, immersion teachers modify their instructional strategies to serve the special language learning needs of majority language students throughout the day, as they teach math, science, and so forth (see Cloud, Genesee, & Hamayan, 2000, and Met, 1998, for descriptions of these accommodations).

Majority language students in immersion-type programs are of relevance to our concerns in this book because some of these students experience learning or language difficulties and may be referred to professionals for diagnosis and remediation. It is important that parents, educators, and other professionals alike understand the typical outcomes of immersion education so that they can distinguish difficulties that can happen when students are educated through the medium of an L2 from those that are attributable to clinical causes. In the following sections, we review what we know about the language and academic development of typically developing majority language students in immersion programs. We then turn our attention to immersion students with language impairment.

How Effective Is Immersion Education for Majority Language Students?

Systematic and comprehensive evaluations of immersion programs for majority language students have been conducted in Canada, Japan, Spain, the United States, and elsewhere (see Christian & Genesee, 2001; Genesee, 2004; and Johnson & Swain, 1997, for in-depth reviews). Thus, we are fortunate in being able to draw on a wealth of scientific information about the development of majority language students who are schooled bilingually. A detailed review of these research findings is beyond the scope of this book (see Genesee, 2004, for a detailed synopsis of this research), but we provide a general overview of the most common findings that have been reported in evaluations of immersion. Specifically, we focus on students' native language, L2, and academic development. We also review evidence concerning the effectiveness of immersion for students from economically disadvantaged and cultural minority backgrounds and for students with language delay or impairment.

Students in General   There has been extensive research on the language development and academic achievement of majority language students in immersion programs. By far the most extensive body of research on these aspects of development has been conducted in Canada on French immersion programs for English-speaking students (Lambert & Tucker, 1972; see also Genesee, 1987, and Swain & Lapkin, 1982). The general findings from the Canadian research have been replicated, for the most part, in other regions of the world in which similar programs with majority language students have been implemented (see Christian & Genesee, 2001, and Johnson & Swain, 1997, for other examples). Our summary draws heavily on the Canadian research.

Research has shown consistently that students in immersion programs who speak a majority language usually develop the same levels of proficiency in all aspects of their native language as comparable students in programs in which the native language is the exclusive medium of instruction. Remember that students in immersion programs are exposed to the native language on a daily basis outside school—at home, in the community, in the media, and so forth. There can be a lag in the development of native language literacy skills (reading, writing, and spelling) among immersion students in the initial years of total immersion programs when all academic instruction is presented in the L2. Parity with comparison students who have been instructed entirely through the native language is usually achieved after 1 year of receiving language arts instruction in the native language, for example, at the end of grade 3 in the case of students whose first exposure to instruction in the native language begins in grade 3. This rapid catch-up is probably due to transfer between the native language and L2. The native language development of majority language students who begin immersion education beyond the primary grades of school (in delayed or late immersion) usually shows no such lags. Students in the latter programs exhibit age-appropriate native language skills at all grade levels.

To make these findings more concrete, consider Samantha—a native English-speaking child who was born and raised in Tucson. Her parents use English in the home, and all of her language experiences in the community at large are in English, except for occasional trips to Mexican restaurants or local grocery stores where Mexican food is sold. Because Samantha's parents wanted her to know another language, they decided to enroll her in the local Spanish immersion program—Buena Vista Elementary, an early total immersion program in which English is not taught until grade 3. Samantha was taught to read and write in Spanish from kindergarten to grade 2 (before receiving formal literacy instruction in English in grade 3), and all of her school subjects (math, social studies, and science) were taught to her in Spanish until the end of grade 2. English was taught for 1 hour per day starting in grade 3, and the amount of English increased gradually so that by grade 6, half the day was taught in Spanish and half in English.

The State Department of Education requires that Buena Vista test Samantha and her classmates at the end of grades 3 and 6 using standardized tests (administered in English), including language, reading, spelling, mathematics, and science subtests. Because the Buena Vista parents were concerned about their children's progress in English, the school decided to extend its testing program and assess the students' English language skills at the end of every grade.

In addition to the language and academic domains that were covered by the standardized tests required by the state, the school also examined the immersion students' speaking, listening, and writing skills in English, using locally devised assessment instruments. These are skills domains that are not usually covered by standardized tests. The school administered these latter tests to classes in a neighboring English language school that had the same demographic characteristics as Buena Vista so that they had a point of comparison for judging the progress of the immersion students at Buena Vista. In order to be extra cautious, they also decided to test the immersion students' mathematics skills, using a standardized test administered in Spanish in grades 1 and 2; the school authorities felt that the standardized test of mathematics in English could underestimate what they had learned in Spanish.

As other early immersion schools across the country and in Canada have discovered, Buena Vista found that Samantha and her classmates tended to score below grade level in kindergarten, grade 1, and grade 2 on the standardized subtests in English-language reading and spelling. This was not surprising because all their language arts instruction had been in Spanish until then; however, their speaking and listening comprehension skills in English did not differ from those of the comparison students in the all-English program in the district. They also noted that, although the students' math scores were below grade level on the English standardized test, they were at grade level, or above, on the standardized math test in Spanish. Most important, and much to their relief, they found that that there was no gap between the English reading and writing scores of the Buena Vista and all-English students by grade 3, after 1 year of English language arts instruction. The Buena Vista students continued to do as well as the comparison students in all their English language skills throughout the elementary grades.

Let's return to our review of the research. Researchers have found that immersion students who receive more native language instruction do not achieve higher levels of proficiency in the native language in the long run than immersion students who receive less exposure to the native language. To be specific, students in early *total* immersion programs score at the same level on standardized tests in the native language at the end of elementary school as students who have been in early *partial* or *delayed* immersion, despite the fact that early total immersion students have less exposure to the native language during the elementary grades than students in other forms of immersion. Therefore, there is no direct correspondence between the amount of native language instruction and native language development in the case of majority language students.

We also noted this pattern for the majority language in the case of minority language students in bilingual programs. It is likely that these findings are due to the compensating effects of extensive exposure to the majority language that students receive outside school. The same factor could explain why immersion students demonstrate the same level of competence in all domains of native language development in comparison with students who have been educated entirely through the medium of the native language.

Researchers have also consistently found that majority language students in immersion programs acquire significantly more advanced levels of functional proficiency in the L2 than students who receive conventional L2 instruction; that is, instruction that focuses primarily on language learning and is restricted to separate, limited classroom periods. This is evidenced by their performance on tests of reading, writing, speaking, and listening comprehension. Although it is difficult to make direct statistical comparisons, impressionistically, many researchers have reported that immersion students' comprehension skills (in reading and listening) are more advanced than their production skills (in speaking and writing). Immersion students' functional competence in the L2 is evident from their academic performance. Majority language students score as well on tests of mathematics, science, and social studies administered in French as comparison English-speaking students on tests administered in English. In order to achieve such high scores, immersion students must have acquired considerable functional proficiency in the L2 to assimilate new academic skills and knowledge.

At the same time, researchers have noted that immersion students seldom attain native-like competence in the target language even after 11 or 12 years of schooling (Genesee, 1991; Lyster, 1987). By native-like competence, we mean performance in the L2 that is identical to that of native speakers. More specifically, immersion students often fail to master important aspects of the target language grammar, such as pronouns, verb tenses, and prepositions (Adiv, 1980; Harley & Swain, 1984). They often exhibit nonidiomatic usage (Genesee, 1991), and they tend to use simplified grammatical forms and show intrusions from their native language. These are the same markers of L2 proficiency that we noted in Chapter 6 are often exhibited by L2 learners. They undoubtedly reflect typical patterns of developing competence among L2 learners.

Returning to achievement in academic domains, such as mathematics, science, and social studies, evaluations of majority language students in immersion programs indicate that they generally reach the same levels of achievement as comparable students in native language programs. This is true whether the comparison students are native speakers of the same language as the immersion students or native speakers of the L2 and are tested in the L2. Parity with native language comparison students is often exhibited even when immersion students receive all academic instruction through the medium of the L2, provided the assessment is conducted in the L2 and modifications are made to take into account that full competence in that language has not been acquired.

Immersion students can appear to have impairments in academic domains if they are tested in the noninstructional language. For example, students in early total immersion programs who receive math instruction in French (their L2), but are tested in English (their native language), may appear to have deficiencies in problem solving. This can be explained by their incomplete mastery of English reading skills because once they receive reading instruction in their native language, these disparities disappear. Moreover, they usually do not exhibit these impairments if tested in the language of instruction. Immersion students may exhibit what appear to be gaps in their learning of academic material if they are questioned about it in the language that was not used to teach it. If students are taught science in French, their L2, but are questioned about their knowledge of science in their native language, they may lack some of the terminology or phrasing needed to fully express what they know. The hesitations that result from these word-finding problems should be interpreted for what they are—word-finding problems—and nothing more. Bilinguals often exhibit dominance or differential proficiency in their languages when it comes to specific domains of knowledge. This is typical and easily remedied, if necessary.

Notwithstanding these qualifications, academic parity with comparison groups is usually exhibited by students in immersion programs at both the elementary and secondary levels and has been demonstrated using a variety of assessment instruments, including standardized norm-referenced tests, official government tests, and locally devised tests. In sum, there is no evidence that instruction in academic subjects through the medium of the L2 impedes the acquisition of new academic skills and knowledge on the part of majority language students in comparison with students receiving the same academic instruction through the medium of their native language.

The general patterns of student achievement that we have just described have been found in diverse sociocultural contexts—Montreal, Toronto, Cincinnati, Los Angeles, Estonia, Japan, Spain, and others. Of note, students in immersion programs fare more or less the same whether they live in communities in which members of the L2 group live. Undoubtedly, immersion students who have contact with native speakers of the target language outside school have the opportunity to extend their L2 learning outside school. It is also noteworthy that these general patterns occur even when typologically different pairs of languages are involved. Researchers have found the same basic results for Japanese and English; Hawaiian and English; Hebrew, French, and English (a trilingual example; Genesee, 1998); Mohawk and English

(Jacobs & Cross, 2001); and Estonian and Russian (Asser, Kolk, & Küppar, 2001). These findings are reassuring from an educational point of view because they indicate that this form of bilingual education for majority language students can be effective in different sociocultural and linguistic contexts.

Academic Ability   With respect to academic (or intellectual) ability, Genesee (1987) systematically examined the performance of both elementary and secondary level English-speaking students in French immersion programs in Canada in relation to their intellectual ability. Students were classified as average, below average, or above average based on their scores on a standardized IQ test. Their school performance was assessed with respect to L1 (English) and L2 (French) development and academic achievement. With respect to L1 development and academic achievement, the below average students in immersion scored at the same level as the below average students in the L1 program on both L1 and academic achievement measures. In other words, the below average students in immersion were not disadvantaged in their L1 development or academic achievement as a result of participation in immersion. In keeping with their at-risk status, the below average students in both programs scored significantly lower than their average and above average peers in their respective programs on the same measures. With respect to L2 acquisition, the below average students in immersion scored significantly higher on all L2 measures than the below average students in the L1 program who were receiving conventional L2 instruction. In other words, the below average students were benefiting from immersion in the form of enhanced L2 proficiency.

Comparisons between the elementary and secondary students revealed interesting and differential effects of academic ability on L2 achievement. Specifically, below average students in both early and late immersion programs scored lower on measures of French language development related to literacy (reading and writing) than average and above average students in the same programs; similarly, the average students in both program types scored lower than the above average students. A different pattern of results was found, however, for measures of speaking and listening. Whereas late immersion students exhibited the same stratification on measures of speaking and listening as they had demonstrated on measures of L2 literacy, there were no differences among the ability subgroups in the early immersion program on measures of L2 speaking and listening. In other words, academic ability influenced the development of proficiency in all aspects of L2 acquisition among secondary school students but had little differential effect on the speaking and listening comprehension skills of immersion students in the elementary school program. Speculatively, acquisition of an L2 when it is integrated with academic instruction is more cognitively demanding at the secondary than the elementary school level and, as a result, calls on the kinds of cognitive skills that are differentially available to older students. In contrast, acquisition of L2 skills that are integrated with academic instruction at the elementary level calls on the natural language learning ability that all students possess during their formative early years. These findings argue that early immersion is more egalitarian than late immersion because it appears to be equally effective for students with different levels of general academic ability. Overall, these results indicate that low academic/intellectual ability is no more of a handicap in bilingual education than it is in L1 programs and, to the contrary, low performing students can experience a net benefit from immersion in the form of bilingual proficiency.

In a related vein, Bruck (1985a, 1985b) examined the role of academic ability in decisions to switch some students out of early immersion. At issue was whether academic ability, or something else, was the primary cause of the students' inability to stay in immersion. More specifically, Bruck compared the academic, familial, and socioaffective characteristics of early immersion students who switched to an L1 program with those of students who remained in an immersion program. She found, as expected, that the students who switched scored lower on a number of achievement measures than most of the students who remained in immersion, but the academic difficulties of the students who switched were no worse than those of a subgroup of students who remained in immersion despite low academic performance. What distinguished the students who switched from those who remained in the program despite their difficulty was the former expressed significantly more negative attitudes toward schooling (and immersion in particular) and exhibited more behavioral problems than the latter. Bruck conjectured that the behavioral problems were engendered by academic difficulties that ultimately led to the decision to switch some students out of immersion in the hope that they would adjust more satisfactorily in an L1 program.

In a follow-up investigation, Bruck noted that the students who switched continued to have academic difficulties and to exhibit attitudinal and behavioral problems. Bruck's results suggest that the ability to cope with poor academic performance may be a more serious problem for some immersion students than poor academic performance alone. Her results also support the argument that academic ability alone does not distinguish students who can benefit from immersion education and those who cannot. In other words, other things being equal, students with low levels of academic ability should be eligible for immersion education.

Socioeconomic Status   Students from families with low SES are usually at risk for failure or poor achievement in school for reasons that are not fully understood. Because of this risk factor, researchers in the United States and Canada have examined the performance of students from low SES backgrounds in immersion programs (Genesee, 1987; Holobow, Genesee, & Lambert, 1991). Canadian researchers have found that socioeconomically disadvantaged students in early immersion programs usually attain the same levels of native language competence as students with comparably low SES in native language programs. SES has been measured in these studies according to the educational level and occupational status of parents and characteristics of the communities in which they live.

At the same time, and as one would predict from their low SES, such students usually score significantly lower on native language literacy tests than their middle class peers in the same program; this is also true for students from low SES backgrounds in native language programs. The same pattern has been found for achievement in mathematics and science. For example, even though immersion students from low SES backgrounds receive all their math instruction through their L2, they score as well as students from low SES backgrounds who have received math instruction through the medium of their native language.

With respect to their L2 development, it has been found that economically disadvantaged immersion students perform significantly better than comparable students in conventional L2 programs on all measures of L2 proficiency. Of particular note, they also sometimes perform as well as middle class immersion students on tests of listening comprehension and speaking, although significantly lower on tests of reading. Recall that Cummins and others have argued that social, interpersonal communication skills develop differently from and more readily than academic language skills (e.g., reading). One could also argue that humans are innately capable of acquiring interpersonal communication skills without instruction. This, then, may explain the differential success of students from low SES backgrounds when it comes to the acquisition of listening and speaking skills in comparison to reading and writing skills in the L2.

Working in the United States, Caldas and Boudreaux (1999) similarly reported that socioeconomic disadvantage is not an obstacle to typical development in immersion programs in the case of English-speaking American students attending French immersion programs in Louisiana. Because these researchers did not have access to information concerning the SES of individual students, they compared entire groups of students in immersion classes with high concentrations of impoverished students (determined by the number of students who participated in a free/reduced lunch program) with groups of students in classes with similarly high concentrations of impoverished students in which the native language was used as the medium of instruction. They found that the immersion students (both white and African

American) tended to score higher than nonimmersion students in the same school district on standardized state-mandated tests of English and mathematics achievement administered in grades 3, 5, and 7.

Taken together, these studies indicate that students from low SES backgrounds can maintain typical levels of native language and academic development in L2 immersion programs.

Ethnic Group Status   Yet another risk factor in school is ethnic minority group status. Students from ethnic minority groups typically have disproportionately high rates of failure in North American schools (Goldenberg, 2003). As a result, one might expect their development to be put at greater risk if they are schooled through the medium of an L2. In this section, we discuss whether this expectation is true, but we do not discuss students from all minority ethnic groups. We have already discussed in the preceding section students from minority ethnic groups who have no or little proficiency in the language of the larger society in which they live. Of interest here is the performance of students from ethnic minority groups who speak the majority language; for example, African American students who speak English but attend French immersion programs in Cincinnati, Ohio (Holobow et al., 1991), or Louisiana (Caldas & Boudreaux, 1999).

Immersion programs that have been developed by indigenous language communities in order to revive their heritage languages are also relevant here because many of these students also speak the majority language but bear the risk of their ethnic group status, for example, English-speaking children of Hawaiian descent in Hawaiian language immersion programs in the United States (Slaughter, 1997) and English-speaking children of Mohawk descent in Mohawk immersion programs in Canada (Jacobs & Cross, 2001; see Christian & Genesee, 2001, for other examples). The students in these programs are doubly interesting because not only are they members of minority ethnic groups, but many also speak a nonstandard variety of the majority language. Many African Americans speak Black Vernacular English, and many children of Hawaiian descent speak Hawaiian Creole English (or "pidgin English"). This is important because it could be said that, in fact, these students are learning Standard English in school as a third language, in addition to a heritage language.

Research in all of these cases indicates that these students, even those who spoke a nonstandard variety of English, demonstrated the same levels of native language development and academic achievement as comparable students in native language programs, and, in addition, they developed advanced levels of functional proficiency in the L2. It must be reiterated that all of the students in these evaluations spoke a variety of English outside school, and, thus, these findings cannot be generalized to children from a minority ethnic group who speak a minority language at home. To summarize, membership in a minority ethnic group that speaks a variety of the majority language, even a nonstandard variety of that language, does not pose an impediment to typical linguistic and academic development if the student is in an L2 immersion program.

First Language Ability   Although the research evidence reviewed to this point indicates quite clearly that majority language students in general, and even students who are disadvantaged due to academic ability, ethnic group membership, and SES, can succeed in L2 immersion programs, the issue we address here is whether students with low levels of L1 ability should be excluded from such programs because they will be differentially disadvantaged in comparison to what they would achieve in an L1 program. Despite the significance of this issue, there is remarkably little systematic investigation of it, one exception being work by Bruck in Montreal. In order to examine this question, Bruck (1978, 1982) identified subgroups of grade 3 immersion and nonimmersion students who were "impaired" (i.e., children with disabilities) or "normal" (i.e., typically developing children) in their L1 development. Classification was based on teachers' judgments, an oral interview, and a battery of diagnostic tests. When Bruck tested the students on literacy and academic achievement measures, she found that the immersion students with disabilities scored at the same level as students with similar disabilities in the L1 program, and both groups scored lower than their typically developing peers in the same programs, as would be expected from the status of the students with disabilities. At the same time, the immersion students with disabilities had developed significantly higher levels of L2 proficiency than both subgroups of nonimmersion students (with and without disabilities) who were receiving conventional L2 instruction.

In sum, and as was found in the case of students with low levels of academic ability, students with low levels of L1 ability have been found to demonstrate the same levels of L1 development and academic achievement in immersion programs as students with similar disabilities in L1 programs. At the same time, participation in the immersion program benefited the students with disabilities with significantly superior L2 proficiency in comparison to students receiving conventional L2 instruction. Although these findings are important and useful, it would be important to examine the progress of students with more specifically defined forms of L1 impairment because, arguably, the operational definitions used by Bruck do not reflect current thinking about language impairment, nor do they capture the full range of language impairment that might cause problems for school children (Leonard, 1998).

KEY POINTS AND CLINICAL IMPLICATIONS

Many minority language and majority language children begin to acquire their L2 when they begin school. For minority language students, it is a matter of being schooled in the majority group language and, thus, acquiring the L2 that is essential for their social integration and economic prosperity in the wider community. For majority language children, it is a matter of choosing to add competence in a second or foreign language to their linguistic repertoire. The L2 may or may not be useful in their immediate community, but it will certainly broaden their horizons. The prospects of greater opportunity that come from knowing another language prompt majority language parents to select bilingual forms of education for their children.

In this chapter, we have sought to identify a number of significant issues pertaining to the language development of such children and, where available, to summarize key patterns of empirical evidence concerning their development. Our goal has been to sketch typical patterns of development of minority language and majority language children who are educated through their L2, in order to better identify those with language impairment of a clinical nature. We would like to help professionals determine if the difficulty reflects the typical challenges that students face when they are educated through the medium of their L2 or is a reflection of an underlying language impairment.

Key Point 1

Minority language students who are educated through the medium of the majority language face the triple challenges of acquiring an L2 for academic purposes, integrating socially into a new community of peers, and acquiring new academic skills and knowledge. Their success in the face of these challenges depends on their ability to acquire the language skills that are required of academic tasks and their ability to bridge the cultural and socio-economic differences between their homes and the school.

Implications

- Professionals should rule out the following factors before concluding that an individual minority language child's language difficulty is cause for clinical concern: 1) lack of acquisition of language skills required of academic tasks; 2) unfamiliarity with the cultural norms that govern school behavior; 3) lack of prior experience with literacy and literacy-related behaviors in the home; 4) hardship associated with disadvantaged SES, such as inadequate nutrition; 5) dysfunctional or disruptive family circumstances; and 6) medical problems.

Key Point 2

Minority language children generally develop the same or higher levels of proficiency in the majority language if they attend additive bilingual programs that provide substantial instruction in academic and language domains through the medium of their native language. At the same time, they maintain and extend their proficiency in the native language. In other words, they become bilingual and biliterate in the native and majority languages. Use of the native language can provide an important developmental scaffold for the acquisition of the majority language, especially with respect to academic language proficiency. L2-only or transitional bilingual programs do not achieve these benefits because they fail to promote high levels of competence in the native language, and, as a result, there are no positive transfer effects from the native to the majority language.

Implications

- It should not be assumed that participation in a bilingual program impedes acquisition of the majority language.

- Professionals should take a developmental perspective and expect that early lags in the majority language due to use of the minority language in school can, and often are, offset by later gains. In other words, minority language students may be behind other students during those grades when the native language is the predominant medium of communication, but they usually show rapid catch-up once the use of the majority language is extended.

- A focus on the majority language is not necessarily the most effective developmental route to promoting minority language children's acquisition of that language, and, moreover, such a strategy compromises development of the native language and, thus, bilingual development.

Key Point 3

Most majority language students, even those from disadvantaged socioeconomic and ethnic groups, acquire typical levels of native language development and high levels of achievement in academic domains in immersion programs. Students from disadvantaged backgrounds often perform at lower levels than students from advantaged backgrounds, but this is equally true for students in bilingual and monolingual programs.

Implications

- Professionals should not assume that the difficulties (linguistic or academic) experienced by some majority language students in bilingual programs are due to participation in a bilingual program. Learning through the medium of another language is not a linguistic, cognitive, or social hardship for most majority language students.

• Professionals should rule out socioeconomic, ethnic group, and family-related factors as possible explanations of individual student's difficulties before seriously considering underlying language or learning impairments.

REFERENCES

Adiv, E. (1980). *An analysis of second language performance in two types of immersion programs*. Unpublished doctoral dissertation, McGill University, Montreal, Canada.

Asser, H., Kolk, P., & Küppar, M. (2001). *Estonian-Language Immersion Programme: Report on student achievement and parental attitudes for the academic year 2000–2001*. Tallinn: Estonian Immersion Centre.

Baker, K.A., & de Kanter, A.A. (1981). *Effectiveness of bilingual education: A review of the literature*. Washington, DC: U.S. Department of Education, Office of Planning, Budget and Evaluation.

Bialystok, E. (2001). *Bilingualism in development: Language, literacy, and cognition*. New York: Cambridge University Press.

Bruck, M. (1978). The suitability of early French immersion programs for the language disabled child. *Canadian Journal of Education, 3,* 51–72.

Bruck, M. (1982). Language disabled children: Performance in an additive bilingual education program. *Applied Psycholinguistics, 3,* 45–60.

Bruck, M. (1985a). Consequences of transfer out of early French immersion programs. *Applied Psycholinguistics, 6,* 101–120.

Bruck, M. (1985b). Predictors of transfer out of early French immersion programs. *Applied Psycholinguistics, 6,* 39–61.

Caldas, S.J., & Boudreaux, N. (1999). Poverty, race, and foreign language immersion: Predictors of math and English language arts performance. *Learning Language, 5*(1), 4–15.

Christian, D., & Genesee, F. (Eds.). (2001). *Bilingual education*. Alexandria, VA: Teachers of English to Speakers of Other Languages.

Cloud, N., Genesee, F., & Hamayan, E. (2000). *Dual language instruction: A handbook for enriched education*. Portsmouth, NH: Heinle & Heinle.

Crago, M.B. (1988). *Cultural context in communicative interaction of young Inuit children*. Unpublished doctoral dissertation. McGill University, Montreal, Canada.

Cummins, J. (1984). *Bilingualism and special education: Issues in assessment and pedagogy*. Clevedon, England: Multilingual Matters.

Cummins, J. (2000). *Language, power and pedagogy: Bilingual children in the crossfire*. Clevedon, England: Multilingual Matters.

Echevarria, J., Vogt, M.E., & Short, D.J. (2000). *Making content comprehensible for English language learners*. Boston: Allyn & Bacon.

Genesee, F. (1987). *Learning through two languages: Studies of immersion and bilingual education*. Rowley, MA: Newbury House.

Genesee, F. (1991). Second language learning in school settings: Lessons from immersion. In A. Reynolds (Ed.), *Bilingualism, multiculturalism, and second language learning: The McGill conference in honor of Wallace E. Lambert* (pp. 183–202). Mahwah, NJ: Lawrence Erlbaum Associates.

Genesee, F. (1998). A case study of multilingual education in Canada. In J. Cenoz & F. Genesee (Eds.), *Beyond bilingualism: Multilingualism and multilingual education* (pp. 243–258). Clevedon, England: Multilingual Matters.

Genesee, F. (Ed.). (1999). *Program alternatives for linguistically diverse students.* Educational Practice Report No. 1. Washington, DC: Center for Research on Education, Diversity & Excellence. Available at http://www.cal.org/crede/pubs/edpractice/EPR1.htm

Genesee, F. (2002). Rethinking bilingual acquisition. In J.M. deWaele (Ed.), *Bilingualism: Challenges and directions for future research.* Clevedon, England: Multilingual Matters.

Genesee, F. (2004). What do we know about bilingual education for minority language students. In T.K. Bhatia & W. Ritchie (Eds.), *Handbook of bilingualism and multiculturalism* (pp. 547–576). Malden, MA: Blackwell.

Genesee, F., & Riches, C. (in press). Literacy development: Instructional issues. In F. Genesee, K. Lindholm-Leary, W. Saunders, & D. Christian, *Educating English language learners: A synthesis of research evidence.* Washington, DC: Center for Applied Linguistics.

Goldenberg, C. (2003). Making schools work for low-income families in the 21st century. In S.B. Neuman & D.K. Dickinson (Eds.), *Handbook of early literacy research* (pp. 211–231). New York: The Guilford Press.

Harley, B., & Swain, M. (1984). An analysis of verb form and function in the speech of French immersion pupils. *Working Papers in Bilingualism, 14,* 31–46.

Holobow, N.E., Genesee, F., & Lambert, W.E. (1991). The effectiveness of a foreign language immersion program for children from different ethnic and social class backgrounds: Report 2. *Applied Psycholinguistics, 12,* 179–198.

Jacobs, K., & Cross, A. (2001). The seventh generation of Kahnawàke: Phoenix or dinosaur. In D. Christian & F. Genesee (Eds.), *Case studies in bilingual education* (pp. 109–121). Alexandria, VA: Teachers of English to Speakers of Other Languages.

Johnson, R.K., & Swain, M. (1997). *Immersion education: International perspectives.* New York: Cambridge University Press.

Kindler, A.L. (2000). *Survey of the states' limited English proficient students and available educational programs and services: 2000-2001 summary report.* Washington, DC: National Clearinghouse for English Language Acquisition & Language Instruction Educational Programs.

Lambert, W.E., & Tucker, G.R. (1972). *The bilingual education of children: The St. Lambert experiment.* Rowley, MA: Newbury House.

Leonard, L.B. (1998). *Children with specific language impairment.* Cambridge: MIT Press.

Lindholm, K. (2001). *Dual language education.* Clevedon, England: Multilingual Matters.

Lindholm, K.J., & Aclan, Z. (1991). Bilingual proficiency as a bridge to academic achievement: Results from bilingual/immersion programs. *Journal of Education, 173*(2), 99–113.

Lindholm-Leary, K., & Borsato, G. (in press). Academic achievement. In F. Genesee, K. Lindholm-Leary, W. Saunders, & D. Christian, *Educating English language learners: A synthesis of research evidence.* Washington, DC: Center for Applied Linguistics.

Lyster, R. (1987). Speaking immersion. *The Canadian Modern Language Review, 43,* 84–100.

Met, M. (1998). Curriculum decision-making in content-based language teaching. In J. Cenoz & F. Genesee (Eds.), *Beyond bilingualism: Multilingualism and multilingual education* (pp. 35–63). Clevedon, England: Multilingual Matters.

Porter, R.P. (1990). *Forked tongue.* New York: Basic Books.

Ramirez, J.D., Yuen, S.D., & Ramey, D.R. (1991). *Longitudinal study of structured English immersion strategy, early-exit and late-exit transitional bilingual education programs for language-minority children* (Final report to the U.S. Department of Education). San Mateo, CA: Aguirre International.

Roseberry-McKibbin, C. (2002). *Multicultural students with special language needs.* Oceanside, CA: Academic Communication Associates.

Rossell, C.H., & Baker, K. (1996). The educational effectiveness of bilingual education. *Research in the Teaching of English, 30,* 7–74.

Slaughter, H. (1997). Indigenous language immersion in Hawai'i: A case study of Kula Kaiapuni Hawai'i. In R.K. Johnson & M. Swain (Eds.), *Immersion education: International perspectives* (pp. 105–129). New York: Cambridge University Press.

Swain, M., & Lapkin, S. (1982). *Evaluating bilingual education: A Canadian case study.* Clevedon, England: Multilingual Matters.

Thomas, W., & Collier, V.P. (1997). *School effectiveness for minority language students.* Washington, DC: National Clearinghouse for Bilingual Education. Available at http://www.ncbe.gwu.edu

Thomas, W., & Collier, V.P. (2002). *A national study of school effectiveness for minority language students' long term academic achievement.* Santa Cruz, CA: Center for Research on Education, Diversity and Excellence.

Diagnosis and Intervention

CHAPTER 8

Assessment and Intervention for Children with Dual Language Disorders

In previous chapters, we describe aspects of typically developing dual language children, but this chapter focuses on issues and recommendations for the assessment and intervention of developmental language disorders in dual language children. The chapter is structured around the eight children that we introduced at the beginning of the book. However, we use these children's stories in this chapter to illustrate how professionals would determine whether each child has specific language impairment (SLI) and to suggest treatment for each.

At various points in the previous chapters, these children were cited as examples of typically developing dual language learners. In this chapter, we make use of the same children in terms of their language background and ethnolinguistic communities, but we have altered one aspect of each profile: we suspect that they have language learning impairments. Our strategy in doing this is to underscore how dual language children with SLI can have the same background as typically developing dual language children. By using the same children in this chapter to represent cases of children who need assessment for language impairment, we are not implying that the children had disabilities in the previous chapters.

In our descriptions of the eight children in this chapter, we make two working assumptions. The first assumption is that the children's language learning difficulties are recognized by their parents, teachers, or health care professionals. Parents often become concerned that their child has a language impairment when the child does not develop in the same manner or at the same pace as other children that the parents know. In Chapter 1, we describe the incidence and nature of SLI or other language learning disorders. Children with SLI may have delayed onset of language, and they are slow to learn the grammatical aspects of their language. At age 3, for instance, they will not use the same kind of verb endings as typically developing children. Their utterances tend to be shorter and simpler than their peers.

Parents who do not have experience with other dual language children may find it difficult to recognize when their child is not learning two languages in the expected manner. The same lack of experience will make the recognition of language impairment difficult for certain teachers. However, teachers with experience teaching bilingual or second language learners can be especially astute in noticing dual language learners with SLI because on a daily basis the teacher can compare a child with SLI with typically developing children in the class who have the same language background. Overall, dual language children with language impairment will not learn verbal material in the classroom or at home as quickly or as well as others.

Our second working assumption in this chapter is that the eight children do not have difficulties in other domains of their functioning. In other words, our assumption is that their primary impairment is limited to their language abilities and that they have typical auditory, visual, cognitive, motor, and social-emotional abilities. For this reason, we refer to them as children with SLI. Readers who are not familiar with SLI should refer to the more in-depth discussion of this form of language impairment in Chapter 1. Our advice for assessment and intervention for these eight children would not be different if the children had other impairments such as hearing impairment or cognitive limitations.

To demonstrate the variation in factors associated with dual language learners with different types of language disorders, we provide a brief description of the eight children. Remember as you read that, for the purposes of this chapter, the children are suspected of having language disorders. Thinking about them as typical language learners as you did elsewhere in this book provides you with a good basis for comparison when you think about how their language-learning situation differs now that they are suspected of having language impairment. The choices for language learning that face parents of typically developing dual language children can differ from the choices facing the parents of dual language children with SLI.

In our descriptions of the children in this chapter, we raise certain assessment and intervention issues that are particular to each of the various types of dual language learners. Just as the eight children vary in their trajectories for typical language learning, they also differ in their language impairment. Such differences imply different approaches to assessment and intervention for each child. When reading our descriptions of these children, be mindful that the children should not be mistaken as stereotypes of their ethnic group. Every child is an individual, and what may apply to one child in a certain linguistic and ethnic context may not apply to another child in that same context.

As we present each child, we point out evident sources of such variation. Our aim is to inform the reader of the child-related and other factors to consider when determining if a particular child has language impairment. There are two subtypes of children in our group: simultaneous bilingual learners and second language learners. Within each subtype are children who are learning languages that have either majority or minority status.

PROFILES OF SIMULTANEOUS BILINGUALS WITH LANGUAGE DISORDERS

James

James is a 5-year-old boy who lives in Montreal, Quebec, with his mother and father. James's mother and father use the one parent–one language rule, so he gets adequate exposure to both French and English at home. Both languages are also used widely in the community, so it is advantageous for James to maintain both languages. James's kindergarten teacher, however, is not sure how to help him. It is now spring of his first year in school, and he is not able to keep up with the other children in her class; he seems slower than most children at this stage of kindergarten. His vocabulary is not as extensive as the other monolingual pupils in the class, and he seems to have trouble finding the right word in English. She wonders if he is having difficulty because he has a language impairment.

Assessment Issues

Dominance   The first diagnostic issue that professionals working with James should address is language dominance. Simultaneous bilinguals like James are likely to have a dominant language, and it is important not to mistake dominance in one language as a disorder in the other language. Because both of James's languages are majority languages, it is not expected that he will be strongly dominant in either of them; however, there are no guarantees that this will be true. If James is dominant in one of his languages and that language is not used in diagnosis, then he may falsely appear to have a delay or disorder. Professionals assessing children like James should expect that the children have one language that is dominant, although the difference may be subtle.

Bilingual Assessment   James should be tested in both languages. Diagnosticians working with James have an advantage because standardized tests exist in both Quebec French and in English. Professionals working with children who speak Spanish and English in the United States may also have this advantage, but it does not exist for professionals working with all children who are simultaneous bilinguals. It is very important to note that there are no standardized tests whose norms are based on bilingual children. This means that at certain stages and on certain components of language learning, simultaneous bilinguals like James may test slightly below the monolingual norms even if they do not have language disorders.

Expected Outcomes   Based on our research, we expect that James will show the same degree and pattern of impairment in his two languages as monolingual children with SLI learning the same languages (Paradis, Crago, Genesee, & Rice, 2003). This should be true regardless of any language dominance he may have. In other words, the type of errors he makes will not depend on whether he is using his more dominant language or his less dominant language. For instance, we would expect him to have difficulties with past tense in both English and French.

Bilingual children with language impairment may exhibit other language-specific patterns because impairment does not manifest itself the same way in all languages (Paradis & Crago, 2001). For example, both monolingual and bilingual French-speaking children with SLI have problems learning and using object pronouns. We expect James to have this same kind of difficulty in French. Thus, it is important for professionals to learn about the language patterns that are symptomatic of monolingual children with impairment who speak the same languages spoken by the bilingual children with whom they are working. As a general rule, expect bilingual children to exhibit the same kinds of impairment as monolingual children with language impairment speaking the same language.

Due to the lack of bilingual norms on standardized tests, we might expect that James would do less well than monolinguals on receptive vocabulary tests because simultaneous bilingual children often have smaller vocabularies in each of their two languages than monolinguals. Another anticipated outcome of diagnostic testing and/or language sampling in James's case is that he would use minimal code-mixing because in Montreal, neither intrautterance nor interutterance code-mixing is frequent. By school age, James will be aware of the norms of his community that discourage both children and adults from mixing the two languages. This would be different if James were growing up in Ottawa, a Canadian city in which code-mixing occurs more frequently in both adult and child speech.

Intervention Issues   Because James is a simultaneous bilingual who lives in an environment where both of his languages have majority status and where educational and clinical services exist in both of his languages, we would strongly encourage his parents, educators, and clinicians to help him maintain his two languages. Suppressing either of his languages could have detrimental long-term consequences for his educational and career prospects in Montreal.

We strongly recommended that James receive his educational and/or clinical intervention bilingually. Unfortunately, this is not a frequent practice even in a bilingual city like Montreal, where many educators and speech-language pathologists actually know and use both French and English. Our opinion is that bilingual intervention and education could be highly effective with children like James and should be encouraged by educational and health care authorities and parents. To mention just one possibility, therapists and educators working with bilingual children with language impairment could make metalinguistic comparisons between French and English (e.g., object pronouns like *it* come after verbs in English, but before them in French) that could be advantageous to this kind of child's language learning.

Bistra

Bistra is 4 years old and lives in Iowa. Her parents are both graduate students at the local university. Bistra's mother is from Bulgaria and has spoken to her exclusively in Bulgarian from birth, and her father, who is American, uses English exclusively with her. Bistra gets lots of exposure to English outside the home but seldom hears Bulgarian because there are few Bulgarian speakers in her local community. Bistra is like a lot of simultaneous bilinguals who are learning the dominant societal language and a minority language with few speakers with whom she can interact. Bistra's parents would like her to be fully bilingual in English and Bulgarian, but they are worried that this may not be realistic or possible. Bistra was slow to talk, and she still seems behind other children her age in her oral proficiency. They have decided to take her to a speech–language pathologist to see if she has a language impairment.

Assessment Issues

Dominance   In Bistra's case, we would expect that she would be dominant in English because she hears it at home from her father, at child care, in the surrounding community, and in the media. Some other simultaneous minority-majority bilingual children like Bistra may not be dominant in English, for instance, when both parents speak the minority language or when the child stays at home with a grandparent rather than going to English-language child care. In these situations, children may be balanced bilinguals or even dominant in the minority language before they begin schooling. We recommend that the speech–language pathologist determine Bistra's level of oral proficiency in each of her languages because this will help the professional judge whether Bistra's language skills are at the level they should be for her overall development. The speech–language pathologist does not know Bulgarian or tests of Bulgarian, but Bistra's parents would be a good source of information about her Bulgarian proficiency because both of them know the language (Juárez, 1983).

Bilingual Assessment   If the speech–language pathologist determines that Bistra is more proficient in English, as we predict, then she could be tested with English-language standardized tests. As a cautionary note, however, it is important to remember that there are no standardized tests that are normed on bilingual populations. Because there are no standardized language tests in Bulgarian, the professionals involved with Bistra will need to rely on a resource person to help them understand how well she speaks Bulgarian. Bistra's mother's education level would make her a good possibility to be such a resource person. Alternatively, a Bulgarian speaker with experience with Bulgarian-speaking children would be especially helpful. These kinds of resource personnel can help characterize how Bistra's language is different from that of typically developing Bulgarian language learners in the same community.

It might be tempting for parents and professionals working with a child like Bistra to do an informal translation of a standardized English language test so that it can be used to test her Bulgarian. It is very important that professionals and parents do not translate standardized measures. The norms will not apply to any translated adaptation. Also, because of the language-specific nature of certain aspects of impairment, each language has different target structures that are difficult for all children learning that language. A translation will not tap those structures and instead will assess aspects of language that are irrelevant for determining if a child who speaks Bulgarian has an impairment.

Expected Outcomes   In general, based on our research on French-English bilingual children with SLI, we would expect Bistra, like James, to experience impairments in both English and Bulgarian. Her degree and pattern of impairment should be the same as that of monolingual children with SLI who speak English and monolingual children with SLI who speak Bulgarian. We would also expect there to be certain language-specific features to her impairment in English that may differ from her impairment in Bulgarian. Generally speaking, if Bistra has SLI, we would expect her pattern of performance in English to look like that of monolingual English-speaking children with SLI.

Because Bistra is likely to be tested for SLI using standardized English-language tests, the speech–language pathologist could interpret Bistra's performance on the English test using the same expectations she would have for monolingual English-speaking children. Of course, she must take Bistra's overall level of proficiency in English into account when she interprets her test performance. In other words, she must allow for the possibility that Bistra could score more poorly if her English is not at age-level. Professionals working with Bistra will have to use their judgment to decide whether her overall proficiency accounts for her test performance or if an underlying language impairment may be to blame. To do this, they should look for the markers they would typically use to identify SLI in monolingual children.

Intervention Issues   Out of necessity, Bistra's education and her clinical intervention will be primarily in English. Clinicians and educators could instruct her parents on certain activities that will promote language acquisition and suggest that her mother carry them out in Bulgarian with Bistra. One of the biggest intervention challenges with children like Bistra is evaluating the importance of continued dual language learning. If Bistra's parents are motivated to have Bistra learn Bulgarian, then continuing to expose her to that language is recommended because there is no evidence that such exposure will harm her English language acquisition. However, there may be reasonably little cost to Bistra if her parents decide not to continue speaking Bulgarian to her.

Professionals working with children like Bistra need to help parents evaluate whether continuing in a language like Bulgarian in the North American context is causing extra stress on the family or child when they already have to deal with the stress of coping with a language disorder. Some of the factors that such families will need to consider include the following: the resources inside and outside the family for the minority language; the effort required to ensure adequate input in the minority language; the social and emotional outcomes for the child, parents, and extended family; and the educational, social, and career advantages of being able to speak the minority language.

Pasquala

Pasquala is 6 years old. She was born and lives in New York City with her two parents. Her mother is a nurse, and her father works for an insurance company. Pasquala's parents and grandparents, who live in the same neighborhood in New York, all speak both Spanish and English in the home and community, although they try to speak more Spanish than English in the home so Pasquala will keep up her Spanish. There are many families of Puerto Rican heritage in the neighborhood, so Pasquala is exposed to Spanish not just in the context of her family, but also in local stores, in church, and with other children on the playground at school. She is in grade 1 in a bilingual school.

Pasquala seemed like a typical playful child until she started school. Now, she is quiet and withdrawn and does not participate much in classroom activities. Her grade 1 English teacher wonders if Pasquala is having trouble because she is bilingual and is unable to keep up with two languages. Based on her experience with other bilingual children, however, she suspects that Pasquala might have a language impairment.

Assessment Issues

Dominance Like James, Pasquala has had a lot of input both inside and outside of her home in both languages, so she should be a balanced bilingual; however, it is important to check her dominance so that this is not a confounding factor in diagnosis. We recommend that professionals carry out the diagnosis in both languages, but, if this is not possible, assessment should be done in Pasquala's dominant language (Guttiérrez-Clellen, 1996).

Bilingual Assessment Like James, Pasquala's languages can be measured with standardized tests because they exist in both English and Spanish. It is imperative to remember that these tests are not normed on bilingual children, so they may give misleading results when used with simultaneous bilinguals like Pasquala. It is also important to determine which dialect of Spanish is used in any given Spanish-language test. There are several distinct features to Iberian, Mexican, Caribbean, and South American Spanish that professionals need to be aware of. Such bilingual testing implies the necessity for bilingual diagnosticians or at least testing in Pasquala's two languages.

Informal translations of English tests into Spanish should be avoided. Professionals who speak only English will need to work with Spanish-speaking resource collaborators when diagnosing children such as Pasquala. These collaborators can be professionals or community liaison workers (Guttiérrez-Clellen & Kreiter, 2003). It is preferable for them to have experience with bilingual children so that they can help compare Pasquala's language to that of other such children. Resource collaborators should be easier to find for Pasquala than for a child like Bistra who lives in a community with only a few Bulgarian speakers.

Samples of Pasquala's language in English and Spanish will be important in order to evaluate not only certain grammatical properties of her language but also her code-mixing. Professionals working with Pasquala should ask her parents about code-mixing in their community to determine whether to expect it in Pasquala's speech. Her parents or other resource collaborators can be helpful in ascertaining whether the types of code-mixing that Pasquala uses are in any way different from what is typical of her community. The kinds of questions that need answering might include: Does Pasquala's code-mixing stand out in some way? Is it more frequent? Is it context insensitive, or does it have peculiar patterns to it? Gathering samples of Pasquala's language in different contexts, inside and outside of school, is also important to ensure valid assessment of her competence. Limiting the assessment of her language to a single context, especially if it is a formal context like school or a clinic, can give a one-sided picture of the language competence of a minority language child like Pasquala. Their full competence is often more evident if they are observed in informal settings with playmates or familiar adults.

Expected Outcomes   A typical balanced bilingual should be at age-appropriate levels in both languages except for vocabulary, which will be below expected level in each language. If Pasquala's language is not at age level, then she may have a language impairment. Unlike James, we would expect Pasquala to code-mix because it is typical of the community of speakers in which she is growing up. However, we might expect it to be different in pattern than that used by more typically developing children of her community. Her code mixing is likely to be less sensitive to speaker context and may have grammatical peculiarities.

Like James and Bistra, we would expect Pasquala to have the same pattern and degree of impairment as monolingual children with SLI in each of their languages. We would also expect her to have certain language-specific forms of impairment in English and Spanish. For example, she may have pronounced difficulty with articles and object pronouns in Spanish but not in English, and she may have difficulty with verb morphology in English but not in Spanish.

Intervention Issues   Pasquala's parents should be encouraged to continue talking to her in Spanish and English. Because both of her languages are spoken in school, in the community, and in her extended family, it would be a great loss for Pasquala to learn only English. In fact, the nature of the family and the community that she lives in might make a decision to switch to one language impossible because Pasquala would continuously encounter Spanish on a daily basis in her social interactions in her home and community.

Pasquala can profit greatly from bilingual education and bilingual clinical intervention. She is fortunate that her school offers a bilingual program, and it is regrettable that similar bilingual educational programs in North America are becoming increasingly difficult to find. It is also regrettable that speech-language pathology services are rarely bilingual. Bilingual children such as

James and Pasquala would be well served by intervention programs in which they receive help in both languages, either from one bilingual speech-language pathologist or two different speech-language pathologists, one French- or Spanish-speaking and one English-speaking.

SECOND LANGUAGE LEARNERS

Samantha

Samantha is a 7-year-old girl who lives in Tucson with her two parents, both of whom speak English. Samantha attended a Spanish-speaking child care center for 2 years and is presently attending a Spanish immersion primary school. Her parents hope that she will learn Spanish as a second language, but they are becoming discouraged by the fact that neither her Spanish nor her English language skills are what they expected after 4 years of schooling. They are worried that they made an inappropriate educational choice for her. Their concerns are shared by Samantha's grade 2 teacher who has suggested to them that Samantha should be assessed by the school's speech-language pathologist.

Assessment Issues

Bilingual Assessment   Speech-language pathologists should diagnose language impairment in second language learners using their first language. In Samantha's case, this is relatively straightforward because her first language is English.

Expected Outcomes   We expect that, if confirmed, Samantha's language impairment will resemble that of a monolingual English speaker with SLI. It is unlikely that there will be interference from her second language on her English because she has been exposed to Spanish only recently. It is not likely that she will speak Spanish with any degree of proficiency until at least grade 2, and we do not expect her to be as proficient in her second language as her typically developing peers. Because her first language is English, a majority language in her country, she is not at risk for losing her first language simply because she is being schooled in a second language.

Intervention Issues   The main question facing Samantha's parents is whether to keep Samantha in a Spanish-language school. There are no contemporary well-documented studies of the effectiveness of second-language education for children with SLI. One of the only relevant studies was conducted in Montreal in the late 1970s and early 1980s (Bruck, 1978, 1982). To date, it is still one of the only studies that has addressed learner outcomes for children with learning disabilities who are educated in a second language. In her study, Bruck demonstrated that second language immersion schooling harmed neither the children's first language skills nor their academic development. At the same time, these children were able to achieve more advanced levels of second language proficiency than children with similar impairments in conventional school programs with more limited exposure to the second language. It would be beneficial to replicate Bruck's results with children with SLI using contemporary criteria and definitions of SLI.

Samantha's family will need to take into consideration the availability of speech-language pathology intervention in both her first and her second language. Bilingual intervention is a rarity. The lack of it in Samantha's case might make continued education in Spanish less desirable. Samantha's parents, like other parents in similar situations, need to examine carefully their motivations for second language schooling. Some questions they might consider are whether they, as parents, can support their child's second language learning, whether there are adequate professional services available in both languages, whether having a second language is important for their child's future opportunities, whether second-language learning will be an additional and unnecessary stress for their child, and the extent to which Samantha will be likely to use her second language.

Professionals working with Samantha will have an important role to play in helping her parents sort through the pros and cons of continuing second language education by weighing the effort and costs involved. Clearly, if the cost of having a second language, no matter how limited it is, is not great, then Samantha's parents will be more motivated to pursue this educational option for their daughter. It is our best guess that learning a second language will not harm Samantha's first-language learning; however, it may be a frustrating experience for her. If this is so, then pursing this educational option will require that the parents firmly believe that the long-term gain of having a second language is worthwhile.

Trevor

Trevor is 6 years old. He is an English-speaking American boy who has moved with his parents to Germany, where his father has a new job. Trevor's parents thought that their time in a foreign country would provide Trevor with a special opportunity to learn a second language. They enrolled him in a German-language school for German children. Trevor is struggling at school, and his parents are becoming worried that their son may not be up to learning two languages, especially because family relatives have pointed out that Trevor's English is not as advanced as his cousins' language was at the same age. Trevor's mother is nervous about whether she will be able to find diagnostic and intervention services in Germany that are appropriate for Trevor.

Assessment Issues

Bilingual Assessment   Trevor, like Samantha, needs to be diagnosed in his first language, English. The major difference is that, as Trevor's mother suspects, Trevor's family may have difficulty in locating the services of an English-language speech-language pathologist in Germany. There are, however, a number of options for this family. Parents we have known in similar situations have brought their children back to North America for a diagnostic evaluation. There is also the possibility of finding professional services through English-language schools, such as an American School in Germany. Trevor's parents may also be able to find a German speech-language pathologist who speaks English well and is willing to work with Trevor's parents to understand the nature of Trevor's language difficulties.

Expected Outcomes   As with Samantha, it is unlikely that the speech-language pathologist will find any interference on Trevor's English from whatever German Trevor has learned because his exposure to German is recent. However, because he is living in a fully German-speaking context, we expect that his German will advance more quickly than Samantha's Spanish. At the point of initial diagnosis, the speech-language pathologist who is assessing him is likely to find that Trevor's competence in his first language will resemble that of an English-speaking child with SLI. If he continues to learn German, there may eventually be some interference from his German in his English. We might also expect to find certain language-specific problems in each of Trevor's two languages. For instance, the placement of the verb in relation to the subject and object in the sentence varies in German, but English has relatively fixed subject-verb-object word order. Misplacement of the verb is a common problem exhibited by children with SLI who are learning languages such as German (Håkansson & Nettelbladt, 1993).

Intervention Issues   We recommend that the primary language of intervention for Trevor be English given that it is his first language and his family's situation in Germany is temporary. Intervention in German would also be desirable if the family intends to continue their child's second language learning. Trevor's family, like Samantha's, needs to evaluate both the opportunities and the costs to Trevor's learning German. In Trevor's case, his family needs to consider not only his intervention possibilities but also his educational possibilities. Bruck's research provides only limited guidance in Trevor's case because it took place with children in immersion programs. Because Trevor is not in an immersion program, it is not clear what his

language learning and academic achievement outcomes will be in an all-German school. His family, like Samantha's, is faced with a series of questions, such as how much they can support his language learning, what professional and educational resources are available to Trevor in Germany, what the long-term desirability of knowing German will be for Trevor once his family returns to the United States, and how frustrating it will be for Trevor to continue being educated in a German-language school.

Carlos

Carlos is the 6-year-old son of Mexican migrant workers who are presently living in California. His family lives in a community of Spanish-speaking people that includes a number of members of his extended family. Carlos attends an English-speaking school along with a number of his cousins. Carlos' aunts have pointed out to his mother that his Spanish is not as proficient as their children's language skills were at the same age. They have questioned how well he will be able to learn English and how well he will do in school because he is so slow to learn Spanish.

Carlos' mother is worried by her sisters' comments and by Carlos's teacher's concerns. At the first parent–teacher meeting of the year, the school translator explained to her what Carlos's teacher thought about his school performance. The teacher, who has many years of experience teaching children of Hispanic migrant workers, told Carlos's mother that Carlos is slower to learn English than many of the other children that she has taught. She is concerned not only that he speaks very little English, but also that he doesn't appear to understand directions after almost a full year in an English-speaking classroom. She would like to refer Carlos to the school's Spanish-speaking speech-language pathologist and a community resource worker familiar with Carlos's cultural background. Carlos's mother is not clear what such professionals will do, but her sisters and friends in the neighborhood think it's a good idea. She hopes that her son will be able to get a good education and find a good job when he finishes school.

Assessment Issues

Bilingual Assessment   The assessment of children like Carlos is particularly challenging for professionals who are not familiar with the Spanish language or with Carlos's social and cultural background. It is imperative to assess Carlos in his first language. For this reason, Carlos is very lucky that the speech-language pathologist who will assess him is Spanish-speaking and that she will work in collaboration with a community resource worker. This is an ideal combination for assessing him. Carlos's experienced kindergarten teacher will be a wonderful adjunct in the assessment process because she has observed children from the same language and social background as

Carlos and can compare Carlos's progress with that of other children in her classroom.

The community resource worker will explain to Carlos's speech-language pathologist any cultural and linguistic practices that might interfere with Carlos's test performance. For instance, children of Mexican background are rarely alone with an adult, so this aspect of traditional language testing can be disconcerting for them. It is also important to note that many children from a rural background in Mexico are from indigenous communities with a different culture than mainstream Latin American culture, regardless of whether they speak the indigenous language. Professionals will also need information on what dialect of Spanish Carlos speaks and any local norms that might be pertinent to his language development.

Fortunately, there are tests in Mexican Spanish that could be used to assess Carlos's Spanish language abilities. However, these tests are not necessarily normed on children like Carlos who have lived in the United States all of their lives. Scores may not be accurate because some Mexican and other immigrant children have quite a bit of experience translating for their parents. As a result, they can score very well on tests because they have more advanced metalinguistic abilities than monolingual children who have never been called on to translate from one language to another.

Expected Outcomes   Carlos's situation is interesting because he was born in the United States but only began learning English as a second language when he started school 1 year ago. He has been raised in a Mexican American community where the cultural norms differ from those of mainstream North Americans. These differences may be misinterpreted by professionals who do not have experience working with children from this background. These children are at risk for both over- and underdiagnosis for SLI because 1) professionals might expect them to do poorly under all circumstances and, thus, fail to notice that a language problem is causing them to do poorly in school, or 2) people might mistake their lack of English ability as a sign of impaired language development because they are not new arrivals to the United States or because their cultural background makes them perform poorly on tests.

We expect Carlos to use very little spoken English at this time and even in his second or third year of schooling in English; however, what English he has may cause some interference with his Spanish. His Spanish is likely to show the same pattern and degree of impairment as a monolingual Spanish-speaking child with SLI. His social class and educational background might contribute to a lower vocabulary level than other children with SLI, even in Spanish. His literacy skills in Spanish are likely to be even more limited than expected for a child with SLI because his entire literacy education is in English.

Intervention Issues Carlos would benefit from bilingual education and bilingual intervention. Because his knowledge of Spanish can support his learning of English, it would be optimal for Carlos to have the services of a bilingual speech-language pathologist and a bilingual teacher. Even though Carlos is not fortunate enough to attend a bilingual school program, it is important for his family to keep using Spanish with him at home. It would be a true loss for Carlos if he could not interact with his family and community in their language. Not speaking Spanish could diminish his relationship with his monolingual Spanish-speaking parents as well as his ethnic identity. In addition, Carlos's parents may not be able to provide much exposure to English in the home. The family should be encouraged to provide as much literacy in Spanish as possible at home. Carlos's mother cannot read, but other family members or friends could read to Carlos in Spanish after he gets home from school.

Bonnie

Bonnie is an 8-year-old girl who lives with her Mandarin-speaking parents in Vancouver, Canada. Bonnie learned Mandarin at home as a child before she began attending her English-language primary school. Her parents are professionals who place a high value on her school performance. They are part of an active Chinese immigrant community where Mandarin is spoken among their friends and overheard in the neighborhood stores and streets. Bonnie was not a fully proficient speaker of Mandarin before she entered kindergarten. Now in grade 2, she is struggling with her reading and writing, and her spoken English is not as advanced as her parents expected. Bonnie's difficulties at school are upsetting to her parents, both of whom have become near–native speakers of English. One of Bonnie's mother's colleagues at work suggested to Bonnie's mother that she take Bonnie to see a private speech-language pathologist because she was low on the waiting list to see the speech-language pathologist at school. Bonnie's mother found a speech-language pathologist through the local Chinese hospital who can assess Bonnie in both Mandarin and English. She hopes the speech-language pathologist can help Bonnie learn English so she can perform better in school.

Assessment Issues

Bilingual/Bicultural Assessment Having a bilingual speech-language pathologist is important because Bonnie needs to be assessed in her first language to ascertain if she has a language impairment. If Bonnie's parents had not been able to find such a professional, they could have worked in a collaborative manner with an English-speaking speech-language pathologist. Another alternative is for a member of Bonnie's community who is familiar with child development to function as a resource collaborator. People with knowledge of typical development will be particularly important during her assessment because we know of no standardized language tests in Mandarin. (There are tests in Cantonese, however.) The speech-language pathologist working with Bonnie will need to resist the temptation to use informal translations of English language tests.

Expected Outcomes   We expect Bonnie to have the same pattern and degree of impairment in Mandarin that a monolingual Mandarin speaker with SLI would have. However, we also expect her to make faster progress in learning to read and write in English than Carlos because both of her parents speak English and, therefore, can help her with her schoolwork. We expect her to have a certain amount of interference from Mandarin in her English and predict that she will learn English slower than a typically developing child with her background. She will profit at school from her parents' education level because literacy will be a familiar part of her home life. We do not expect cultural bias in the testing situation because children from her background are accustomed to responding to adults' requests for performance. For this reason, she would probably find the testing situation more comfortable than Carlos would.

Intervention Issues   Bonnie is very fortunate that her parents were able to arrange the services of a bilingual speech-language pathologist who can provide intervention in her two languages. It would certainly be preferable to have a bilingual school program, and such programs are becoming increasingly available in Western Canada. As with her assessment, if there had been no speech-language pathologist who could provide her with services in Mandarin, a resource collaborator who is a native speaker of Mandarin would have been very important. Because her Mandarin language skills can support her English language development, Bonnie's speech-language pathologist would probably recommend, as we would, that her parents continue to use Mandarin with her at home. This will also help to maintain her family and community ties and, in so doing, bolster her ethnic identity. Speaking Mandarin in Bonnie's context may well have economic advantages for her in the future.

Pauloousie

Pauloosie is an 8-year-old Inuk boy who lives in a tiny remote Inuit community in Northern Quebec. He comes from a family where he has several sisters and brothers. For the past 3 years, he has been in an Inuit-run school in which he was taught exclusively in Inuktitut, his native language. This year, in grade 3, he has started to learn English from an English-language non-Native teacher who has just moved to his community from southern Canada.

In grade 1, Pauloosie's Inuk teacher recommended that he be tested by a visiting Inuk special education counselor because she found his vocabulary and grammar in Inuktitut very weak. The counselor confirmed that his Inuktitut was not as proficient as other children from his community. She suggested to his teacher that she keep Pauloosie close to her in the classroom and make sure he overhears the spoken language of the other children in his class and sits near an excellent student so he can learn by observing this child's work.

This year, Pauloosie is becoming very agitated at school. The calm support of his experienced Inuit teacher is not paralleled in his new, inexperienced teacher from the South. Due to his restless behavior in class, the teacher has made him sit by himself, and he feels alone and unsupported by his peers. Both Pauloosie and his teacher are uncomfortable. The teacher wants the school's English-speaking speech-language pathologist and visiting Inuk special education counselor to assess Pauloosie. She wants to know the source of his frustration and how she can help.

Assessment Issues

Bilingual/Bicultural Assessment   We recommend that Pauloosie be assessed in his first language by someone who is familiar with his culture. Chapter 2 recalls our mishaps as researchers in Inuit communities before we understood how striking our cultural differences with Inuit were. Pauloosie is fortunate and unlike many native children in that his assessment can take place in Inuktitut by someone who is familiar with his culture—the visiting Inuk special education counselor. Pauloosie, unlike many North American native children, is able to speak his native language fluently. He is also being educated in a school with a school board run by Inuit where he can be assessed by a trained Inuit special education counselor using testing materials in Inuktitut that have been normed on children from Nunavik, the territory in which he lives. This situation is ideal for indigenous language–speaking children like Pauloosie, and it is one that is rare not only in North America but also in the world at large.

Both the Inuit special education counselor and her English-speaking colleague understand that literacy is not a common practice in many Inuit homes. They also understand that Inuit children are very reluctant to speak to adults. For this reason, they will use more comprehension tasks rather than expressive tasks when assessing Pauloosie. Both of these counselors know that silence and averted eye gaze are positive developmental indicators in children of Pauloosie's age.

Expected Outcomes   We expect that Pauloosie has grammatical and vocabulary shortcomings in his Inuktitut and that these will be accurately diagnosed by the experienced special education counselors because of their linguistic and cultural familiarity and special training. Our research has shown that certain difficulties that Pauloosie will have in his Inuktitut are language-specific and different from those experienced by English-speaking children with SLI (Crago & Allen, 2001). Other aspects of Pauloosie's impairment will be remarkably similar to certain impairments shown by English-speaking children with SLI.

We also expect that he will be a relatively poor second language learner because his impairment will manifest itself in both of his languages. Pauloosie's Inuktitut is likely to interfere with his English. For instance, he is not likely to easily distinguish *he* from *she* in his spoken English because Inuktitut does not make this distinction. Inuit adults who work with Pauloosie may find that he is too talkative or that his eye gaze is too direct. Behaviors such as these might be considered appropriate by unfamiliar non-Inuit professionals, but for many Inuit, they will seem inappropriate and, therefore, may be taken as indicators of a learning disability.

Many native North American children living in cultural and linguistic circumstances that differ from Pauloosie's are likely to be both over- and underdiagnosed in much the same way that children like Carlos are. Some inexperienced professionals will expect little of such children in language development, resulting in their being overlooked for language impairment. Other inexperienced professionals, however, will overdiagnose native children as having language impairments because they are not aware of their cultural or linguistic differences and, therefore, will consider their behavior as an indication of a disorder when it is not.

Intervention Issues   Pauloosie is particularly fortunate when it comes to intervention and education. Although, or perhaps because, his community is remote, the Inuit-controlled school district has made sure that there are trained Inuit special education personnel in all of its schools. Because Pauloosie's language impairment is severe, the counselors are likely to recommend that he be placed in a special class for children with learning disabilities in which he will have an Inuk teacher who is bilingual and who will educate the children in both English and Inuktitut. His teacher in the special class, like many Inuit teachers who participated in our research, will be particularly skillful at integrating children with disabilities into an inclusive classroom framework where they do not stand apart from their classmates (Brophy & Crago, 2003). Pauloosie's family will be encouraged by the school counselors to continue speaking Inuktitut at home. Having attained a certain degree of literacy in his first language, Inuktitut, will be helpful to Pauloosie as he learns to read and write in English.

Pauloosie's situation provides an optimistic picture of what is possible for certain native North American children when community control of schools is in place and native languages are still spoken by members of the community. It is profoundly regrettable that the rich language and cultural resources that can be found in Pauloosie's community are not available to more native children or, for that matter, to more minority-language speaking children elsewhere in the world.

For native children who are less fortunate than Pauloosie, it is important to assess the child's language dominance. Because most speech-language professionals will not be competent in the child's native language, this will call for a community collaborator who is a native-language speaker. This person will preferably be someone who has experience with other children who speak the native language so that he can gauge the language of the child who is suspected of having language impairment in comparison to children of the same age who are acquiring the language typically. Such a collaborator should also be familiar with the culture of the child so that testing and subsequent intervention can be done in a culturally sensitive manner.

If the child is dominant in English and if a professional is not available to provide intervention in the child's native language, then we recommend intervention in English. At the same time, we encourage parents and other adults in the child's life to continue to use the native language to the extent they can so that the child does not lose a valuable part of his cultural and personal heritage. Furthermore, native children living in urban environments are often overdiagnosed as having learning difficulties long after they no longer speak their native language, in part because they may still retain many cultural communication patterns such as averted eye gaze and reticence to speak to adults. Even more regrettable are the generally low educational expectations that exist for this group of children. Such lowered expectations on the part of non-native professionals can be erroneous and can represent a form of either conscious or unconscious ethnic and racial bias.

SUMMARY

To summarize, assessment, diagnosis, and intervention for dual language children with language impairment is a complex, multidimensional process. To date, we do not know of any unique markers that distinguish typically developing dual language learners from those with impairment, so a lot of judgment is called for in making decisions. It is important to collect information about the children's competence in both languages, if possible, and, if not, to collect it in their more dominant language so that one has an indication of their relative strengths. It is also highly recommended that the child's language use be observed in multiple settings and, in particular, that the child be observed outside clinical settings as well as in clinical settings. Children often have a range of competencies that is not expressed when they are observed in formal, adult-dominated contexts; this can be especially true for children from minority cultural backgrounds.

To work effectively with dual language learners requires multiple competencies on the part of responsible adults. In many cases, a single speech-language professional will not possess all the competencies she needs to do the job right. In these cases, it is important to call on collaborators who know the child's language and culture so they can assist in getting a complete and accurate picture of the child. Obviously, it is best if the collaborator is also experienced in some way with language and language disorders or, at least, is familiar with what other children who speak the same languages can typically do when they are the age of the child under assessment.

Clearly, the all-too-frequent advice given by many professionals in the past, that children with SLI should learn only one language, is not appropriate to most children. Each child's situation is different and colored by many factors. Parents and professionals alike should not have stereotyped assumptions about the value of bilingualism for children and about children's capacity to learn two languages. We know that in appropriate circumstances, children, even those with language impairment, have the capacity to learn two languages. Professionals and parents need to assess whether the circumstances that a given child is in are conducive to dual language learning. They should never automatically assume that having two languages is the exclusive domain of children with typical development.

Finally, it is always important to realize that dual language learning itself is not a cause of language impairment. Everything we know about children tells us that they are capable of acquiring more than one language, simultaneously or successively. Furthermore, our own work on bilingual French-English children with SLI as well as Bruck's earlier work on school children with language impairment attest to their ability to learn more than one language. This research also shows that children with SLI will be challenged in learning two languages, just as they are challenged in learning one language. Our task is to create the optimal conditions that will make this possible given the capacities that children with and without impairment have. When children have impaired capacity for language learning, it is our task to use caution and sensitivity in our assessment of them and to give them the extra care and attention in our clinical and educational interventions with them so that they can achieve their personal best.

REFERENCES

Brophy, A.E., & Crago, M. (2003). Variation in instructional discourse features: Cultural or Linguistic? Evidence from Inuit and non-Inuit Teachers of Nunavik. *Anthropology and Education Quarterly, 34*(4), 1–25.

Bruck, M. (1978). The suitability of early French immersion programs for the language disabled child. *Canadian Journal of Education, 3,* 51–72.

Bruck, M. (1982). Language disabled children: Performance in an additive bilingual education program. *Applied Psycholinguistics, 3,* 45–60.

Crago, M., & Allen, S. (2001). Early finiteness in Inuktitut: The role of language structure and input. *Language Acquisition, 9*(1), 59–111.

Guttiérrez-Clellen, V. (1996). Language diversity: Implications for assessment. In S.F. Warren & M.E. Fey (Series Eds.) & K.N. Cole, P.S. Dale, & D.J. Thal (Vol. Eds.), *Communication and language intervention series: Vol. 6. Assessment of communication and language* (pp. 29–56). Baltimore: Paul H. Brookes Publishing Co.

Guttiérrez-Clellen, V., & Kreiter, J. (2003). Understanding child bilingual acquisition using parent and teacher reports. *Applied Psycholinguistics, 24,* 267–288.

Håkansson, G., & Nettelbladt, U. (1993). Developmental sequences in L1 (normal and impaired) and L2 acquisition of Swedish syntax. *International Journal of Applied Linguistics, 3*(2), 3–29.

Juárez, M. (1983). Assessment and treatment of minority-language-handicapped children: The role of the monolingual speech-language pathologist. *Topics in Language Disorders, 3,* 57–65.

Paradis, J., Crago, M., Genesee, F., & Rice, M. (2003). French-English bilingual children with specific language impairment: How do they compare with their monolingual peers. *Journal of Speech Language and Hearing Research, 36,* 113–127.

Paradis, J., & Crago, M. (2001). The morphosyntax of specific language impairment in French: An extended optional default account. *Language Acquisition, 9*(4), 269–300.

Glossary

additive bilingual environments language learning environments (including family, community, and/or school settings) that encourage the acquisition of children's native or home language at the same time that they acquire an additional language. Acquisition of a second language in an additive bilingual environment does not occur at the expense of maintenance and development of the native language. Such environments also usually embrace dual cultural identity; this is characteristic of the language learning environments of children from majority ethnolinguistic groups who learn more than one language. This environment results in bilingual proficiency and is also sometimes referred to as *additive bilingualism*.

Anglo-Western culture culture that is based on or is derived from English-speaking cultures and/or broader Western cultural values and traditions; for example, Canada, the United States, Australia, and New Zealand have distinct mainstream cultures but share values and beliefs that are similar because they are derived from their common historical links to England and other Western cultural traditions.

bilingual children see *simultaneous bilinguals*

bilingual education/programs K–12 programs for language minority students in the United States in which both English and the students' native language are used for academic and literacy instruction during several grades.

canonical babbling   babbling that consists of repeating the same consonant–vowel combination over and over (e.g., da-da-da). This babbling is
characteristic of infants 6–8 months of age.

child-directed talk   adult talk that is directed to children who have not
yet mastered language. In certain cultures, the adult will attend to or share
in children's activities and talk directly to them about such activities. Child-
centered talk can include modifications, such as lexical and grammatical
simplifications, that make the words different from the way adults would
typically talk to older children or other adults. This form of talk is typical
of the white middle-class culture in North America and is also referred
to as child-directed speech or language or "motherese."

code-mixing   use of elements from two or more languages of a bilingual
in the same utterance or stretch of conversation. The mixed elements may
be phonological, lexical, or morphosyntactic. Mixing that occurs in a single
sentence or utterance is called *intrautterance mixing*. Mixing that involves
a switch from one language to another from one turn to another in the
same conversation is called *interutterance mixing*. Examples of each are
provided in Chapter 5. Code-mixing is a common form of language use
in both bilingual adults and children. It is grammatically and socioculturally
constrained; that is to say, it does not occur randomly. It is also sometimes
referred to as *code-switching*.

cognitively demanding communication   verbal communication that
calls for active cognitive involvement on the part of the speaker because
the subject matter is complex, abstract, or unfamiliar, and thus, the language
skills that are necessary to make meaning comprehensible have not been
fully automatized. This communication is characteristic of language use
during academic instruction; for example, explication of the methods and
results of a scientific experiment or arguments against nuclear disarmament
are complex and abstract and, therefore, cognitively demanding. Effective
communication in these cases requires careful use of language to explicate
one's intended meaning or point of view.

cognitively undemanding communication   verbal communication that
requires language skills that have been overlearned and, thus, require little
cognitive involvement on the part of the participants. Characteristic of
face-to-face communication about familiar subjects and topics; for example,
talking about a football game while watching the game draws on familiar,
overlearned language skills and makes few cognitive demands on the
speaker because the speaker is highly familiar with the game, players, and
terminology used to talk about the game.

context-embedded communication   verbal communication during
which the participants can actively negotiate meaning directly through

feedback to one another, and the meanings they seek to convey are supported by shared context. Context may be shared by virtue of common past experiences or by the immediate setting in which communication is taking place. Context-embedded communication is characteristic of much day-to-day social language use (e.g., a face-to-face conversation about a movie that two people have seen, talking about a football game that both speakers are watching).

context-reduced communication careful and explicit use of language to convey complex and novel meanings in situations when the intended meaning is not supported by shared experiences or immediate social context. This communication is characteristic of much language use during academic instruction in school (e.g., a lecture on homeostatis and its role in survival of living organisms). It has been argued by some that success in school depends critically on students' context-reduced language skills.

contingent query conversational activity in which someone asks a question that elicits a direct or contingent response. It is a frequent pattern in the conversational interactions of adults and children in certain cultures (e.g., white middle-class North American culture).

crosslinguistic influence interactions between the bilingual child's two languages during development. These interactions result in target-deviant structures in one language that reflect structural properties of the other language. Crosslinguistic influence is distinct from the concept of a Unitary Language System because the target-deviant structures do not result from across the board blending of the two languages but instead are limited in scope. The target-deviant structures that result from crosslinguistic influence are not pervasive, and many researchers have found that they are not permanent in a bilingual child's language, but occur as part of the typical bilingual developmental process. This concept is also called *crosslinguistic transfer* or *crosslinguistic interference*.

delayed immersion bilingual immersion programs for majority language students in which use of the second language for academic instruction is delayed until the middle elementary grade (e.g., grade 4 or 5). At that time, usually about 50% of academic instruction is presented through the second language and the remainder through the students' first language.

developmental bilingual programs bilingual programs for language minority students that aim for full bilingual proficiency and grade-appropriate standards in academic subjects. English and the student's native language are both used to teach literacy and academic subjects throughout the elementary grades and sometimes through the secondary grades.

developmental errors target-deviant structures produced by second language learners in their interlanguage that are typical of all learners of that target language regardless of their first language. The source of these errors cannot be traced to the first language of the second language learner; see also *transfer errors*.

dominance   the condition of bilingual people having one language in which they experience greater grammatical proficiency, more vocabulary, and greater fluency than the other language. This language may also be used more than the other language. Most, if not all, bilingual children and adults experience dominance, and the preferred language is referred to as the *dominant language*. The dominant language can change throughout the life span, and a bilingual person can be slightly or highly dominant in one language. In bilingual children, dominance can affect language choice (choosing to use the dominant language more than the nondominant language) and rate of language development (the bilingual child's competence in the dominant language more closely resembles that of monolingual children who speak that language).

dominant language   see *dominance*

Down syndrome   chromosomal abnormality caused by the presence of an extra 21st chromosome. This condition results in a distinctive physical appearance and moderate to severe mental retardation. It can also affect language development.

dual language learners/children   simultaneous bilinguals and second language learners of preschool or school age.

dual language learning   the acquisition of two languages simultaneously from birth (or beginning within the first year of life) or the acquisition of a second language after the first language has been established, usually taken to be around 3 years of age.

dual language system hypothesis   theory about early bilingual development that claims that when an infant is presented with dual language input, he or she constructs two separate linguistic representations from the outset, such as two vocabularies and grammars. According to this view, there is no period in development in which a child exposed to two languages cannot be considered bilingual, and there is no discernable stage in development in which the child's language system has to differentiate or separate into two. This view has been the majority view among researchers since the 1990s and contrasts with the *unitary language system hypothesis*.

early partial immersion   immersion programs that begin in the elementary grades and provide up to 50% of instruction through the medium of a second/foreign language. The number of years of partial immersion and the initial grade level in which immersion begins varies among programs.

early total immersion   immersion programs that begin in kindergarten and provide 90%–100% of instruction through the medium of a second/foreign language for a minimum of 2 years. Instruction through the native language of the students is introduced in grade 2 or higher. The percentage of instruction in English varies among programs.

English language learners   language minority students in the United States who are learning English, the majority language, for social integration and educational purposes (e.g., Spanish-speaking, Vietnamese-speaking, and Korean-speaking children residing and being educated in the United States). These children were previously referred to as *limited English proficient (LEP)* students; this term continues to prevail in federal and state legislation but is not widely used by educators and researchers because of the pejorative connotations of the term *limited*.

English-only programs   see *second language–only/English-only program*

errors of omission/commission   terms referring to two kinds of *target-deviant structures* that appear in the developmental language of both first and second language learners. An omission error is one in which an obligatory element, such as a grammatical morpheme, has been left out (e.g., *Robin Ø going there* instead of *Robin is going there*). A commission error is one in which the learner has supplied an element but chosen the wrong one (e.g., *Robin am going there* instead of *Robin is going there*). In the first and second language acquisition of English, omission errors are more common than commission errors.

family bilingualism   situation in which the immediate family is bilingual (e.g., the parents speak two languages to their children), but one of the two languages is not used in the community. Many children being raised in *one parent–one language* families experience family bilingualism.

50/50 two-way immersion programs   two-way immersion programs in which approximately 50% of instruction (including language and academic instruction) is presented through the medium of the non-English language and 50% through English during the elementary school grades. Approximately 50% of the students in two-way immersion classrooms are native speakers of English, and 50% are native speakers of the target non-native language, often Spanish.

first language (L1) attrition   process whereby proficiency in the native language declines as the second language becomes dominant. This process can result in restricted communicative competence in the first language compared with the second language and/or complete loss of the first language. Attrition can take many forms: decay or stagnation in size of the first language vocabulary, reduction in fluency/spontaneity in the first language, transfer of grammatical rules from the second language into the first language, or borrowing vocabulary from the second language into the first language. When the first language is a minority language, whether a child is bilingual or a second language learner, there is a risk of first language attrition.

formulaic language see *telegraphic language*

grammatical morphology morphemes that mark grammatical functions such as past or present tense and contrast with content morphemes like nouns, verbs, and adjectives. Grammatical morphemes can be inflectional morphemes (e.g., the plural *-s,* or past tense *-ed*), which are attached to words, or free-standing words such as articles (*the, a*) or auxiliary verbs (*is* in *she is eating*).

heritage language a term used to refer to the minority language spoken by members of a minority ethnolinguistic group or the language associated with that group. This term is often used when describing immigrants and their children and may refer to a language that is no longer spoken by members of the group in the community in which they are currently living. Examples include Italian in the case of Italian adults and children living outside Italy; Spanish in the case of Mexican American children who have migrated to the United States; and Turkish in the case of children living in Europe.

immersion programs K–12 educational programs for students who are members of the majority ethnolinguistic group in which at least 50% of curriculum instruction is provided through the medium of a second or foreign language for one grade or more. The grade level when instruction through the medium of the second language begins varies from the primary grades (kindergarten or grade 1) to the middle grades of elementary school (around grade 4) to middle or early high school grades (grade 7 or 8). As well, the duration of immersion instruction can vary from 1 to several years. These types of program are also referred to as *second/foreign language immersion programs*.

inflectional morphology see *grammatical morphology*

interlanguage intermediate language of second language learners that does not correspond either to their first or second language and appears "errorful" from the perspective of the second language. Interlanguage is thought to be a viable language system, even if it is not exactly like the target language (i.e., the second language). In other words, interlanguage is a rule-governed systematic language that is dynamic in nature because it is continually developing toward the second language. This term was first coined by Selinker (1972).

interutterance code-mixing see *code-mixing*

intrautterance code-mixing see *code-mixing*

L1 attrition see *first language (L1) attrition*

L2-only/English-only programs see *second language–only/English-only programs*

language aptitude ability or potential that an individual has for learning language. Language aptitude is distinct from general intelligence and includes skills such as the ability to rapidly and accurately decode unfamiliar speech into phonetic units and parts of speech (e.g., nouns, verbs, adjectives). Language aptitude predicts success in second language learning better than personality, social, or attitudinal factors. It is considered to be an intrinsic ability and not a learned skill.

language crossing   term used by Ben Rampton (1995) to describe the language use practices of adolescents in multiethnic schools in England. These young people would borrow certain phrases and expressions from each other's first languages and integrate them into their own first language. This kind of intentional language mixing created and represented a kind of social bond between them.

language socialization   study of language socialization that has as its goal the understanding of how children become competent members of their social groups and the role language has in this process. Language socialization, therefore, concerns two major areas of socialization: socialization through the use of language and socialization to the use of language (Schieffelin, 1990).

late immersion   educational programs for language majority students that provide at least 50% of instruction, including reading, writing and academic subjects, through the medium of a second/foreign language beginning in middle or high school.

lexical gap hypothesis   theory that children and adults mix words from one language into an utterance in another language when they do not know or cannot easily access the word in the appropriate language (e.g., if a Spanish speaker is trying to say, "I lost my wallet," but does not know or cannot remember the word for *wallet* in English, he may insert the Spanish word *cartera*).

limited capacity hypothesis   theory that infants and children have the ability to acquire one language completely, but the acquisition of two or more languages exceeds their innate ability. As a result, it is argued, acquisition of two languages simultaneously during infancy and early childhood or the acquisition of a second language during childhood (after a first language has been learned) will result in reduced levels of first and/or second language proficiency. The parents of children who are suspected of having specific language impairment are often counseled to limit the child to one language on the assumption that the child's impairment is related to (and perhaps even caused by) excessive demands on the child's language learning ability.

majority ethnolinguistic community   community of individuals who speak the language spoken by most of the members of the community and/or are members of the ethnic/cultural group of most members of the community. The community may be as large as a country, or it may be a state or province within a country or some smaller unit. The majority language and culture usually have special recognition as the official language and culture of the community. In other cases, they are regarded unofficially as the high status language and culture in the community. The majority language is the language used in most newspapers and other media, in the courts, and by political bodies in the community. Examples are Anglo Americans in the United States; English Canadians in Canada; and native German speakers in Germany. We also use the term *majority group.*

majority group   see *majority ethnolinguistic community*

majority language   language spoken by members of a majority ethnolinguistic group.

majority language students   K–12 students who speak a majority language and/or are members of a majority ethnolinguistic group (e.g., English-speaking students from mainstream sociocultural backgrounds in the United States, English-speaking Canadian students with mainstream sociocultural backgrounds).

mean length of utterance (MLU)   common measure of language development that is often inferred to reflect grammatical development. It is the average length of utterances produced by children spontaneously. MLU may be based on average number of words (including bound morphemes) or average number of separate morphemes, bound and free. The former is a more conservative estimate of development because it does not count bound morphemes separately; this estimate is often more appropriate when comparing development of languages with different morphological complexity.

metalinguistic awareness   conscious awareness of and the ability to manipulate the elements of language, including sounds, words, and grammatical structures (e.g., ability to count the number of sounds in a word or to remove, add, or otherwise manipulate the sounds of words; ability to identify words and the characteristics of words). Some metalinguistic skills, especially phonological awareness, have been shown to be highly correlated with reading and writing ability.

middle immersion   see *delayed immersion*

minority ethnolinguistic community   community made up of individuals who speak a minority language and belong to a minority culture. The language and culture may be in the demographic minority or may be in a minority status by virtue of their relatively low social, economic, and political power. Examples include Spanish speakers or individuals of Hispanic background in the United States, speakers of Inuktitut or Chinese in Canada, speakers of Navajo or Hopi in the United States, and Turkish speakers in Holland and Germany. We also use the term *minority group.*

minority group   see *minority ethnolinguistic community*

minority language   language spoken by members of a minority ethnolinguistic community.

minority language students   K–12 students who speak a minority language and/or are members of a minority ethnolinguistic group (e.g., Spanish-speaking students with central or south American sociocultural backgrounds in the United States, or Chinese-speaking Canadian students with Chinese sociocultural backgrounds).

MLU   see *mean length of utterance*.

multimorphemic utterances   number of utterances used by a speaker that are two or more morphemes long (e.g., *the cat, the lazy dog*). Counts of multimorphemic utterances are used as an estimate of a child's level of development in a language, with larger counts suggesting greater development. They are also sometimes interpreted as indicators of syntactic development on the assumption that longer utterances involve more complex morphosyntactic constructions. Morpheme counts can be made by separating free and bound morphemes (e.g., *cats* would be counted as two morphemes) or by counting only stand-alone words whether they include bound morphemes or not (e.g., *cats* could be counted as one morpheme). Counts based on stand-alone words provide a more conservative estimate than counts based on individual morphemes.

90/10 two-way immersion programs   two-way immersion programs in which approximately 90% of instruction (including language and academic instruction) is presented through the medium of the non-English language and 10% through English during the first two or three grades of elementary school. The amount of instruction in and through English increases, usually beginning in grade 3, until it is approximately 50% of daily instruction by the end of elementary school. Approximately 50% of the students in two-way immersion classrooms are native speakers of English, and 50% are native speakers of the target non-native language, often Spanish.

nondominant language   the language for many bilingual children and adults that is less proficient than the other. Children usually have smaller vocabularies, are less fluent, and have less advanced grammatical skills in the nondominant language. Children may also code-mix more when trying to use their nondominant language because they have less well-developed proficiency in that language and thus draw on the skills of the dominant language to fill gaps in their proficiency. Dominance is often, but not always, related to the child's exposure to each language, and the nondominant language is the language the child has had less exposure to. It is important to assess dual language children who are suspected of having language impairments in the dominant language to get an estimate of the child's maximum ability with language.

nonverbal period   stage children go through early in their acquisition of a second language when they do not speak or speak very little in the presence of speakers of the second language. Children accumulate receptive knowledge of the second language in a school or preschool setting and communicate mainly with nonverbal gestures, but they produce very few or no words in that language. The nonverbal period can last a few weeks to a few months; in general, younger children stay longer in this stage than older ones.

one parent–one language rule   pattern of parental language use in bilingual families in which each parent uses only, or primarily, one language (usually his or her native language) with the child. This pattern is often recommended to parents on the assumption that by keeping the languages separate, parents will make it easier for children to distinguish between the two languages and to keep them separate as they learn them. There is little systematic evidence to support or contradict this possibility. Nevertheless, this pattern helps parents manage language use in the family. Parents still need to decide which language to use with one another and with visitors in the home.

partial immersion   immersion programs for majority language students in which 50% of academic instruction is presented through the medium of the students' first language and 50% through the medium of the second language. These programs usually begin in kindergarten or grade 1 and continue until the end of elementary school.

phonemic   acoustic/articulatory differences in *segments* (speech sounds) that signal a difference in meaning in *minimal pairs*. Minimal pairs are pairs of words in which all of the segments are the same except for two segments that contrast (e.g., *bat* and *pat*). Which segments contrast phonemically differs crosslinguistically. For example, the acoustic/articulatory difference between /l/ and /r/ makes a difference in meaning when these sounds are used in minimal pairs in English (e.g., *rice* and *lice*). This difference is not phonemic in Japanese, and thus, Japanese speakers often have trouble hearing and producing this contrast when they listen to or speak English.

prosody   intonation contour of speech, including pauses and changes in stress and pitch.

second language (L2)–only/English-only programs   K–12 programs for language minority students in the United States in which all instruction is provided in English. Language minority students may be provided with some English as a second language instruction by trained specialists; otherwise, all instruction is provided by general classroom teachers.

second language learners/children   children who begin to learn an additional language after 3 years of age; that is, after the first language is established.

segmental features   see *segments*

segments   individual speech sounds, or *phones,* that make up the phonetic/phonemic inventory of a language. For example, [b], [p], [g], [I], [u] are all segments in the phonemic inventory of English. The International Phonetic Alphabet is used to transcribe the segments or phonemes of the world's languages because there are many more speech segments than can be written with the Roman alphabet.

semilingualism   label for the state of linguistic knowledge of a second language learner whose first language abilities have significantly eroded and whose second language abilities have not yet reached a proficient level. These individuals are sometimes labeled *semilingual,* meaning they do not possess full native speaker competence in either language. The existence of semilingualism has been challenged on both conceptual and empirical grounds, and it has become a controversial label, for second language children in particular.

simultaneous bilingual children   children who learn two or more languages from birth or begin learning both languages sometime during the first year after birth. In effect, simultaneous bilinguals have two first languages. Simultaneous bilinguals can be exposed to languages in different ways—from their parents or siblings in the home; from child care workers in the home or in child care centers; or from grandparents or relatives. We also sometimes refer to these learners as *bilingual children.*

sink-or-swim programs   see *submersion programs*

specific language impairment (SLI)   developmental disorder in which children have delayed or deviant language development. Children with SLI have typical intelligence, hearing, and social-emotional behavior, and they have no frank neurological impairment.

submersion programs   K–12 programs for language minority students in which the majority language is used for all instruction (including literacy and academic subjects); typically, no or limited adjustments are made to instruction to accommodate students' special language and cultural characteristics. This type of program is also referred to as *sink-or-swim.*

subtractive bilingual environments   language-learning environments (including family, community, and school settings) that are associated with loss of the native language as a result of acquisition of a second language. Bilingual children in these environments usually lose identification with the culture associated with the native language and family. This process is referred to as *subtractive bilingualism* and occurs in children from minority ethnolinguistic groups, such as immigrant, refugee, or indigenous group children, when they acquire a majority group language. In the long run, subtractive bilingualism usually results in monolingual proficiency in the majority language.

suprasegmental features   components of the sound system of a language that transcend individual phones or segments; see also *prosody.*

target-deviant structures   inaccuracies that first and second language learners produce in their phonology and grammar of the target language. For example, a young child might say, "Me no want broccoli," when the target adult form is *I don't want broccoli*. The child's form is *target-deviant* because it is not identical to the adult model. Calling these constructions *errors* could imply that the child is doing something wrong when, in fact, producing these kinds of sentences is a typical and natural part of the process of language acquisition for all learners.

telegraphic language   type of language children produce when they begin speaking the second language after the silent period. Children's utterances in the second language at this early stage are imitative, contain little original content, and/or seem stripped of anything but the core content (like a telegraph). Children at this stage will produce one-word utterances labeling object or colors or memorized phrases such as *I don't know* or *What's happening?*

threshold hypothesis   theory proposed by Jim Cummins to explain different cognitive and linguistic consequences of bilingualism. According to this hypothesis, children who acquire relatively high levels of competence in two languages are likely to exhibit higher than average levels of general cognitive and language ability, whereas children who acquire relatively low levels of ability in their two languages are likely to experience lower than average levels of general cognitive and language ability. No significant positive or negative cognitive or linguistic consequences are likely to result from the acquisition of levels of bilingual competence that fall intermediary between the upper and lower thresholds.

total immersion programs   see *early total immersion*.

transfer errors   target-deviant structures in a second language learner's interlanguage that are due to influence from the first language. For example, a second language speaker of English whose first language is Spanish may put an *e* before *sp* in words (e.g., *Spanish* becomes *Espanish*; *stop* becomes *estop*). In this example, second language speakers appear to have transferred a phonological rule from their native language to their second language; see also *developmental errors*.

transitional bilingual/immersion programs   programs for language minority students that use the students' native language to teach literacy and some academic subjects during the primary grades for at most 3 years, at which time the students are transitioned into mainstream classes in which all instruction is provided in English. These programs aim for full proficiency in English only and grade-appropriate academic standards.

translation equivalents   words in a bilingual speaker's vocabulary in one language that have a corresponding word in the other language that means virtually the same thing (e.g., *zapatos* in Spanish corresponds to *shoes* in English).

two-way immersion/bilingual programs   bilingual programs in the United States in which half the students are from a minority language group (e.g., Spanish) and half are from the majority language group (i.e., English). Both English and the minority language are used to teach literacy and academic subjects throughout the elementary grades and sometimes through the high school grades. These programs aim for full bilingual proficiency and grade-appropriate standards in academic subjects. The most common forms of two-way immersion are referred to as the *90/10* and the *50/50* models because they provide 90% and 50%, respectively, of instruction through the medium of a minority language and the remaining instruction through English.

unitary language system hypothesis   theory about early bilingual development that claims that when an infant is presented with dual language input, he or she does not construct two separate linguistic representations at first, but instead melds the dual language input into a single system that must undergo a process of differentiation. After differentiation, which is thought to occur around 3 years of age, the child is considered to be bilingual. Researchers Virginia Volterra and Traute Taeschner articulated the most detailed model of this view in 1978. This hypothesis contrasts with the *dual language system hypothesis.*

variegated babbling   babbling that consists of strings of nonreduplicated sounds (e.g., ba–da); characteristic of infants around 8–10 months of age until and during early stages of first word productions. This stage contrasts with the earlier *canonical babbling* stage in which infants can only repeat the same syllable in a string.

Williams syndrome   Williams syndrome (also known as Williams-Beuren syndrome) is a neurogenetic developmental disorder occurring in approximately 1 in 20,000 live births. Physically, it is characterized by a specific heart defect (supravalvular aortic stenosis), craniofacial dismorphology, and scoliosis. Cognitively, it is marked by impairments in key cognitive domains including conceptual reasoning, problem solving, arithmetic, and spatial cognition, alongside relatively preserved abilities in four specific domains: social drive, face processing, language, and music.

word tokens   total number of words used by a speaker during a stretch of conversation. Word tokens can include repetitions of the same type (e.g., the word *cat* might be used five times and would be counted every time as a token). Word token counts are used as estimates of a speaker's volubility or the sheer amount of talk.

word types   number of different words used by a speaker or known by a speaker. Repetitions of the same word are not included in word type counts (e.g., if the word *cat* were used five times, it would be counted as only one word type). Word type counts are used as estimates of a speaker's vocabulary knowledge.

Index

Page references followed by *t* or *f* indicate tables or figures, respectively.